The Rat Pack

The Rat Pack

The Hey-Hey Days of Frank and the Boys

Lawrence J. Quirk
and William Schoell

TAYLOR PUBLISHING COMPANY
Dallas, Texas

Published by Taylor Publishing Company
1550 West Mockingbird Lane
Dallas, Texas 75235

Library of Congress Cataloging-in-Publication Data

Quirk, Lawrence J.
    The Rat Pack : the hey-hey days of Frank and the boys / Lawrence
J. Quirk and William Schoell.
        p.   cm.
    Filmography: p. 344
    Includes bibliographical references and index.
    ISBN 0-87833-992-2
    1. Entertainers—United States—Biography. 2. Sinatra, Frank,
1915– . 3. Singers—United States—Biography. 4. Bogart,
Humphrey, 1899–1957. 5. Motion picture actors and actresses—
United States—Biography. I. Title.
PN2285.Q58   1998
791'.092'273—dc21
[B]   98–10808
                                     CIP

Printed in the United States of America

10   9   8   7   6   5   4   3   2

This book has been printed on acid-free recycled paper.

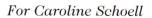

For Caroline Schoell

Contents

Introduction

It surprised no one when Frank Sinatra decided to do a "spectacular" benefit for Father Dismas Clark's Half-Way House for ex-convicts. (Apparently it didn't occur to Clark to collect funds for the convicts' many victims.) Sinatra had been friends with a variety of big-time mobsters and their small-time cronies for most of his life. Throughout his life Sinatra made up for various public and private malfeasances by doing Good Works, and this particular cause seemed made-to-order for Ol' Blue Eyes: a) it was a bona fide Catholic charity, and b) it was for mugs like him, guys who wound up in stir, where Sinatra himself might have resided had it not been for the gift of his golden voice and the encouragement of his sainted mother.

So Frank sent out the command and the members of his Rat Pack came running: Sammy Davis Jr., ever anxious to please; a reluctant if willing Dean Martin, who'd lost one stooge and wasn't about to become another; and Joey Bishop, who said he'd come but hurt his back—and pissed off Frank—at the last minute. His replacement as emcee of the whole shebang was a relatively young and new Johnny

Carson, only a few years into his tenure as host of *The Tonight Show*. As for Peter Lawford, Sinatra had not spoken to him for years.

On Father's Day, June 20, 1965, at the Kiel Opera House in St. Louis, the spectacular was broadcast live via closed circuit to a number of movie houses across the country. This bit of forgotten tape resurfaced in 1997 when the Museum of Television and Radio unveiled a special ninety-minute version of the spectacular for audiences in its New York and Beverly Hills screening rooms. (The entire three-hour tape was also available for private screenings.) Billed (mistakenly, as it were) as the only existing footage of the Rat Pack at work and play, it demonstrated the members of the clan at their best and worst.

Sammy Davis Jr. (not to mention Joey Bishop and Peter Lawford) had never been given much to do in the various Rat Pack movies, but here he was given a chance to shine—and to prove that he was arguably the most talented member of the group. Sammy not only sings and dances well, but does dead-on impressions of Dean Martin and a host of other singers; he is an irrepressible ball of energy. After a shaky start doing jazzy numbers for which his voice is not appropriate, Sinatra does what he does best: superb renditions of the old standards that he helped make famous and vice versa. Dino is not much of a singer, really, but his drunk act—which later was no longer an act and no laughing matter—is amiable and amusing. Carson can barely get a quip in edgewise.

The Museum prefaces the screening of *The Rat Pack Captured* with a politically correct disclaimer of some of the dated (read: racial) humor of the presentation, which pretty much misses the point: these guys were products of their period. In any case, there is nothing that offensive on the tape. Seeing the Rat Pack today, however, some people will find it hard to believe that they were ever considered the epitome of "cool." Still, there's a certain timelessness to their talent and versatility, the sheer fun they had in entertaining, even if much of their shtick was strictly for the rubes.

In the late fifties when the individual members of the clan started working together in twos and threes and, finally, a Pack, America seemed a land of almost stifling middle-class conformity. Sammy and Frank and Dean—the most important members of the Pack—were the Hollywood antithesis of that conformity. (In skin-tight pants and tight black skin, Sammy was the most outré of the lot.) Although all three had (several) wives and children, they essentially lived like playboys. They went to bed when most of the world was getting ready to go to work. (This was true of most entertainers, but the Rat Pack made it a part of their whole mystique.) They had such fun on stage that there was no difference between work time and party time, something that was hardly true for most Americans. Women were attracted to their devil-may-care demeanor; men wanted to be just like them, drinking and laughing the night away together and ending up with a different "broad" each night.

Various social movements of the past few decades have combined to make the Rat Pack passé, which is just what makes them so appealing to those who wish they could be politically incorrect. The Surgeon General has taken the joy out of smoking; AA has done the same for drinking; and if they hadn't your doctor would have. The nutritionist says you can no longer eat red meat, and AIDS and other STDs means that indiscriminate sex with bar pickups isn't safe for straights or gays. Staying up late just gets you bags under the eyes. At least the members of the Rat Pack could never be accused of getting too much sun, which in any case gives you skin cancer and skin like leather. (Frank and Dino were health addicts and didn't even know it.)

The members of the Rat Pack were not sensitive men of the nineties, but they had fun and they had money—and power—to burn, which is what some women like about

them. Women had a place in their lives, but they didn't control them, which is what some men like about them. They
were not really nonconformists in any true sense of the
word, not radicals or revolutionaries or—heaven help us!—
deep, original thinkers (only Sammy was ahead of his time
in any particular fashion, though it must be said that when
it came to civil rights, Frank wasn't far behind him), but to
the insurance salesman home from a job he hated in a house
he couldn't afford with a wife he couldn't relate to, their lives
must have seemed quite idyllic: i.e., cool.

Then there was the dark side. The shamefully neglected
wives and children. The cast-off lovers. The ties to the Mafia
and corrupt politicians. The way they spent and spent and
then resented giving any portion of their millions to the IRS.
Not one member of the Rat Pack went overseas during World
War II or saw a bit of the combat that killed so many
American boys who could neither sing nor dance. (Joey and
Sammy at least were in the Army, but they never left the
States.) Feuds and fusses and arguments galore. And a lot of
broken-down livers.

But there was also their talent and exuberance, the
sheer joy they gave millions of people, the hit records and
movie roles by the dozens, the dizzying cavalcade of women
and celebrities and politicians that made up their fascinating
supporting cast, the influence they had on dress and style
and even, incredibly, social movements in this country, that
irrepressible energy that seemed to electrify and galvanize
everyone around them. It was a wild ride while it lasted.

Come along and see how it all happened.

PART ONE

The Early Years
1915–1957

1

Bogie and the Original Rat Pack

It was called the Holmby Hills Rat Pack, and Frank Sinatra was one of its leading members. But it was not his Rat Pack; it was Bogie's. Humphrey Bogart. His friend and idol—and rival in love. Bogart was already sixteen years old when Sinatra was born. He'd made his first film over a decade before Sinatra made his. But he made quite an impression on the singer. Sinatra liked Bogie's style; he liked his attitude; he liked, in particular, Bogart's wife.

When pretty nineteen-year-old Lauren Bacall found out that her mentor Howard Hawks was thinking of putting her in a picture with either Cary Grant or Humphrey Bogart, she said to herself, "Cary Grant—terrific! Humphrey Bogart—yucch!"

Humphrey DeForest Bogart had been born in New York City in 1899. He came from a good family: his mother was an illustrator for top magazines and his father a prominent surgeon. They had big plans for their boy—precollege studies at the exclusive Phillips Academy in Massachusetts, then on to a medical degree at Yale—which were stymied by Humphrey's expulsion from Phillips for bad behavior and the encroachment of World War I. Legend has it his trademark lisp resulted from a facial injury he endured in the Navy when his ship was torpedoed. While this injury may have affected certain nerves around the mouth—giving him that tight, clipped way of speaking—he may well have lisped since birth.

When Bogie was twenty-one and had spent some time doing assorted tasks for a Broadway producer who was friends with his parents, he decided that what he really wanted to do was act. He went back and forth from Broadway to Hollywood in a succession of supporting roles that did little to further his career. It was his role in the play *The Petrified Forest* by Robert E. Sherwood in 1935 that got him his first big break. Warner Bros. wanted somebody else to play Duke Mantee in the film version of the hit play, but star Leslie Howard—who was set to repeat his stage role in the film adaptation—insisted Bogart be cast instead of Edward G. Robinson.

Still, Bogart was not an overnight success. There followed many more gangster roles in "B" movies, nothing that would put him over the top. However, roles in such films as *High Sierra* (1941), *The Maltese Falcon* (1941), and, of course, *Casablanca* (1942), finally made him a household name and a major Hollywood presence. Arguably Bogart made his strongest impression in *Falcon*, at his best when he's being all angry and moral with his murderous client Mary Astor.

Bogie was always an odd choice to become a movie star. His homeliness and rough manner (at least on-screen) belied his uppercrust background, and the lisp hardly added to his appeal. He could be extremely effective in certain pictures that were within his range or employed his peculiar abilities, such as *The Maltese Falcon* or *The Caine Mutiny*, but no one could seriously claim that he was ever a truly great actor. He was an anomaly in Hollywood: he had the looks of a character actor but the talent of a star. (The reverse is equally infrequent.)

Bogart had been married three times before he met Lauren "Betty" Bacall and was still married to wife number three, Mayo Methot. His first wife was a Broadway actress named Helen Menken, but they ran into difficulties when she spent—as far as he was concerned—too much attention on her career. A similar situation occurred with wife number two, Mary Philips. Third wife Mayo Methot was another actress. He had had a quickie affair with Mayo during a prolonged separation from Mary, but his guilt only lasted until he discovered Mary was having an affair with her co-star in Chicago, Roland Young. After his and Mary's divorce, Bogart felt marrying Mayo would be the right thing to do. It wasn't.

Bogart had had difficulty with his early wives' successes when he was still a struggling actor, but now the situation was reversed. Bogie became a star while Mayo's career limped along. Before long she was a hopeless alcoholic and a hellcat par excellence. She would accuse Bogie of having affairs with each and every one of his leading ladies, get into drunken arguments—and physical brawls—with him, and even tried to literally stab him in the back with a kitchen knife on one occasion. Mayo could also be counted on to start humiliating public scenes whenever they went out. All of Hollywood knew them as "The Battling Bogarts."

This situation wasn't helped at all by Bogart's being cast in *To Have and Have Not* (1944). His co-star was a pretty teenager who was the protégé of producer/director Howard Hawks: Lauren Bacall. Hawks at this time was a bespectacled, white-haired, middle-aged-going-on-elderly man who pretended, at first, that his interest in Lauren was strictly professional. Bogart first met Lauren when Hawks brought her to the set of *Passage to Marseille*, which Bogart was doing for director Michael Curtiz. "There was no clap of thunder, no lightning bolt, just a simple how-do-you-do," Bacall remembered. Bacall thought that Bogart was friendly enough, but other than that he made little impression on her.

That all changed once the two of them began working together. Bogart saw two screen tests that Lauren did and approved her for his leading lady, although she would have had to have been pretty bad for him to turn her down considering how high Hawks was on using her—not to mention how high he was on Lauren period. Later on this would cause major problems for Bogie and Bacall.

During the days of rehearsal in Hawks's office for the second screen test—another actor sat in for Bogart as Hawks worked with Lauren—Hawks really became Bacall's Svengali. He chose her clothing, her makeup, suggested how she should say her lines and react to the actor standing in for Bogie. "Who knew what kind of Frankenstein's monster he was creating?" Lauren wondered. But it was this second screen test that really impressed Bogie, who told her, "We'll have a lot of fun together." (The scene chosen for the second test was the famous "You know how to whistle. Just put your lips together and blow" sequence.)

The Svengali-Trilby bit continued as filming proceeded, but some things Lauren came up with on her own. She was so nervous she trembled, and the only way that she could keep it from showing was to hold her head down, her chin low, and look upward at Bogart from that position. (This was later known as "the Look.") She found that working with Bogart was a tremendous help. "He did everything possible to put me at ease," she said, and she swore that there was no flirting off-screen between the two whatsoever during those early days. On-screen, however, Hawks noticed how much chemistry the couple had and scripted a few more scenes of sexual badinage for them to engage in. Hawks, of course, had his own off-screen plans for Lauren, but never dreamed that anything might happen between her and Bogie once the cameras stopped whirring.

The casual relationship between the two stars began to change one day after filming when Bogart gave Bacall a quick impulsive kiss as a way of bidding her good night. He asked her for her phone number in a friendly sort of way. Before long Bogart would be calling Lauren on the phone at all hours after he'd had a few drinks following one of his unceasing battles with jealous Mayo. From these late-night calls and meetings, they worked their way around to going off for weekends together and having dinner with some friends of Bogie's who lived in a trailer. At first Lauren would go off and meet Bogart wherever he was calling from, but eventually he simply came up to her apartment to talk and everything else two lovers did in privacy.

Eventually talk of the affair reached the supporting players. Lauren's mother was appalled: Bogart was not only forty-four years old to Lauren's nineteen, but he was a married man! Howard Hawks told Lauren she was making a fool of herself—Bogart would eventually drop her and she'd be devastated—and told her she'd be through in pictures if she continued seeing him off the set. "I'll wash my hands of you," he threatened. Of course, Hawks—who was also married and hadn't yet built up the nerve to make a pass at her—was furious and jealous that she was going out with Bogart. He had expected to find competition from handsome young guys, but Bogie? Unfortunately, the rather rodentlike features of Hawks were even homelier than Bogart's, and he was also much older. Hawks felt that both of his leading actors had somehow betrayed him, and he did his best to make life miserable for the both of them.

The worst reaction was from Bogart's wife. Although Bogart rationalized that it was Mayo's drinking that was driving him into another woman's arms, his not-so-discreet affair with Lauren was what really made her hit the bottle more than usual. Feeling washed up, overlooked, rejected by her husband and in his shadow, worried about her looks and wondering if anyone would ever really love her again, Mayo was always depicted as a shrew (particularly by the self-serving Bacall), but she was actually a pitiable figure. At nineteen Bacall was much too callow to see the wife's side of things and too naive to realize that, however enduring her relationship with Bogie was to become, he was really just another aging man who wanted a younger woman. It's debatable whether at first Lauren was ever maturely in love with Bogart (or vice versa), but she did become very attached to him. She saw him as a kind, masculine father figure (her own father, separated from her mother, had always been a distant figure) who needed love and loyalty and help in his battle against the horrible selfish dragon he was married to.

Meanwhile the on-screen chemistry between the two became, understandably, even hotter than before. Bogie only had eyes for Bacall. A subplot wherein Bogie's character sort of falls for Dolores Moran's was left on the cutting-room floor. Moran was not crazy with this development—the pretty blonde had hoped the film might lead to better things—and was often vocal with her disapproval, suggesting that of course Bacall would be favored when she was sleeping with both Hawks (not true) and Bogart (true). "I thought she was ugly," Moran said later. "She looked almost Oriental but not in a pretty way. Her eyes were so funny. She was really weird looking, but she had something and she wasn't ashamed to use it. Shame isn't in that gal's vocabulary."

As Bacall waited for her first picture to be released, her affair with Bogie waxed and waned. One day he was going back with his wife—Mayo swore she'd get treatment for her alcoholism and he wanted to stick by her—the next he was through with the hell-raising harridan and thought of no one but Lauren. Bogie was deeply worried about the difference in their ages, but Lauren assured him that that didn't matter. Bogart had just about made up his mind to leave Mayo for good when she was hospitalized. He felt it would be crummy to leave her when she was at her lowest ebb. When Mayo left the hospital she swore she'd be a good girl and stop drinking, but before the week was up she was back on the bottle, battling with Bogart worse than ever. Lauren began receiving phone calls not only from Bogie but from his wife, who would drunkenly berate her and call her ugly names. Howard Hawks was furious with the whole matter and kept threatening to sell Lauren's contract to bargain basement Republic Pictures.

Eventually Bogart made up his mind to leave Mayo once and for all and ironed out an enormous settlement with her. Mayo went down to Reno to establish residency there so she could get a quickie divorce, but once or twice came back to L.A. and would have to return to Reno to start all over again. Bogart moved into the Garden of Allah, a complex of bungalows with several famous residents, to wait it out. Bacall waited with him.

In the meantime they worked on *The Big Sleep* (1946), their second film together, also directed by (a much tenser) Hawks. *To Have and Have Not* was released first and turned Bacall into an overnight sensation. Since she was a star now too, her relationship with Bogart became tabloid fodder in much the way Sinatra's marriage to Ava Gardner—two more stars in conjunction—would a few years later.

Bacall's first picture got a lot of attention when it was released—for obvious reasons—but *To Have and Have Not*, which was clearly inspired by *Casablanca*, isn't a very good picture. It would probably be completely forgotten today (it never quite became a classic) were it not for the chemistry of its famous players and their off-screen antics. All of those *Casablanca* elements were in place: the tough (if lisping) hero, foreign locale, a nightclub ambiance, and so forth. Bogart plays a boat renter who displeases the Vichy officials by bringing in two "illegal aliens." Sultry Bacall, most people agreed, was perhaps more personality than actress, but what a personality! Following the smitten Hawks's directions for each and every movement, she leers, wiggles, and "eyes" her way through the role with obvious star presence and considerable command. Although there are a few good scenes in the movie, the climax the audience has been patiently expecting for nearly two hours never materializes. Instead Bacall just sort of boogies her way out of the nightclub and that's that. Cute, but so what? It's the Bogart movie that few people list as their favorite.

For years the rumor persisted that Andy Williams dubbed Bacall's singing voice in the movie. Actually Bacall recorded "How Little We Know" and lip-synced to it in the movie. "Howard was satisfied with the recording, though he thought one or two notes might have to be dubbed later on," wrote Bacall in her memoirs. It was these off-key notes that Williams overdubbed and which gave rise to the only half-true rumor.

Walter Brennan worked on *To Have and Have Not* and was amused by Bogie and Bacall's relationship and Hawks's reaction to it. "Everyone could see something was going on with those two," he said some years afterward, "but I think Howard desperately wanted to believe it was just the chemistry they had as performers, all for the good of the picture, that sort of thing. Finally it dawned on him what had already dawned on everybody else—it was so damned obvious—Bogie and Betty were falling in love. He was furious—and not as easy to work with after that."

Although it's not as well-known as the first two, perhaps the best Bogie-Bacall collaboration was *Dark Passage* (1947), which was directed by Delmer Daves. In this film Bogart, who was falsely arrested for murdering his wife, escapes from prison and gets plastic surgery to change his features. He hooks up with Bacall, who helps him hide out as his face heals behind the bandages. Meanwhile the two try to determine who the real killer is. Although the plot is highly improbable, it features some nice twists and emerges as a suspenseful and absorbing mystery. This is all capped by a hair-raising scene in which Agnes Moorehead falls out of a highrise. Delmer Daves wanted to do a fight scene Bogart had in one long take, but Bogart insisted they film it piecemeal, punch by punch, because he was afraid if he got too energetic the toupee he'd just started wearing might fall off.

By this time Bogie and Bacall were married. Bogart had never been able to entertain much while married to Mayo— she always caused such awful scenes when she was drinking, which was practically all the time—but when he moved to the Garden of Allah he became the host with the most. He loved to be surrounded by his friends, people having a good time, people he could relax with and who had fame and good career fortune in common with him. Bogart preferred private parties to going out, where he might be set upon by "the Hollywood gossips and leeches." Like many a star before and after him, Bogart enjoyed all the trappings and privileges of success but wanted no part of the negative aspects that came along with it.

After their marriage, the couple moved from the Garden of Allah bungalow to a house in the Hollywood Hills. When Bacall got pregnant, they decided it might be better to move to an area with more spacious grounds, so they transferred to a place in Benedict Canyon in the Holmby Hills. Hedy Lamarr had been the original owner. She told Bogie she'd let him have the house for free if only he'd co-star in a picture with her, but Bogie decided it would be better to give her the cash. It was in this house that the original Holmby Hills Rat Pack truly began.

When Bacall became part of Bogie's world she discovered how many fascinating, famous friends he had. There was producer Mark Hellinger, who had originally been a newspaper columnist. It was at Hellinger's house that Lauren first met Mike Romanoff and his wife. Romanoff was a restaurateur who had had a brief career as an actor. Back in those days he pretended to be an actual Russian Prince who'd escaped the revolution by the seat of his pants, but he really came from Brooklyn. He was one of the fabulous phonies Hollywood was always taking to its breast; now his restaurant was one of the "in" places to be.

Bogie also knew such writers as Dorothy Parker, Robert Benchley, and John O'Hara, all of whom had bungalows at the Garden of Allah. At Ira Gershwin's home Lauren met such luminaries as Oscar Levant, Groucho Marx, Lena Horne, John Huston, and Judy Garland, who became an important member of Bogie's group, along with her husband Sid Luft. Then there was Irving Lazar, who would one day become the famous literary agent "Swifty" Lazar, almost as well-known a bullethead as Otto Preminger. Lauren became friends with Spencer Tracy because his regular booth at Romanoff's was adjacent to hers and Bogie's. Bogart was also good friends with David Niven and his wife Hjordis.

There were a few honorary, temporary, and visiting (from the East Coast) members, but the main constituents of what was shortly to become Bogie's Rat Pack were Bogie and Betty, the Nivens, the Lufts, the Romanoffs, Swifty, and one other very important person. That person was Frank Sinatra.

Frank Sinatra had been brought to the group by best pal Jimmy Van Heusen and Swifty Lazar, who lived in the same apartment building. At the time Frank first met Betty and Bogie he was at the beginning of a long, hard climb up from rock bottom.

How he'd gotten there was quite a story. . . .

2

Hoboken Romeo

At the very beginning, nobody even thought Francis Albert Sinatra had a particularly good voice. His mother, a mid-wife and ex-abortionist named Dolly, pushed her son to sing at weddings and in local clubs in Hoboken, New Jersey, where he was born, but people would cringe in negative anticipation as he stepped up to the microphone. "He had no training," someone who once worked with him in the early years said on a guarantee of anonymity. "He had no vocal coach, nobody to tell him where he was going wrong. Just his mother—and she didn't know shit about music. His range was limited, his voice was too high-pitched. It was terrible. Most people didn't think he had any talent. They would have been blown over if they'd known that someday he'd make it big. Who would have guessed?"

Francis was born to Dolly and Martin Sinatra on December 12, 1915. His father was as retiring and quiet as his mother was loud and boisterous, determined that her boy would amount to something no matter what the cost. The boy was supposed to be named after his father, but the priest made a mistake and christened him Francis after his godfather, an Irish newspaperman named Frank Garrick. Shy Martin just stood there and said nothing. Dolly, who was only twenty at the time, was home recovering from the difficult breech birth.

Years later Garrick hired young Frankie to bundle copies of the paper for the delivery truck, but this wasn't good enough for Francis or Dolly. When a sportswriter was killed in a car accident, Dolly demanded that Frank go see Garrick—who only handled circulation—and convince him to somehow get Frank the dead writer's job. As Garrick was out for the day, Frankie simply took over the writer's desk and acted as if the position were already his. When the editor found out about this, he was furious: the dead writer hadn't even been buried yet. Garrick was forced to fire Frankie, adding that had he waited until he could have spoken to the editor about him, he may well have gotten the job. Frankie flew into a rage that was positively frightening, an early instance of his formidable, almost maniacal, temper. Even though Garrick was the boy's godfather, and had gotten him a job in the first place, Dolly never spoke to him again. Ditto for Frank, who only broke his silence half a century later after his mother had died.

Now Frankie had no job, only an eighth-grade education, and little interest in anything but music. He organized a small high school band and played for school dances, vocalizing all the hits of the period. Most people agreed that his singing was pretty awful, but to his mother he was a veritable Caruso. She accepted that since singing was the only thing that really interested him, the only thing she could do was support this interest and hope it could somehow parlay him into the big time. She seemed not to notice the many times he hit the wrong note or sang off-key.

Dolly was a big fish in the small pond of Hoboken—Manhattan was just across the river but a whole universe away—and she used her influence to get Frankie a job as a singer at the Union Club. He was twenty years old at the time. It was while doing gigs at some other social clubs in Hoboken that he met a group who called themselves the Three Flashes. Not one to miss an opportunity, Frankie made friends with the trio, and offered to drive them to whichever club they were playing. It wasn't long before the Three Flashes became known as the Hoboken Four, with Francis Sinatra as the fourth member.

His stint with the Hoboken Four led to an appearance at the Capitol Theater in 1935 for Major Bowes's famous amateur contest, the *Star Search* of its day. They did so well that Bowes signed them up for a tour, and also put them into film shorts presented collectively as *Major Bowes' Theater of the Air*. In such one-reelers as *The Night Club* and *The Minstrel*, Frank and the other boys would dress up in blackface and tuxedos and sing a song or two in mini-sketches. The shorts were filmed at the Biograph Studios in the Bronx.

Frank's appeal to women began manifesting itself about this time, and the other members of the group reacted with jealousy. Fred Tamburro, the group's baritone, not only resented Frank's sex appeal, but the fact that Frank often giggled on stage and on at least one occasion caused the other boys to crack up so much they had to cut short the performance. He began to take out his frustration by beating up Sinatra on a regular basis. On many occasions, one of the other members would join in. Frank was skinny and slight; he could hardly hold off one attacker, let alone two. Things got so bad that, nursing his bruises, he finally left the tour and the group for good.

Years later when Frank was a star and Tamburro was struggling to get by as a singer, Tamburro came to Frank and asked him for a job. Frank replied that he could always use someone to shine his shoes. Tamburro refused to be his valet, but a year later he was back begging for a loan, which Sinatra turned down. While this story is often used as evidence of the cruel side of Sinatra's nature (which certainly exists), it shouldn't be. Considering that Tamburro beat Frank so badly that he had to leave the Hoboken Four and go home in disgrace, Tamburro had a lot of gall in expecting anything from his victim. Why should Sinatra have given him anything?

In 1938 Sinatra wanted a job at the Rustic Cabin, a club in the Jersey Palisades. His mother had to use her influence to get past the bandleader, Harold Arden, who had no use for Frankie on either a personal or professional level. Frankie was thrilled with the gig, but his personal life was about to take a turn for the worse. He got enveloped in women trouble, not for the last time in his life, and wound up arrested on morals charges.

There were two women involved, the first of whom was twenty-five-year-old Antoinette Francke, who was separated from her husband. The second was twenty-one-year-old Nancy Barbato, whom Frank had known for three years and who was to become his first wife. During his long courtship with Nancy, Frank saw many other women, but the most volatile of them all was Antoinette, whose nickname was Toni.

Dolly was crazy about Nancy, but she couldn't stand Antoinette, whom she thought came from a low-class background. Dolly argued with Frankie over seeing her, but Sinatra was attracted to this forbidden fruit, and before long Toni was pregnant. When she told him the news, at first he offered to do the right thing, but once his mother started to work on him, he told Toni that she was screwing up his chances of becoming somebody. He stopped calling her and stopped coming by to see her. There was a brief reconciliation when Toni had a miscarriage, but this didn't last long. Dolly's propaganda had been too lethal.

Toni would have none of this. She called Frank one

night at the Rustic Cabin. Nancy answered the phone and got snippy. Finally Toni drove out to the Rustic Cabin, where she planned to make a scene if Frank didn't talk to her. Nancy became enraged when she saw Toni walk in and head toward Frank. Trying to head her off, she grabbed Toni and got a slap for her trouble. Nancy called Toni a whore and started pulling her hair, and Toni responded by grabbing Nancy's dress and giving it a good yank, practically tearing it off her. When Frank told her that Nancy was now pregnant and he would have to marry her, Toni became even more livid; half-drunk patrons of the Rustic Cabin merrily watched as the fight between the two hellcats continued. Finally Sinatra and some club workers were able to tear the two women apart.

This was only the beginning as Toni sought revenge any way she could. In November she had Frank arrested on morals charges, claiming she had been pure and chaste when Frank made love to her. Frank sat in jail as Toni fumed, saying that the only way she'd drop the charges would be if both he and his mother apologized for their treatment of her. Dolly swore that she would do so once Frank was released, but she actually had no intention of saying she was sorry to this creature who was causing her son so much trouble. When Toni showed up at her house to have the satisfaction of Dolly apologizing to her face, Dolly not only didn't apologize, she threw her down the basement stairs and locked her in the cellar until her screaming brought the police. Hoboken was Dolly's town, not Toni's, so Toni was herself arrested for disorderly conduct. Although given a suspended sentence, Toni decided Frank must pay for this new affront upon her dignity and this time had him arrested on charges of adultery, as she was still married to her husband. Toni's family, who detested Dolly and the other Sinatras, convinced her to drop these charges as well.

Although Nancy wasn't really pregnant as Frank had

told Toni—and she and Dolly had conspired to tell Frank— Dolly suggested firmly that her son marry Nancy before he got into any more trouble with grasping females. In early 1939 they tied the knot, but for Frank the most important occasion of the year wasn't his wedding, but his being hired to sing for the Harry James band. Frank was now twenty-four years old and on his way.

James wanted to change Sinatra's name to "Frankie Satin," but Dolly would have none of that. Sinatra was so anxious for major success that he probably would have gone along with it, but his mother convinced him to tell James it was Sinatra or nothing. Although Frank was soon playing major venues with the band and even cut a few records, he thought his journey to the top was moving too slowly. One of the problems was that James's band was a little more raucous and swinging than some club owners and patrons were used to; another was that Frank was only an adequate singer at this point, with little to truly distinguish him from a hundred others. He wasn't the Voice yet.

That began to change when Frank left the James band— nice-guy Harry James tore up his contract without making any trouble for him—and became a vocalist for Tommy Dorsey. Dick Haymes replaced Sinatra with the James band. A few months after switching from one band to the more popular one, Sinatra had his first hit record, "I'll Never Smile Again." His already formidable ego bolstered by new confidence, Sinatra made it his mission to become the only star with the band besides Dorsey himself.

This did not sit well with drummer Buddy Rich, who resented seeing Frank's picture on posters for the band. Rich tried to get Frank off his game by changing the tempo of a number in midstream. For his part, Frank was nasty to the female vocalist, Connie Haines, and often would crowd her off the mike when they were supposed to do a duet. Frank didn't want to share the mike with anyone and told Tommy Dorsey he had to choose between him and Connie. Annoyed at being given ultimatums, Dorsey fired Sinatra, but when Frank said he was sorry for causing so much trouble—backstage fights between "the talent" were often horrendous—Tommy took him back. Frank liked and admired Dorsey and emulated him in many ways, carousing and womanizing like his idol did. And Tommy gave Frank many suggestions that greatly improved his singing. It was while he was with Dorsey's band that he appeared (albeit only as an unbilled vocalist) in his first full-length motion picture, *Las Vegas Nights*. He followed this up with a similar part in *Ships Ahoy*.

While in Hollywood Frank met a woman named Alora Gooding, who threatened to unseat Nancy (she had already given Frank their first child, Nancy Sandra, by this time) as the major woman in his life. A Hollywood starlet, Alora was the first truly glamorous female that Frank got involved with, and their affair lasted—on and off—for some years. Gooding was not the only woman Sinatra dallied with during the next few years. There was a debutante from Long Island named Mary Lou Watts, who helped Frank polish up his speech and manners, and tempestuous romances with such major stars as Lana Turner and Marilyn Maxwell. It was at a party with Maxwell that Frank met future fellow Rat Packer Peter Lawford, who later co-starred with him in *It Happened in Brooklyn*. When Sinatra's publicist urged Maxwell not to attend a fight at Madison Square Garden with Frank—such a public flaunting of their affair would be bad for Frank's image—it wrote finis to the relationship, much to Nancy's relief.

As Frank became more and more successful, he spent less and less time at home. He would make promises to be home for dinner, to spend an evening with Big Nancy and Little Nancy, as they were called, but increasingly these were promises he never kept. Nancy gave him a son, Frank Jr., in January 1944, and in summertime four years later presented him with their second daughter, Christina ("Tina"). Sinatra was always somewhere else when the children were born. Nancy was perfectly aware that her husband was frequently spending time with other women, and she didn't like it. Dolly didn't like it, either, and for a time she and her daughter-in-law, whose relationship had never been easy in the best of times due to Dolly's unhealthy interest in and influence on her son, found themselves in an uneasy alliance. But Dolly was to find that when it came to the willing women who practically threw themselves at his feet, even she couldn't tell her son what to do.

In their 1941 poll, *Billboard* magazine named Frank the top band vocalist of the year, and he displaced Bing Crosby on another poll put out by *Downbeat* magazine. By this time Sinatra was becoming known simply as "the Voice," which had become a blend of ultra-smooth vocalizing with sharp, perfect phrasing and that "dreamy" romantic quality that so excited his fans. Frank had begun to refine the technique that was to serve him in such good stead over the years regardless of the vicissitudes of the instrument itself. Sinatra not only sounded good, he could deliver a song with a matchless combination of sophisticated élan and masculine assurance. The hint of Hoboken that was still in his voice never took away from the essential lyric poise. He made it seem so easy that many styled him a musical genius.

Frank felt that it was now time for him to break out as a solo. He didn't want to spend his whole career known as Dorsey's crooner. But what would he do about Tommy, with whom he still had a contract? He knew that Dorsey would turn on him the minute he found out Frank wanted to leave. In fact, once Frank made clear to Dorsey that he was going to leave in six months and that was that, Dorsey stopped speaking to him, just cut him dead every time he saw him. Frank left everything up to the lawyers and his new managers at Music Corporation of America (MCA), who haggled down Dorsey's original buyout price of one third of Frank's gross earnings for the next ten years—virtual indentured servitude—for a settlement of $60,000.

Dorsey's most famous quote about his ex-vocalist was, "He's the most fascinating man in the world, but don't stick your hand in the cage." Dorsey had always scratched his head at the way women carried on about a man whom he thought of as somewhat homely and undeniably scrawny. Some years later he said, "I knew Sinatra had something or I never would have hired him, but I honestly didn't think he'd last very long once he left my band. He made me out to be the villain all the time, but I tried to play straight with him when I don't think he gave a damn about that; he was just out for Frank. He even took my arranger with him when he left, but I still offered to give him an advance because I'd no longer be paying him every week once he stopped singing for me and it would be a while before he'd be drawing any salary from somewhere else." (This advance would be in exchange for the aforementioned 33 percent of Frank's future earnings, it should be noted.) "It surprised the hell out of me when he agreed. I deliberately made such an outrageous offer because I honestly wanted Frank to stay. Did I carry on when he stopped paying me and made it out to the papers that I was practically an extortionist? When he got the big guns at MCA to renegotiate, I went along, didn't I? I admire Frank's talent, but he was a real son of a bitch, let me tell you."

After Tommy Dorsey, the man most responsible for Sinatra's success was his publicist, George Evans, who also represented Dean Martin and Jerry Lewis, among many other top acts. It was Evans who hit upon the way to move Frank up from the front ranks into a class by himself. He came upon the idea when he saw how some of the girls at Frank's concerts seemed to swoon and get carried away by his singing. That was it! He would turn Frank Sinatra into the love dream of every teenaged girl in America!

"It was kind of comical," he said years later, "turning this gawky guy into a love god, but I saw that he did have a certain effect on a lot of young girls. All I did was capitalize on it, enhance it a bit, and it worked."

What Evans did was hire a dozen girls to sit in the audience when Frankie sang at the Paramount, his first big post-Dorsey appearance. Before the concert, Evans coached the girls on every move they would make. They would sigh when he began his ballads, scream every time he sang the word "love," shudder in ecstasy when he held his arms out toward them, and even faint dead away on certain song cues. They were instructed to carry photos of Frankie and kiss them all through the concert. Before they crowded around Sinatra at the stage door and showered him with kisses, they were to put on plenty of fresh lipstick. Evans reasoned that the tabloids wouldn't be able to resist a funny, sexy photo of Sinatra with lipstick all over his face. Evans also had his associates hand out plenty of free tickets to teens so that they'd be assured of a capacity crowd.

The ploy worked even better than Evans expected. The twelve girls may have started the ball rolling, but before the concert was over dozens more were screaming, sighing, fainting, and painting their lips in anticipation of planting a personal trademark on Frankie, who was "the most." Evans and his associates were staggered by the reaction. The hysterical reactions of the bobbysoxers created a kind of audience participation that wasn't really duplicated until Elvis, and then the Beatles, came along.

Social critics of the period were appalled, just as they later were by Presley, the Fab Four, and their fans' reactions.

It was suggested that most of Sinatra's fans—at least the obsessive, overly hysterical ones—were overweight, plain girls from lower-income homes who had few if any dates and little likelihood of ever having a boyfriend of their own. Sinatra became their surrogate boyfriend. They dripped tears when they saw him because he represented the unattainable, the dream prince who was forever out of reach just as every boy—even the freckled-faced boy next door—was out of reach. So they cried because they knew that that ultimate happiness of loving and being loved in return would never be theirs. The same theory was applied to the Presley fans of the fifties and the Beatles fans of the sixties.

Frankie also represented the dream of the common man, the boy who came from nothing and made good. To that end, Evans manufactured a new and entirely false biography for Sinatra. First he turned him from a twenty-eight-year-old into a twenty-six-year-old, pushing his birthdate up two full years. Then he transformed the high school dropout with no academic achievement or interest in sports into an honors student and all-around athlete. In Sinatra's revised life story, he hadn't been a paper bundler fired for trying to replace a dead reporter, he had been employed as a genuine sports-writer. His childhood of relative ease and privilege had now been a constant struggle against hunger and neighborhood street gangs, the wolf knocking against the door as Frankie strived always for his dream. Dolly was portrayed as a strug-gling, heroic mother, not someone who had once given neigh-borhood abortions and wielded enormous power in her town. And Frankie's marriage was happy and fulfilling. "Frankie adores his fans, but he needs no other women," the publici-ty machine would say as Sinatra was figuring the angles on his latest conquest. "When he's not performing, he loves to be home with his wife and children."

Life could not have been better for Sinatra at this point,

but an ill wind was blowing in his direction. Teenage girls and even older women may have wanted to take him home with them and mother him and more, but their menfolk weren't so thrilled with this Hoboken Casanova. By now the United States had entered World War II, and many men Frank's age were being drafted, sent overseas, and dying in record numbers while Sinatra the crooner was kissed and cuddled by their women back home.

It was a volatile situation that could only get worse.

3

The Varsity

Sinatra liked to surround himself with hangers-on and lackeys, good-time Charlies who would put up with his mercurial temperament for a chance to pal around with a star of his magnitude and share in all the perks that went along with fame and success, such as the best tables in clubs and the hordes of willing women who were attracted to Frankie and all that he represented. A guy could make out like a bandit just by picking up Sinatra's castoffs or rejects. When you were with Sinatra you went first class, you had only the best of everything. Sinatra found that many of the guys from the old neighborhood in Hoboken and environs would be pleased to carry out his demands if it meant they had a chance to be a part of his world. He knew that they knew there would probably be no other opportunity for them to rise—even second-hand—above their station in life.

Some of the men Sinatra hung with were petty criminals or even gangsters, who held a strange fascination over him. Others were minor celebrities who had established a reputation in other or related fields. Collectively these men were known as the Varsity, the forerunner of the Rat Pack. Unlike the Rat Pack, none of the members besides Frank were superstars.

The Varsity included Nick Sevano, a childhood friend of Frank's, who became his personal assistant and all-around gofer; boxer Tami Mauriello, whom Frank owned an interest in; bodyguard and sometime prizefighter Al Silvani; Ben Barton and pianist Hank Sanicola, who started a music company with Frank; sportswriter Jimmy Taratino; record company president Manie Sacks; the songwriting team of Jimmy Van Heusen and Sammy Cahn; and Frank's arranger/conductor—stolen from Tommy Dorsey—Axel Stordahl. Many of these fellows enjoyed all the perquisites of working for and hanging out with Frank while at the same time resenting his demanding nature and air of haughty superiority that went fist in glove with an "I'm just one of the guys" earthy humor and camaraderie (particularly when he was drinking).

Jimmy Van Heusen and Axel Stordahl shared a bachelor pad at the Wilshire Towers, which served as unofficial headquarters for the Varsity. There Frank could get away from the demands of his wife and children and spend time with his buddies, indulging in every whim and fancy. His mother wasn't there to wag her finger at him. The boys would drink and carouse until all hours, and a parade of women marched in and out of the bedrooms. An apocryphal story has it that Frank once showed up with no less than Marlene Dietrich in tow. Reportedly, Dietrich kept her cool when she saw all the men sitting there and just walked with Frank into the appointed bed chamber, leaving—still unflustered—about an hour later.

But no matter how much Frank partied, one thing that couldn't be ignored was the rising anti-Sinatra sentiment in the country, all because he had avoided the draft. He had been classified as 1-A, but the fact that he was a father (before the bombing of Pearl Harbor) and that another child was on the way was enough to keep him out of service. When members of the press and young soldiers began heckling him over this, he went for a second exam by the draft board and this time, conveniently, was classified 4-F, ostensibly because of a punctured eardrum suffered during childbirth.

Frank knew he would lose hundreds of thousands of dollars in contracts if he were to be drafted, not to mention the cushy lifestyle he was leading. The young girls who screamed at his concerts were thrilled that their Frankie would be staying home, but everyone else was infuriated.

In 1945 Sinatra was examined again, and this time reclassified as 2-AF. Congress had passed a bill stating that able-bodied men either fought overseas or worked at home in an occupation necessary to the national interest. Sinatra would still have been disqualified due to his eardrum, but this time he was also exempted because of his career. When news of this hit the papers, it sparked a firestorm of controversy. Columnists, mothers, and soldiers alike all wondered why a crooner for bobbysoxers was considered "essential" for the national interest. Everyone wondered why famous actors, entertainers, and athletes were allowed special consideration when ordinary Joes had no choice but to fight and die for their country. Most people felt that Sinatra's stumping for Roosevelt had something to do with his exemption. Sinatra issued statements saying that he wanted to fight but the draft board wouldn't let him, but he didn't even go overseas to entertain the fighting men until he was practically forced to.

His publicist George Evans knew that the public outcry against his client could toll the death knell for his career. Frank's girl fans were not in the least critical of him—they were overjoyed he could stay safe and sound with his family and on the stage where he belonged—but sooner or later even they would be influenced by public opinion, especially when their brothers and male pals started dying. Evans announced that Frank was going to join a USO tour in May 1945. Of course, by this time the Germans had already surrendered, so it was seen by most as an empty gesture. Frank made matters worse by insisting that room be made for him on a plane from Los Angeles to New York where he was to meet up with the rest of his group. To make sure the celebrity had a seat, a soldier who had fought at Iwo Jima was denied his own. When news of this got out, people were outraged. In spite of all this, Sinatra won over most of the troops by making fun of his scrawny appearance and his unlikely role as a national loverboy.

Phil Silvers was pulled off of his honeymoon to organize the USO tour, which featured Frank as its centerpiece. During an interview he gave during the run of his very popular *Sgt. Bilko* TV show some years later, he talked about those days with Sinatra.

"There was no way I could just call him out on the stage and say to those grunts, 'Look, guys, here's Frank Sinatra!' I mean, he was not one of their favorite people, if you understand me. The gals back home were crying, 'Don't let our Frankie go to war,' and here these guys are overseas in the middle of the fighting and the mud and all the other crap. So I suggested—carefully—that we present him like a real schmoe, nobody the guys could possibly get jealous over. We put him in clothes two sizes too big to emphasize how skinny he was. I made jokes like where I looked Frank up and down and said, 'I know there's food rationing back home but this is ridiculous,' that sort of thing. We kept it up until I felt the guys were warming up to him, sympathizing with him. Before too long they were yelling at me to shut up and let the poor guy sing!"

George Evans—via Phil Silvers—had pulled off the impossible: making Frank Sinatra likable to thousands of combat troops. (The fact that the fighting was over, however, certainly contributed to the ease with which this was accomplished.)

Meanwhile Frank's film career had begun in earnest in

1943 with the release of *Higher and Higher*, which he made for RKO. (He appeared in *Reveille with Beverly* for Columbia that same year, but only to sing one number, "Night and Day.") Of course, *Higher and Higher* wasn't much of a stretch for Sinatra since he played himself. The plot had a scullery maid (Michele Morgan) masquerading as her broke employer's daughter so that she might attract a wealthy husband and put her, her employer, and the rest of the staff in the chips again. Also in the cast were Victor Borge, Mary Wickes, and Frank's future rival for Ava Gardner, singer Mel Torme, also known as the "Velvet Fog." The picture is amusing and light-hearted if a bit syrupy at times.

Mary Wickes recalled in the seventies what it was like working with Sinatra on *Higher and Higher*. "I found him very intense, but pleasant. He was coming under fire then for not being in the service, and I think even he realized how frivolous this fluffy movie we were in was compared to what was going on overseas. But that's why we were making it; to help people forget, to help women forget for a little while all their worry over their men. I told Frank that—that he served a purpose—and he seemed very appreciative—if unconvinced."

Frank's next film for RKO was *Step Lively* (1944), a musical remake of the Marx Brothers' *Room Service* that was an inevitable disappointment. In addition to Frank, George Murphy as a broke producer stalling for time in a swank hotel, and chipmunky Gloria De Haven as the love interest, there were a host of good character actors but no one to replace Groucho, Chico, and Company. By this time, however, Sinatra had absorbed every lesson he had ever learned about singing from Dorsey and others and had finally developed the Voice, which would make him a legend in his own time. His singing is the highlight of the picture, as it would frequently be in the movies that followed.

Eventually Sinatra had his MCA agents get him a five-year contract at the world's biggest movie studio, Metro-Goldwyn-Mayer. His annual salary—from pictures alone—was to be $260,000. He wisely held on to the publishing rights of any songs he might sing in the MGM movies, thus adding to his coffers. Adding his concerts and records and radio show fees to that meant that Sinatra was soon a millionaire many times over.

There were some problems, however. By this time Sinatra had hit the big three-oh and his looks—such as they were—were already fading. Imperfections that weren't so noticeable from the first row at the Paramount were magnified a hundred times by the movie camera. Sinatra didn't like it, but if there was one thing MGM knew, it was how to turn ordinary people into Movie Stars. His hairline was receding, so he was fitted with a hairpiece. He had small scars on his face, which had to be covered with heavier makeup than usual. Adding to his indignity, he had to wear a padded appliance under his trousers because it had been discovered that he had absolutely no behind. When a wag in wardrobe jokingly asked Frank if he'd also like an appliance to build up his "basket" in front, Frank exploded and had to be pulled off the man. About certain things, Sinatra had no sense of humor.

His first MGM picture was *Anchors Aweigh* (1945), in which he and Gene Kelly played two sailors on leave. Kathryn Grayson was a wanna-be singer with a little boy who wants more than anything to be a gob. The mammoth 140-minute length of the pedestrian film works against its trite charm and lightweight quality. Grayson was to work with Sinatra again, although she never cared for the man nor found him especially attractive (making their love scenes in 1948's *The Kissing Bandit* a chore for her). The film is chiefly remembered today for Kelly's cute and innovative dance with Jerry the cartoon mouse.

Sinatra was reteamed with Kelly in *Take Me Out to the Ballgame* (1949) and with Grayson in *It Happened in*

Brooklyn (1947). *Ballgame*'s director, Busby Berkeley, had his hands full getting Sinatra to obey his dictums, as Sinatra may have respected the man's talent but found him too epicene and flamboyant to take seriously; Kelly was a dancer, sure, but to Sinatra he was more of a man. Frank got along better with *Brooklyn*'s director, Richard Whorf, who had also been at the helm of *Till the Clouds Roll By* (1946), in which Sinatra sang a number as a "special guest star." Whorf recalled that "directing Frank is a revelation. He blends in more than you'd think with the other cast members. He once said to me, 'When everyone else is in top form, they improve my form.' He believed in teamwork."

Sinatra's final MGM film of the forties was *On the Town* (1949), the film adaptation of the Broadway musical scored by Leonard Bernstein. Gene Kelly was not only Sinatra's co-star this time, but the co-director (with Stanley Donen) of the movie. Since the film dealt with three sailors on leave in "New York, New York" (the film's most famous song), it was decided to do a lot of location filming, something MGM was not known for, in Manhattan. Because much of the film's length was simply taken up with exuberant dancing, Kelly would direct and choreograph all those city sequences where his expertise could come into play.

Kelly did not have an easy time of it working with Sinatra in *On the Town*. Sinatra was moody, childish, often late and irresponsible, fun and light-hearted one day and sullen and obstreperous the next. Gene noticed that Frank had a natural gracefulness (although this fact embarrassed Frank), but was not a trained dancer, so he choreographed movements for him that he would find easy to do and that would make it look as if he were working harder than he really was. Sinatra did not enjoy rehearsing, however, which made things difficult. He especially disliked rehearsing the non-dancing dialogue sections, figuring his acting would seem more spontaneous if he went into it totally fresh.

Despite all of this, *On the Town* became one of Sinatra's most acclaimed pictures, an honor it has never really deserved. Frankly, the picture is so silly and awful at times that it's hard to sit through; even at its liveliest it's more frenetic and desperate than genuinely amusing. In fact, it's really no better than the dozens of bad, sappy "gobs on leave" films that came after it (or ones like the aforementioned *Anchors Aweigh*, which predated it but was probably inspired by the Broadway show). Bernstein's score, written in his pre-*Candide* and *West Side Story* period, has always been one of his most forgettable—only "New York, New York" stands out. Of the cast Frank and Betty Garrett come off the best, with a nice bit of work from Alice Pearce.

Sinatra's contract allowed him to do an outside film once in a while, and one of these was *The Miracle of the Bells* (1948) for RKO, in which he played, of all things, a Catholic priest. This came about because of the further machinations of his publicist, George Evans, who, as usual, was worried about all the bad press Frank was getting. Some of the press had to do with Frank's palling around with mobsters; the rest was over his home life—or lack of same.

When Frank and Nancy had moved lock, stock, and barrel to California, Nancy's five married sisters went with them. Even though they each had their own homes, it was only natural that they come visit Nancy at her more palatial estate, if only to see the occasional famous person they might find in the living room. Now Frank not only had to contend with wife and kiddies, but a plethora of sisters- and brothers-in-law and their kids as well. It was a situation that he would not tolerate for long. Sinatra didn't need an excuse to see other women, but he undoubtedly justified his affairs with the old "my home isn't my own" excuse. He walked out on Nancy for the first time in 1946, but she refused to divorce him. He went back to her, only to walk out again and again in the hopes she would finally accept that, as far as he was concerned, the marriage was over. Nancy refused to let go even when Frank had his widely publicized affair with bombshell Ava Gardner (whom he eventually made his second wife).

So George Evans thought that all would be forgiven by the public, and his client's home-wrecking, mob-loving image somehow set right, if he played a man of the cloth in a major motion picture.

The Miracle of the Bells was an oddball movie concerning an actress (Alida Valli) who manages to finish the picture that will make her a star (*Joan of Arc*) after she's been diagnosed with an unspecified fatal illness. When Fred MacMurray learns that the studio has decided not to release the picture after her death, he accompanies her body to her hometown and cooks up a publicity stunt to revive interest in the movie: he has the bells of all the churches in the town ring continuously in an attempt to attract the press and the power they represent. At the end of the film some statues in a church move by themselves (or was this caused by a minor earthquake?), creating a bona fide "miracle" and thereby accomplishing MacMurray's task. *Joan of Arc* will be released and Valli will become, posthumously, a great star. The screenplay for this mess was co-written by Ben Hecht—on a bender, obviously.

As the priest whose church is the scene of the aforementioned miracle, Frank had only a small scene with MacMurray. Although one could argue that he is ludicrously miscast, he really isn't bad in the part. The role did nothing to make the public forget his Hollywood hell-raising, bad-boy image. The movie itself was earnest in intentions but all too superficial and forgettable.

Another late RKO release was *Double Dynamite* (1951), in which Frank was teamed with Groucho Marx and buxom Jane Russell. This grade-C comedy with forgettable song numbers featured Frank as a bank teller who wins big at the races just when the bank he works for notices a large cash shortage—and guess who they blame for it. During this picture Frank began a professional friendship with supporting player Don McGuire, who later wrote a screenplay for him and became a key member of the Varsity. The on-screen situation of Frank and Don vying for the attentions of Jane Russell basically repeated itself off-screen, but hard-as-a-diamond Russell could handle anything Sinatra threw at her and then some. Neither gentleman got to first base with her.

But *Double Dynamite* was a far cry from "A" productions like *On the Town* and *Anchors Aweigh*, whatever their relative quality. There was, sadly, no prestige anymore in co-starring with the likes of Groucho Marx. Frankie's records weren't selling as well as they used to and the girls weren't screaming as loud. Sinatra had weathered the World War II scandals, but it seemed even George Evans couldn't help him through this latest crisis. Frank was simply getting old (certainly by bobbysoxer standards), and time was catching up with him. He could not go on being a teen idol forever.

Even Evans couldn't protect him from what was coming—the darkest, most desperate period in Francis Albert Sinatra's life.

4

Downslide to Eternity

Frank's shenanigans with the ladies, particularly with the voluptuous Ava Gardner, kept his publicist hopping like crazy to keep unsavory stories out of the papers. Frank hated anyone interfering in his personal business, and he resented it when George Evans told him he ought to cool it with Ava. But the man who bore the brunt of Sinatra's terrible ire was actually Evans's West Coast associate, Jack Keller. After a particularly harrowing time covering up an incident when Frank and Ava descended upon a sleepy California desert town, got drunk, and started shooting out streetlights and such with some pistols Sinatra had in his car, Keller had to report to his partner that things were getting way out of control. Hearing Keller's sordid report of what had happened, George called up Frank and gave him hell.

Even though Keller had done a lot to save Frank's already seedy reputation, Sinatra felt no gratitude. Instead he blamed him for Evans's tirades and told Evans that it was either him or Keller. If George didn't fire Keller, Frank would fire George. Sinatra was Evans's biggest client—they were still friends—but he had no intention of firing another good friend and associate (who had done nothing wrong—in fact, he had done his job all too well) just to placate Sinatra. So after many years of being together, after all that Evans had done to make Frank Sinatra who he was, Evans reluctantly told Frank that he would have to hire another publicist. It was over. Some months later Evans, still acting the press agent, got into a lather when somebody attacked Frank's morals and the next morning suffered a fatal heart attack. Frank's number-one booster and buffer against the world was gone for good.

In the meantime Frank's records weren't getting anywhere on the *Downbeat* and *Billboard* polls, and his movies weren't doing so hot at the box office. Columnists theorized that his original fans had grown up and were too mature to holler and scream as they used to, and the teenage girls of the late forties had their own, younger idols; they didn't care about Frank Sinatra. There were even those who suggested that all Frank had ever been about was what today we'd call "hype." Shorn of his hysterical, gyrating bobbysoxer syco- phants, all the "excitement" of Frank Sinatra had seemed to dissipate. At this point there still weren't enough people who took him seriously as a vocalist.

All the bad press had worked against him, too—staying out of the service, partying with mobsters, being pho- tographed with Lana Turner and too many other women who weren't his wife. Now the Ava Gardner mess was the latest disaster. Frank's young fans may have desired him, but they still liked to think of him as the boy next door, unattainably married but wholesome just the same. But as Frank got older both his appearance and his behavior worked against it. The boy next door did not hang around—and Lord knew what else—with the likes of Ava Gardner.

Ava had already been married twice, to Mickey Rooney and Artie Shaw, when she met Frank Sinatra. At first she was not very interested in him, but her extreme dislike for his apparently rather sexy arrogance soon turned into wary intrigue and finally uninhibited lust. These were two people who lived on the edge, who took what they wanted and damn the consequences. Ava finally saw something in Frank that reminded her of herself, that told her this might be the one man who could match her if never tame her. Their affair was one of the most tempestuous in Hollywood history.

Ava was furious that Frank was taking forever to finally get rid of Nancy. Frank was enraged that Ava still received expensive gifts from so many male admirers and former lovers. He was particularly hung up on Howard Hughes. Frank had heard all the stories about Hughes's homosexual dalliances but didn't believe them, not while there were women like Ava and Jane Russell to testify to Hughes's heterosexual bedmanship. The truth—which had been known by the gay grapevine and anyone with access to it for years—was that Hughes was bisexual, perfectly adept at pleasing both men and women, but he was hardly likely to tell a satisfied Jane Russell or Ava that he'd had sex with a man the night before (especially not in an era when attitudes were unsophisticated and bisexuality was considered improbable if it was considered at all). In any case, Frank found Hughes a formidable rival and would blow up whenever Ava mentioned his name.

But Ava went far beyond speaking about Hughes. She bristled when the still-married Frank demanded that she see no other men, and retaliated against this dictum by dating every sexy Italian type—younger, handsomer—that she could find.

Frank tried to placate Ava by going public with their affair, which she knew would hasten his divorce. He had an engagement to open a new hotel and asked her to accompany him to Houston, where she sat in a front table during his show and went out with him every night afterward to the busiest, brightest restaurants in that part of Texas. The night after George Evans's funeral, which Frank had attended, they were spotted at Sorrento's, where they were dining with Jimmy Van Heusen and Houston's mayor. The story hit the papers and was picked up from coast to coast. When Nancy heard about it she threw everything of Frank's that she could find out on the front lawn of their house and ordered the locks changed immediately. This was one separation that would turn out to be permanent.

Nowadays the public is fascinated and a little bit thrilled by the peccadilloes of its stars, but in the 1940s and '50s there was a somewhat more straitlaced attitude among the press and public. Most of the country reacted the way Nancy did, with shock and outrage. Married men just didn't carry on with other women and flaunt it the way Frank did. They did not dine with their paramours in public restaurants with the mayor as if what they were doing was perfectly respectable. Sinatra began to lose the few fans he had left. He took such a drubbing from the papers over Ava that he began ribbing certain periodicals and columnists in his act, a habit he would continue for decades to come, culminating in the infamous incident when he told a nightclub crowd that "(gossip columnist) Maxine Cheshire is a cunt."

Sinatra's stormy on-again, off-again relationship with Ava Gardner was always exacerbated by the fact that their love affair was played out against the backdrop of Sinatra's inevitable downslide. Ava became a symbol to him, the perfect woman who would be his alone, even as his fans and friends deserted him, as he fell off the charts and out of the movies; he would know he was worthy because Ava would willingly belong to him and only him. With Ava at his side he knew he would be able to make it back to the top.

So it was not just the thought of losing Ava but his severe career travails that had him both threatening and attempting suicide several times over the next few months. And his career was truly in the doldrums.

Perhaps the biggest blow came in April 1950 when Frank was told—with extreme delicacy by an agent—that MGM had decided to terminate his contract even though he'd worked for the studio only four of the five years originally stipulated. If his days as a teen idol were over, Frank had figured he always had the movie career as backup; it would earn him a whole new set of fans. Now it looked as if he were washed up in pictures, too. MGM agreed to compensate him with $85,000.

Sinatra tried to put a brave face on it, saying that he was glad he now had the freedom to accept all the other offers that had come in over the past few months, only there were hardly any offers. Frank had made too many enemies; the public disliked him, and those who booked talent on TV and radio shows were well aware of this. What's worse, his own agents at MCA thought he was a stinker—they were tired of his nasty remarks and hostile attitude—and didn't spend a lot of time trying to dig up assignments for him. Frank had nobody else to blame, although he blamed everyone else in sight.

Meanwhile, his wife was trying to put a freeze on what little income he had, and Ava was having a well-publicized fling with a bullfighter while making a picture overseas, pushing Frank into fits of rage and torment. He found little solace in his work. His record company eventually dropped him and so did MCA, leaving him out at sea, treading water, counting on his nightclub contacts to get him guest spots. Attempts at TV and radio shows were dismal failures, cancelled after only a few weeks. It was about this time that Sammy Davis Jr., who was on top of the entertainment world, saw him walking down Broadway without a soul stopping him for an autograph or even recognizing him. People Frank had treated badly over the years—and there were many—took no pity on him. The tide had turned, and he was only getting what he deserved. He had never been, they felt, that great to begin with.

Eventually all of this negation had a serious psychological and physical effect on Sinatra. He had somehow managed via old connections to get booked into the Copa, where everyone hoped his few remaining loyal fans would show up. But when he opened his mouth to sing at one point, nothing came out of it. His vocal cords had been affected by a condition known as hysterical aphonia. Desperately trying to produce sound after he fled in horror to his dressing room, Sinatra worsened the situation by developing a submucosal hemorrhage. He would not be able to sing for at least two weeks, and with the aphonia, there was no guarantee he would ever be able to sing again at all. In the meantime, Nancy's lawyers were making demands, and Ava, busy with her toreador like a latter-day Carmen to Frank's Don Jose, wasn't returning his phone calls.

Frank had already staged a suicide attempt some months before. He had called Ava and, while she was listening on the other end, fired a gun into a pillow, dropping a heavy box on the floor to make it sound like his body had fallen. She was attending a party hosted by her ex-husband Artie Shaw, and Frank was throwing a childish temper tantrum out of jealousy. Hearing the gunshots, Ava fled the party and rushed to the Hampshire House Hotel where he had a suite, only to find him alive and well and denying all.

Now all of the career pressures, combined with the thought that he had lost Ava too, caused him to take an overdose of sleeping pills at a lodge in Lake Tahoe after a bitter fight with Gardner at a restaurant. Ava had sworn that she was through with him and rushed off. He went to his cabin and decided it would be better to end it all. Without his singing, without Ava, nothing seemed to matter. Luckily his valet found him in time, noticed that he didn't seem to be sleeping off a simple drunk, and called a doctor. Sinatra was induced to vomit and then had his stomach pumped to remove all the poison. By the time reporters got wind of the incident, Frank was back with Ava and once again denying everything. He told everyone he'd had a bad case of food poisoning and nothing more.

Recognizing that he would lose Ava for good unless he married her, he finally got a divorce from Nancy in Nevada. But Nancy's lawyers phoned his lawyers and vowed that she would not agree to the divorce unless certain financial arrangements were made and back alimony immediately paid. Nancy got her own divorce in Santa Monica, charging Frank with flagrant acts of "mental cruelty." Her settlement was massive, leaving Frank effectively broke and dependent on Ava, a position that was difficult for the overly proud man to swallow.

Still, if he had to depend on Ava for his drinking and gambling money it would be better to be married to her. But even when they went out to dinner and a nightclub the night before the wedding, Frank couldn't resist chatting up a pretty blonde at the next table. James Mason, who'd starred with Ava in *Pandora and the Flying Dutchman* (1951), had been invited to dine with the "happy" couple that night, along with his wife Pamela. Years later Mason wryly recalled the evening.

"It was like a three ring circus. We started out with Frank and Ava like two lovebirds, the four of us happily chatting—or rather Pamela and I watching Ava and Frank make googly eyes at one another—and then all was chaos. At the club I went to a nearby table to say hello to someone, and when I got back Ava and my wife were in deep conversation, Pamela trying to calm Ava down while Frank—who was oblivious to them—talked to this lovely woman at the next table. I thought she was someone he knew, but apparently Ava was livid that he had dared to flirt with this pretty girl on the very night before their wedding. Pamela was trying to convince Ava not to take it so seriously. Men are men, and all that.

"The next thing I knew Ava was shrieking at Frank, hitting him, throwing ashtrays or something at him, and he was shouting right back at her. She took off her engagement ring and said, 'Let's call the whole thing off!' and threw the ring across the room. By now everyone in the place was watching. Pamela and I didn't know where to look, so we just looked at this—accident—going on in front of our eyes. Then Ava threw a drink at Frank—he threw his drink at her—and then both of them tore out of the nightclub and left the two of us sitting there amid the ruins. Pamela just looked at me and said, 'I hope we're never dining with those two again.'"

Incredibly, Ava and Frank got back together again, although it took a lot of doing on the part of their friends. James Mason was one of those who counseled Ava. "I told her that Frank had spent so many years being the object of adoration from women that it was difficult for him to just turn it off, to turn off that need to respond to this adoration—because he knew that women were responsible for his success. That might not excuse his flirtation, but it explained it a bit. I told Ava that as an international sex symbol there would be times when her fans—mostly men, mind you—would stare and start to talk to her in a restaurant and if she didn't want Frank hysterical she would have to see his side of it." Then Mason laughed and added, "Frankly, I was winging it. I wasn't so certain she ought to marry Frank in the first place. I guess I was right."

So the two were married on November 7, 1951 in Philadelphia. Right from the start there was trouble, primarily caused by the fact that Ava's career was now flourishing while Frank's was in a dangerous state of stagnation. She was making movies like the highly touted second film adaptation of *Show Boat* while he was stuck in stuff like *Meet Danny*

Wilson, a picture he did for Universal just before his marriage to Ava.

It was considered at the time that Sinatra had somehow "lucked out" by winning the leading role in *Meet Danny Wilson*, but it was luck that he created for himself. Actor-friend Don McGuire, who'd been in *Double Dynamite* with Frank, wanted to move to the other side of the camera and to that end had put together a screen treatment about a singing star. He and Frank would sit around and dream up incidents for the picture, many of them taken from his own life story, which the screenplay greatly resembled as it developed. There were those who thought Sinatra still had some name value, and a thinly disguised biopic about him, his famous temper, jealousy, and mobster ties, might have some prurient interest. Taking the whole package to Universal—Sinatra as star, McGuire as writer—McGuire was able to get a deal.

Hollywood wondered why Sinatra would want to play in a film that seemed to expose and almost parody him, but no one knew how big a hand Frank had had in the screenplay. If using his own life got him back into the movies, made him a great star again, what did he care? He was desperate. As *Time* magazine put it, "The story cribs so freely from the career and personality of Frank Sinatra that fans may expect Ava Gardner to pop up in the last reel."

In the film, the Danny Wilson character (Sinatra, of course) is a totally self-absorbed singer who skyrockets to fame but so neglects wife Shelley Winters that he doesn't even realize she's fallen for his best friend and manager (Alex Nicol). Sinatra isn't bad, but Raymond Burr comes off best as a mobster who owns Wilson's contract and has a financial stranglehold over him. The movie is entertaining but much too superficial, as if Frank was willing to expose himself but only so far. All of the film's conflicts are resolved much too neatly.

Everyone had a terrible time making the picture. Frank's troubles were so overwhelming that he could barely concentrate and snapped at anyone who interrupted his brooding. Advisors, including Catholic priests, would visit him daily on the set, bringing production completely to a halt. One day he and co-star Shelley Winters had such a monumental quarrel that Winters hauled off and slugged him. (To be fair to Sinatra, Winters is known to bring out the worst in her co-stars.) Universal executives had to talk Winters into returning to the set and blamed Frank's love for Ava Gardner and concern over his deteriorating voice for his temperament. They asked her to show compassion.

Winters returned to the set, but in their first scene together Sinatra deliberately changed some dialogue so that it would be insulting to Shelley. Once again, Shelley walked off the set. She only returned when Nancy Sinatra, of all people, begged her to go back to work so that she and the children could seize the money that Frank was to be paid when the picture was in the can. For that reason, Winters was happy to finish *Meet Danny Wilson* with "that bastard, Sinatra!"

Knowing how badly her husband needed to be on top again, and how much it would help his self-esteem and hence their marriage, Ava went to Joan Cohn, the wife of Columbia Pictures head Harry Cohn, and begged her to do what she could to get Harry to cast Frank in the upcoming major production of *From Here to Eternity*, based on James Jones's bestseller. Frank now had representation at the William Morris Agency and also begged his agents there to do whatever it took to get him the part of Angelo Maggio, the scrappy little guy who gets beaten to death. Everyone thought the odds were against Frank; the front runner for the role was Eli Wallach, who had stage training and whose screen test for the part impressed everyone who saw it. The only problem with

Wallach, as Joan Cohn saw it, was that "he's not skinny, he's not pathetic, and he's not Italian;" i.e., he had too muscular a physique to be the scrawny Maggio. Nevertheless, everyone felt Wallach would give the finest performance of all those tested and the part was offered to him. Sinatra was out.

But to everyone's—especially Harry Cohn's—amazement, Wallach turned the role down. He had been offered the lead in Tennessee Williams's new play *Camino Real* and knew it was too good an opportunity for a serious actor to turn down. He had already made a commitment to the piece in any case. Cohn couldn't understand how Wallach could make this choice, because as far as he was concerned every actor had only one thing on his mind: being in the movies. As far as Wallach was concerned, a role in a new play by America's premiere playwright was of much more importance.

Besides Sinatra, there was only one other serious contender for the role, Harvey Lembeck, who was considered to be too "funny" and was passed over in favor of Sinatra. Lembeck went on to play Erich Von Zipper in a dozen "Beach Party" movies while Sinatra got the plum role and an Academy Award. For years afterward the rumor would fly that Sinatra had exercised mob pressure on Cohn and others connected to the picture to get him the part, but this unsubstantiated charge has been denied by everyone involved in the production who would be in a position to know.

Sinatra was coached on the role by co-star Montgomery Clift, who took him through each line and movement until a real performance began to emerge and Sinatra's own personality was somewhat subdued. Sinatra returned the favor by helping out Clift whenever the actor—who was alcoholic and addicted to drugs at this point in his life—collapsed on the set and had to be taken to his trailer and sobered up. For the most part, Sinatra behaved himself during filming, obeying director Fred Zinnemann's dictates, but they had a terrific disagreement about how to do a particular scene on the last day of shooting, and Harry Cohn himself had to drive to the set to restore order.

As *From Here to Eternity* did so much for Sinatra's career, it is worth reevaluating the film today. The story takes place primarily at Schofield Barracks in Hawaii in 1941. Robert E. Lee Pruitt (Clift), a bugler, has been transferred to the outfit but earns the enmity of the men by his refusal to box (he inadvertently blinded his last opponent, so he has hung up his gloves), denying them a coveted championship. His friend and fellow soldier Maggio (Sinatra) himself earns the enmity of Sergeant "Fatso" Judson (Ernest Borgnine), who dislikes the fellow's manner and can hardly wait to get him in the stockade, where Judson is boss. Pruitt falls for a woman (Donna Reed) who works at a nearby "social club" while Sergeant Warden (Burt Lancaster) has an affair with the neglected wife (Deborah Kerr) of his captain. When Maggio later dies of injuries sustained at the hands of Fatso, Pruitt hunts the latter man down and kills him in a knife fight, later going AWOL. After the Japanese attack Pearl Harbor, Pruitt is found dead. A philosophical Warden oversees the removal of his body.

What once seemed a masterpiece now seems contrived, a bit dull, and strangely unmoving. The whole business with Pruitt refusing to box and the rough treatment he receives from the other men because of it is rather trivial, and overshadows the two love stories in the first half of the film. (In fact, the love stories and the Army story never really jell.) To begin with, the entire situation is never believable. While there are certainly conflicts among enlisted men at times, soldiers also tend to pull together, and it doesn't make sense that not one of the other men would see Pruitt's side of it, understand the guilt he felt over blinding someone with his fists, and cut him some slack. The way the captain willfully allows Pruitt's mistreatment is also unrealistic, making the picture less a "typical" depiction of Army life and more of a "what if?" story, where renegade officers and soldiers-on-the-fringe are the rule rather than the exception. The screenplay tries to emphasize how atypical these soldiers are at the end when the captain is reprimanded for his actions, but by then it's too little, too late. Another suspect development has the MPs failing to find the AWOL Pruitt when all they had to do was go to his girlfriend's apartment.

Another problem is that all of the characters are distinctly unpleasant people; there's no one to root for or sympathize with, not even Sinatra's Maggio, who brings all of his troubles upon himself (as the actor playing him did off-screen). Transforming what was supposed to be a whorehouse into a "social club" was a ludicrous sop to the production code, but the inappropriate moments of humor during the climactic air raid are even worse. More melodrama than incisive, meaningful drama, *From Here to Eternity* manages to trivialize one of the worst events in American history.

There is some good dialogue scattered throughout the picture, however ("Nobody ever lies about being lonely," Clift says to Donna Reed), and the fight scene between Clift and one of the soldiers who wants him to join the boxing team is very well orchestrated. On the technical side, Fred Zinnemann's direction is first-rate, as is the editing and photography by Burnett Guffey. Zinnemann, Guffey, and screenwriter Daniel Taradash all won Oscars, as did the movie itself.

Sinatra won a Best Supporting Oscar (as did Reed), which was given more out of admiration for his pluck and sympathy for the near-has-been status Hollywood had accorded him than for his acting. (Screenwriter Taradash once said of Frank's screen test, "It was good—better than expected—but it had none of the consummate acting ability of Eli Wallach.") His performance is good, but not quite worthy of an Academy Award. Coached by Clift, he gives very good line readings, and he does manage to register a certain vulnerability (similar to, if not as goofy as, the vulnerability he and Phil Silvers exploited to win over the soldiers on the USO tour). He is very good in a drunk scene at a hotel with Clift and Reed, demanding whiskey, banging on the bar (as he probably often did in real life). Just before his death scene, however, when he escapes from the stockade and encounters Clift, he's a bit too self-conscious as he has that dramatic conversation with his buddy. Working so hard with Frank must have rubbed off on Clift, because when he does a drunk scene he seems to be imitating Sinatra.

Frank's coworkers seemed to think a lot of Frank and his performance. Fred Zinnemann said in 1955 that "Frank was wonderful to direct. He knew the part of Maggio was important to him, and he really got into it, under the skin of it— that's what made it come so alive. He deserved his Oscar." Burt Lancaster opined, "Frank has a humility you wouldn't suspect. Once he asked me if I thought he hit the right note in a scene; he seemed genuinely concerned that he get it right. I told him no one could have done it better. He beamed at me like a happy kid who's just won the spelling bee."

Donna Reed said that Frank "was very affecting in his lighter scenes, like when he's kidding with Monty and me in the bar. There was a kind of wistful-puppy quality to him in scenes like that." According to Ernest Borgnine, "I wasn't playing a very nice guy in *Eternity*, but Frank always had a smile for me when the shot was over. 'Now you can go back to being the nice guy you are,' he'd say."

From Here to Eternity was hugely popular in its day and made over eighty million dollars, and it started Frank back on the road to the top. But it would be a road strewn with difficulties and heartbreak. His relationship with Ava Gardner, his new bride, would not go smoothly.

One evening his friend Jimmy Van Heusen and neighbor Irving "Swifty" Lazar took Frank along with them when they went to a certain house in the Holmby Hills. There was a weekly party there, a gathering, and the other guests were all dying to meet "Maggio."

So Frank found himself attending a meeting of Bogie's Rat Pack, where Lauren Bacall was waiting for him.

5

The Holmby Hills Rat Pack

Sinatra had, of course, already run into Humphrey Bogart and Lauren Bacall casually at the studio and at Romanoff's, the restaurant owned by "Russian Prince" Mike Romanoff, before being invited to one of their famous soirees. But this evening was the first chance the three had to really get to know one another. Frank had always idolized Bogie, who seemed—on-screen, at least—like the kind of tough guy Sinatra had always tried to be. (Actually, Bogie's image and background were as fabricated as Frank's.) For Lauren, Frank felt another kind of idolatry. As Bacall put it in her autobiography, "There must have always been a special feeling alive between Frank and me from the earlier days." What Bacall didn't put into her memoirs was the fact that the romance between her and Sinatra began long before Bogart's death in 1957.

But now it was 1953, and Frank was slowly making his climb back to the top. He was preoccupied with thoughts of Ava Gardner and his disintegrating marriage to her. Shortly she and Bogart would begin filming *The Barefoot Contessa*, in which Bogie played a director who turns Spanish dancer

Gardner into a movie star. Everyone knew that Ava's volatile marriage to Frank would implode at any moment, but Lauren was waiting in the wings. She loved her husband, but he was middle-aged, homely, and complacent. Frank represented danger, romance, and excitement to Bacall. According to one friend at the time, "Lauren pursued Frank with a vengeance. She tried to help him patch things up with Ava whenever they had one of their innumerable quarrels, but she was always hoping that this time they wouldn't make up and she'd have Frank for herself. She was perfectly willing to stay married to her main man Bogie and have Frank on the side." Frank and Lauren grew especially close while their respective mates were off shooting *Barefoot Contessa*.

In the meantime, Frank found welcome companionship with the Holmby Hills Rat Pack. According to Bacall, in order to be a member, "One had to be addicted to nonconformity, staying up late, drinking, laughing, and not caring what anyone thought or said about us." Sinatra was the "packmaster"; Sid Luft was the "cage master." His wife, Judy Garland, was the "first vice president," and Swifty Lazar the "recording secretary." Lauren Bacall served as the "den mother" and Bogart was in charge of public relations. Nathaniel Benchley, the group's "historian," sketched out an insignia for the group which consisted of dozens of rats of different sizes going in every which direction. Members without titles included, as mentioned previously, Jimmy Van Heusen, David Niven and his wife Hjordis, Mike and Gloria Romanoff, and "honorary rats" such as Spencer Tracy. Mike Romanoff had everyone to the private dining room at his restaurant so they could elect these officials and draw up a charter.

Although they were never official "rats," Bogie was also good friends with writer Louis Bromfield and his secretary George Hawkins, actor Clifton Webb and his mother (and permanent date) Maybelle, and even flagrantly homosexual Noel Coward. (Somehow one could not imagine Frank

Sinatra admitting some of these people into *his* Rat Pack.) Others who came to the Holmby Hills gatherings were John Huston, John O'Hara, Adlai Stevenson, singer/writer Kay Thompson, and the cartoonist Charles Addams (of "Addams Family" fame).

Van Heusen, who was Frank's best friend and the one who got him out of nearly as many jams as his publicist George Evans had, was actually born Edward Chester Babcock. According to Shirley MacLaine, Chester was "a pilot and a daredevil, bald, rather rotund" and "the man Frank secretly wanted to be." As Frank had always had a fear of heights, one assumes Shirley was referring to Frank's envy of Van Heusen's daredevil abilities and not his rotund appearance. It was just as likely that Van Heusen was envious of Frank's way with women and voluptuous wife, Ava.

Babcock was born in Syracuse in 1913 and was two years older than best buddy Frank. He signed up with Paramount Pictures in 1940, where he composed many scores and songs for their musicals, first with lyricist Johnny Burke, then Sammy Cahn. During the war he was a test pilot for Lockheed Aircraft, something that acrophobic Sinatra could hardly have conceived of. Many of Van Heusen's songs became standards, including several composed for Frank Sinatra movies, such as "All the Way" in *The Joker is Wild* and "High Hopes" in *A Hole in the Head*. Other famous numbers include "Swinging on a Star" from *Going My Way* and "Call Me Irresponsible" from *Papa's Delicate Condition*. He also did full scores (often including songs) for a number of Sinatra starrers, such as *Young at Heart* (1954), *The Tender Trap* (1955), and *Robin and the 7 Hoods* (1964). In fact, Van Heusen's association with Sinatra was very good for the former's career indeed.

Judy Garland, the group's "vice president," had been born Frances Gumm in 1922. After earning an MGM contract at age thirteen, she stole scenes with her singing in a number of films before emerging a star in her own right in *The Wizard of Oz* (1939). First taking pills to combat a serious weight problem, Judy later relied on drugs for sleeping, waking up, and just to get through the day. By 1951 she had married and divorced two husbands, bandleader David Rose and director Vincente Minnelli, father of Liza. Tired of her mercurial behavior caused by depression, pill popping, and a private life in a state of upheaval, MGM fired Judy in 1950.

At the time she became a member of Bogie's Rat Pack, Judy, like Frank, was fighting her way back to the top with the help of her third husband, Sid Luft, who became her manager. He orchestrated her comeback with history-making engagements at the London Palladium and the Palace Theater in New York. In 1953, she was preparing for the film that would make her (briefly) a Hollywood player again, *A Star Is Born*. During her Holmby Hills days she was often preoccupied and thoroughly self-absorbed with her own problems and her need to reestablish herself.

James David Graham Niven had come into the world in Kirriemuir, Scotland in 1909. He went to military school, joined the Highland Light Infantry, and bummed around the world doing an assortment of odd jobs from lumberman to bartender before winding up in Hollywood at the age of twenty-five. He appeared in a variety of features, moving ever upward until he was cast as Edgar in William Wyler's production of *Wuthering Heights* (1939). There followed a variety of starring roles trading on his urbane manner and polished wit, which he employed to great effect in both comedic and light dramatic parts. During World War II he did not avoid service as Sinatra did, but rather became a lieutenant with the commandos of the British Army, one of the first Hollywood stars to wholeheartedly embrace the Allied war effort. At the time Sinatra joined Bogie's Rat Pack, Niven was just finishing up a series of featherweight romantic pictures, the latest of which, Otto Preminger's *The Moon Is Blue* was steeped—incredibly—in controversy because of sexual innuendos that would be less than mild by 1998 standards.

According to David Niven, it was Betty Bacall who gave the Rat Pack its name. Jack Entratter, who owned the Sands hotel in Las Vegas (Sinatra also owned an interest and always played there), threw a party at Romanoff's in honor of Noel Coward's appearance at the hotel. At each table there was to be a little white rat as a kind of outre party decoration, but the rats escaped from their cage and fled the upstairs banquet room to run amuck among the regular diners downstairs. The origin of the term Rat Pack came later that evening, when most of the members went out on the town and came back to Bogie's place after hours of drinking and carousing. Lauren took one look at them and said, "You look like a pack of rats." The name stuck and the Rat Pack was born.

Bogie's—and later Frank's—Rat Pack grew so legendary that many other people later claimed to be members of it. Most of these simply attended a few "meetings"—a.k.a. parties—at Betty and Bogie's but were not regulars. These included Dean Martin and his wife Jeanne, who claimed that the Bogarts were among their first friends and biggest supporters when she and Dino first moved to Hollywood. Still, while Dino became a bona fide member of the second Rat Pack, he was not in the Holmby Hills group, although surely he was at the Bogart home on more than one occasion. The same was true of Tony Curtis, who'd had a cameo in *Meet Danny Wilson* with Frank, and his then-wife, future *Psycho* victim, Janet Leigh. Sammy Davis Jr. was another sometime member of the group, although many years later he would try to inflate his relationship with Bogart practically to best-friend-and-devoted-buddy proportions.

Star-struck Sammy first met Bogart when he and his father and uncle—known professionally as the Will Mastin Trio—opened at the trendy Slapsy Maxie's club in Los

Angeles. His good friend Frank Sinatra arranged for several of the major stars in Hollywood (Spencer Tracy, Douglas Fairbanks Jr., Judy Garland) to be in the audience. Bogart and Betty came backstage with Frank, where Bogie told Sinatra that he must bring Sammy "up to the house sometime." That led to Sammy becoming, in his words, "a fringe member of the elite centered on the Bogart household." As Bogart got to know and like Sammy better, he, like Sinatra, would call up important people and make sure they attended the Trio's performances.

Like Sinatra, Sammy idolized Bogie, but found he could be blunt, particularly when he would offer unsolicited but generally constructive criticism of his act. One night, backstage at Ciro's after the Trio had performed, Bogart was rather merciless with the two older men—father and Uncle Will—working with Sammy. "The show was great," he told Will Mastin, "but you're too damned old for the business. Why don't you retire? The kid's the whole show!" When Bogart, who undoubtedly had to be drinking heavily to be so unforgivably tactless, saw the shocked, hurt look on Mastin's face he apologized, but told Mastin that he had to face reality, that he and Sammy's father were doing less and less with each show and "the nostalgia's wearing a little thin, y'know." He suggested that a real showman would know when it was time to retire.

Sammy felt a little intimidated by all the high-powered talent, the movers and shakers at the house in Holmby Hills—he was not yet a major star—but he got into the groove by doing what he did best—entertaining. There was a lot of impromptu singing and dancing at the Holmby Hills gatherings: Sinatra and Noel Coward doing numbers together; Judy singing her heart out through her boozy tears; Bacall reprising a song from *To Have or Have Not* without benefit of Andy Williams. It was a heady time for all of them.

Besides entertaining one another with songs, jokes, and snappy stories, the Rat Packers did a great deal of drinking. Betty Bacall rarely indulged in this, but when she did, Bogie didn't like it. After a live telecast of *The Petrified Forest* that Bogie and Betty did with Henry Fonda (in the Leslie Howard role), Betty got so drunk at the celebration at Holmby Hills afterward that Bogart found her curled up on the rug with Fonda. Whether he was annoyed at her inebriated state—or the position he found her in with an equally intoxicated Fonda—is another story. At other times people would get so drunk they'd have to be left behind to sleep it off when the group went off for their usual dinner at Romanoff's, which is what happened one night to Sid Luft, comfortably curled up on an empty bookshelf where he was found the next morning.

The Rat Pack members all thought they were being unconventional and glamorously out of control, "thumbing their noses at Hollywood," as Bacall put it, but they were also being monumentally silly. (And rather vapid: "We were all terribly young and terribly witty and terribly rich," said fringe member Kay Thompson.) And not everyone in Hollywood was enamored of their antics. For one thing, most of the Rat Packers were card-carrying liberals; Hollywood conservatives such as John Wayne and William Holden were appalled.

Holden had worked with David Niven on *The Moon Is Blue*, but he had no great interest in partying with the man or his friends. Publicly he stated, "It is possible to have social intercourse and drink and do anything without resorting to a rat pack. People have worked for years to lend some dignity to our profession, and the rat pack reflects [negatively] on the community and on my children and on their children and everybody's children." Privately, Holden once said of the group, "I haven't been invited to their gatherings and I never will be, and wouldn't go if I were asked. The Rat Packers are only interested in being with people who think exactly as they do. You have to believe in the same things, support the same political candidates, have the exact same politics. If that's being a 'liberal,' you can keep it."

Meanwhile, Frank Sinatra was busy trying to keep his marriage to Ava Gardner afloat. They went on a second honeymoon combined with a European singing tour for Frank, but on both levels the trip was a disaster. Sinatra was slowly making his way back to the top in the United States, but in Europe nobody cared about him. Wherever he went, he played to half- and quarter-filled houses. Short running times and overpriced tickets didn't help matters. Frank canceled the tour and took out his anger on Ava, who wasted no time telling Frank what she thought of him. She told him the whole marriage had been a mistake. Their quarrels became so operatic in quality, quantity, and volume that soon the "Battling Sinatras" had replaced the "Battling Bogarts" (Bogart and former wife Mayo) in legend as Hollywood's noisiest and least fun couple. Not only did each of their careers conflict with the quality time they could spend with one another, but they both discovered that a serious marriage was hard work, something neither of them had realized beforehand or been prepared for. Neither Frank nor Ava were really ready for a serious commitment to another human being. Both wanted to party too much: Ava with her bullfighters and wiry Italians; Frank with the Rat Pack and Betty Bacall.

While making *The Barefoot Contessa* with her, Bogart asked Ava why she fiddled with men "in tights and capes and slippers" when she was married to a man so many women would have loved to be with. Ava couldn't help but note the irony of a man who lisped calling into question the manhood of her brave and handsome bullfighter lover (Luis Miguel Dominguin, by name), but she only told Bogart to mind his own business. She had found her husband a lot sweeter when he was down and out, but now that things were turning in his favor again, he was the same arrogant SOB that she had despised back at MGM.

The jealousy between Ava and Frank was so all-consuming that there was no way their union could last. Ava was the first to pull out; she had MGM publicists issue a statement that she and Frank were separating for good while she sought a divorce. Frank had opportunities to meet with her and try to talk her out of this decision, but always at the last minute his pride wouldn't let him go. How dare a woman decide to leave him, Frank Sinatra! Who the hell did Ava think she was? But deep down he was devastated at the thought of losing her. As Lauren Bacall put it, "I do believe it was the first and only time that someone else had done the leaving."

Ava tried to get back to her old life without Frank, which included seeing old friends. During her marriage to Frank, at least when they were both in the same city, she had never seen anyone without Frank being in tow, and she would never have considered dining alone even innocently with a male friend for fear Frank would find out and put the wrong construction on it. (Perversely, Ava was less careful when she was really sleeping with the male in question.) Now that she was about to get rid of Frank for good, she didn't care who she had dinner with or where.

One afternoon she had lunch with her business manager at a popular Los Angeles eatery named Frascati's. Also having lunch there were Peter Lawford and his friend and associate Milt Ebbins. Peter, who had known and briefly dated Ava many years before—the two had remained friends—took Milt with him to Ava's table to say hello. As Ava couldn't interrupt her business lunch for long, she suggested that she, Milt, and Peter all have drinks later that day at The Luau restaurant where she was meeting her sister, Bea.

Peter had misgivings—what would Frank think?—but he agreed to go. The four of them had one or two drinks a piece and spent less than one hour together. Peter and Ava were never alone for one minute.

Nevertheless, spies of Louella Parsons, the famed gossip columnist, told her of what they'd seen, and she ran a trumped-up story about Ava Gardner's "date" with Peter Lawford: "Are Things Heating Up Again for Ava and Peter?" she asked.

Early in the morning Peter got a hysterical phone call from an inebriated Frank Sinatra, who threatened to break his legs and cut off his private parts either personally or via some goon friends of his if Peter didn't "lay off" Ava. "I was never so scared in my life," Peter said some years later. "I think Frank really meant it. He didn't let me get a word in edgewise. I had no chance to explain that it wasn't a date or that Ava and I were with Milt and Bea and it was all very innocent. He knew Ava and I were friends, but he just wouldn't listen. He was hysterical, a rabid dog. Very frightening. I was genuinely terrified that he'd get one of his friends to kill me."

When Peter told Milt Ebbins what had happened, Ebbins called Jimmy Van Heusen, who was rapidly losing patience with his best buddy. He suggested Milt call Sinatra himself. When Ebbins got through to Frank he explained what had really happened, and it seemed as though Sinatra believed him. But it didn't do any good. Frank said not one word to Peter Lawford for the next five years.

Little did Peter realize at the time that he was just as well off, because Frank was making it difficult for the people he *was* talking to. He was absolutely uncontrollable when it came to Ava, drinking too much, alternately raging and crying, and even attempting suicide again. Jimmy Van Heusen kept an apartment in Manhattan and was stunned one

evening when he came home and found Frank on the floor
of the building elevator with blood dripping out of his
slashed wrists. Van Heusen paid off the doormen and such
and rushed Frank to Mt. Sinai. The chunky Van Heusen had
been a nonjudgmental friend of Frank's (Frank had given
him many opportunities, for one thing), but he was convinced that all the stress and strain over Frank and his love
troubles with Ava would give him, Jimmy, a stroke or a
heart attack. He told Frank that he never wanted to see him
again unless he swore to get psychiatric counseling. Frank
agreed and made an appointment—perhaps unfortunately—
with the same shrink who was seeing the even screwier
Marilyn Monroe.

If his heartbreak over Ava did nothing else, it added a
new dimension to Frank's singing, particularly when it came
to ballads of love and loss. He was recording for newcomer
Capitol now (no other record company would have him)
where Nelson Riddle's arrangements did a lot to establish a
new Sinatra style and bring him back to the stratosphere
again. By 1954 *Billboard* was once more naming him top
male vocalist. But just as his downsliding career pressures
had affected his voice in the late forties, his upset over Ava
would have a similar effect in the fifties. And, as usual, Frank
would blame everyone but himself.

Nothing Frank did would get Ava back. On one occasion
he flew to Spain to see her; they billed and cooed over dinner, but the reconciliation lasted exactly one day before they
were back to throwing things and screeching at one another.
On another occasion Frank learned that Lauren Bacall was
flying to Rome to see Bogie, filming *The Barefoot Contessa*
with Ava, and importuned her to carry a fancy coconut cake
to Ava as a peace offering. Although she could not have cared
less if Ava and Frank got back together, Lauren did her duty
and made sure the cake arrived at Ava's flat in one piece,

where it sat in its box, unopened, as Ava gave her a highly unenthusiastic thank you. Ava wanted nothing to do with Frank, and that included his cake.

Ava officially filed for divorce from Frank in 1954. The female members of the Holmby Hills Rat Pack were having romantic fantasies about the soon-to-be-single Sinatra, who was so disgusted over what had happened with Ava that he now saw women as something to have sex with and little else. Lauren was certainly available, but there was Bogart to be considered. And Judy Garland began sniffing around him again.

Judy's relationship with third husband Sid Luft was problematic at best, and the two were always separating on and off until the time of their divorce and the bitter custody battle it engendered. Judy had had a relationship with Frank right after she divorced Vincente Minnelli and before she married Sid, but it ended the night she invited him for dinner, cooked the meal and set the table, and sat there the entire evening getting drunk and crying as he stood her up. Frank did not want to become the third Mr. Judy Garland. Now things were falling apart between her and Sid, and Ava had left Frank for good . . . did she have a chance now? Was the timing right? Clearly it wasn't, because the success of *A Star Is Born* and the birth of her son Joey temporarily cemented her relationship with husband Sid. By the time Frank was on her mind again, his mind was very much elsewhere. Judy was too neurotic for Frank, even though he himself could hardly be called emotionally stable during this period.

Bogart was blunt with Judy and wouldn't put up with her whining about how talented yet unappreciated she was for long. It was Bogie who told her that her talent was useless if she didn't employ it to her benefit, who told her to get off her duff and make things happen. When Judy whined to Frank,

Frank would just turn off. He had no patience for her. Sadly, the only men who did were those who were out to use her. Years later Sinatra would completely cut Garland out of his life when she dared to perform at a Las Vegas hotel other than the Sands.

As for the male members of the Rat Pack, they all got along with Frank even if they found him a pain in the neck at times. Van Heusen found it easier now that his pal was pouring out his problems to a shrink instead of to him, and their neighbor, the diminutive, bullet-headed Swifty Lazar, was becoming the butt of Frank's often elaborate practical jokes. One day Frank hired someone to plaster up Lazar's clothes closet and on another occasion had Lazar's favorite hat added to a recipe for shirred eggs and served to him for breakfast.

Bogie himself was always amused by Sinatra, who he saw as a weird "kind of Don Quixote," always getting into unnecessary fights with people who really didn't want to fight him and had nothing whatsoever against him. Bogart was also amused because Frank was so physically ill-suited to be a constant scrapper. The way Sinatra almost deliberately took things people said the wrong way and took umbrage at everything made him feel (correctly) that Sinatra was emotionally stunted, still an angry young boy at heart instead of a full-grown man. Bogart was never fooled as to why Frank came so often to his Holmby Hills house; he knew it wasn't to see him, even if Frank was genuinely fond of Bogart. Bogart knew that Frank was attracted to Lauren, and he may well have suspected how much the feeling was mutual, even if he chose to ignore it most of the time. Friends reported that occasionally Bogart would make angry allusions to the attraction when he was inebriated.

Some years after his death Frank was to say of Bogie, "He was an original—no one like him, ever. They broke the mold when they made Bogie. He was taken from us much too soon. We (the second Rat Pack) ganged up, I felt, sort of to keep Bogie, his spirit, alive, to give us the feeling he was still there for us."

Particularly now that Ava was out of his life, Frank spent more and more time with the original Rat Pack and practically turned the Bogart domicile into his home away from home. If the Bogarts were receiving (to a privileged few) they would leave a light on above the front door. Lauren made sure the light was on most nights, and Frank was sure to drop by for a nightcap no matter where he'd been before. Frank was lonely and restless. He'd had some brief flings with anonymous women since the Ava debacle, but no one intrigued him as much as Lauren did.

When Frank traveled, he liked to take the Rat Pack with him, such as when Noel Coward was booked to do an act at the Sands. Most of the members of the Rat Pack were not really into the Las Vegas scene—"gamblers and mobsters, it was all rather declasse," David Niven once said—but Sinatra was determined to show them a good time. Frank took care of all the arrangements, which included suites for each couple or single, a well-stocked bar in each suite, free dinner and drinks each night, and chips worth a hundred dollars for each of the ladies just to start them off in the casino. There was a front table stocked with its own booze for Noel's opening night. Frank didn't bring a date to the show, as if he were trying to convince Lauren that he wasn't a love 'em and leave 'em kind of guy. He was quite smitten with the lady.

On another occasion Frank flew everyone down to his place in Palm Springs for New Year's, but was disconsolate when Bogie and Betty said they were leaving early with the Nivens. Lauren was bothered by Frank's hangdog expression and asked Bogart if they had done the right thing by going when Frank so obviously needed them to stay with him. In essence Bogie told his wife, "I'm sorry Frank's lonely, but we have our own lives. We can't spend all our time holding his hand." Bogie felt that Frank had brought his loneliness upon himself by his failure to sustain a mature relationship with any woman.

Bogart started to feel poorly while Lauren was working on *Written on the Wind*, so he went to see his doctor. After a number of tests spread out over a number of weeks he was diagnosed as having throat cancer. At a weekend at Frank's place in Palm Springs, Betty and Bogie told everyone the bad news but were confident that the surgery Bogie was scheduled for would take care of the problem. Bogie was in good spirits, making jokes, and his Rat Pack rallied around him. He was on the operating table for nine and a half hours. Unfortunately, the cancer was not defeated and after awhile, wasting away, Bogie took to his bed at home to wait for the end.

All the members of the Rat Pack—plus Katharine Hepburn with Spencer Tracy—came to see Bogie practically every day. Sinatra came too, which was a mixed blessing. He always had the effect of cheering Bogie up, but as Bacall later admitted in her memoirs, her husband was also jealous of him. Frank was a vibrant, attractive man probably in love with his wife—and possibly vice versa—while he was bedridden and utterly incapable of bestowing the kind of physical affection that a woman of Bacall's nature required.

During this time Lauren and Frank grew closer as each faced the terrible thought of a life without Bogie. Frank could hardly stand to see his idol shriveled up in bed the way he was, a shadow of himself, his arms as thin as sticks, his face gaunt and pale. Yet Frank knew that he could always make Bogie laugh and bring him out of his gloom for awhile, so he went to see him whenever he could. The same was true of Swifty Lazar (who truly hated any sick room or anything smacking of germs), and the Nivens and Romanoffs as well. David Niven wouldn't even bother taking off his makeup as he came directly from the studio after each day's shooting.

Eventually Bogie fell into a coma and passed into the Great Darkness a few hours later on Monday, January 14, 1957.

It was the end of an era, and the beginning of a new one for Frank Sinatra. In the meantime, the rest of what would become his Rat Pack—Dino, Sammy, Peter, and Joey—were leading lives of their own. . . .

6

Stud and the Geek

The man who would become known as Dean Martin was born Dino Crocetti in Steubenville, Ohio on June 7, 1917. His father was an immigrant barber named Gaetano (later Guy) and his mother a seamstress named Angela. Although Dino would have made a fine high school athlete, he, like Sinatra, was more interested in singing. He dropped out of school when he was sixteen and took to soaking up local color in pool rooms and boxing a few matches at the community center. He hung out drinking with characters that had some people predicting a dire fate for Dino. But singing was to be his salvation.

When Dino was seventeen he sang in public for the first time at Craig Beach. It was 1934 and Dino had learned everything he knew about singing from the recordings of Bing Crosby, from whom he adopted his basic singing style. Throughout his career every note he sang was derived from Crosby, although Dino was to add a certain suggestiveness, a vocal leer if you will, that Crosby would never have considered or needed. Still, many appreciated his sensually romantic way with a song. Gradually Dino worked his way into nightclubs like the Half Moon, the Rainbow Gardens, and dozens of cheap gin joints and beer halls from Columbus to Cleveland.

One night a bandleader named Ernie McKay caught Dino's act and hired him as vocalist under the almost prophetic name "Dino Martini." Billed as a new "singing sensation," Dino played a variety of restaurants, bars, and supper clubs with McKay and his band. But Dino had bigger fish to fry and sent a cheap recording he made to Cleveland's top bandleader, Sammy Watkins. Watkins liked what he heard on the tinny record and agreed to hire Dino as main vocalist with featured billing as the more American-sounding "Dean Martin."

It was while appearing at tonier nightclubs with Watkins's orchestra that Dino—now Dean—met a woman named Elizabeth (Betty) Anne McDonald and fell in love. A whirlwind courtship was followed by a hasty wedding—everyone assumed Dino had gotten Betty pregnant—and the two spent their honeymoon on a bus touring the midwest with Sammy Watkins's band. Virtually nine months later to the day Betty presented Dean with a baby boy named Stephan Craig Martin. As this was 1942, Dean received "greetings" from the draft board, but if the baby wouldn't have disqualified him, his double hernia would. He was classified 4-F.

Dean signed a new contract with Watkins that would guarantee him the sum of sixty-five dollars a week for as long as the orchestra was playing. It also stipulated that Watkins could have a cut of any money Martin earned by performing on his own when the orchestra wasn't playing. It was a lousy contract, but Martin did nothing about it until the day he heard from a fancy Manhattan club called the Riobamba, which was owned by mob hit man Louis Lepke. Frank Sinatra, for one reason or another, had canceled his engagement there and they were desperate for another good-looking crooner to cover. Was Dean interested? Dean was not only interested, he saw this as the biggest break of his career so far, but what could he do about Watkins? He decided to cross that bridge when he came to it. He let the management at the Riobamba know that he was their boy and left Cleveland in the middle of the night.

When he heard his vocalist had fled town, a furious Watkins followed Martin to Manhattan. He still had a contract with him whether Dean liked it or not. Dean agreed to meet with Watkins, but made it clear that under no circumstances would he return to Cleveland with him. Watkins then handed him a new contract, in which he agreed to let him go to sing at the Riobamba under the condition that Martin sign over 10 percent of all future income to him for the next seven years. MCA (Music Corporation of America), which represented Sinatra at that time, agreed to represent Dean (they had engineered the Riobamba deal), but also wanted a 10 percent cut. Literally the night before he was to open at the Riobamba, Martin signed the contracts, cursing Watkins under his breath.

Martin got very mixed reviews at the Riobamba—he was compared (unfavorably) to everyone from Crosby to Sinatra—but the audience seemed to like him and his stay was extended. Dean and Betty got an apartment in Chelsea and borrowed from their friends to get by. Minus the 20 percent he was supposed to pay Watkins and MCA, Dean was still making enough money, but he and Betty spent too much to furnish the apartment and indulge little Stephan. Dean also was profligate in buying booze for himself and his buddies and losing at poker. By the time his daughter Claudia was born in 1944, Betty was fed up with skimping and saving because of his out-of-control spending and not too crazy about the stories she heard about him and other women. During a trip back to Steubenville she left the children with her mother-in-law and took a train to Philadelphia and her own mother.

By this time Dean was about to be evicted from his Chelsea apartment and MCA was wondering where their 10 percent commissions were. (In those days entertainers received the checks and paid their agents 10 percent out of pocket instead of the agent receiving the check and forwarding 90 percent to the client.) Dean had never forwarded a dime to Sammy Watkins and figured the hell with him, but he had been paying MCA until he could no longer afford to do so. To earn extra money he resorted to driving a cab days and other part-time work, but he hated it and knew he had to find another way.

Dean's "other way" was to sell off percentages of himself to a succession of agents and managers while continuing to pay—or at least owe—10 percent to MCA and another 10 percent to Sam Watkins. First there was a new "personal manager" named Dick Richards who got 20 percent; then there was Lou Perry of the American Guild of Variety Artists, who got a whopping 35 percent, and finally Lou Costello of Abbott and Costello fame, who got another 25 percent. This, of course, added up to 100 percent of himself that Dean had signed away, but none of his assorted agents, managers, representatives, and advisers ever caught on to it until later. Dean would also have the gall to offer yet another 10 percent to an arranger named Jerry Sears and would occasionally con club owners out of extra advance money by offering them a percentage, too. As one wag put it, "More people had a piece of Dino than Heinz had pickles."

Lou Costello, who had caught Dean's act at a club called the Harlequin, thought the kid really had something and wanted his manager, Eddie Sherman, to sign him. But Sherman heard stories about all the different people who had a piece of Dean and all the money Dean owed and wanted no part of him. Lou, who gambled, drank, and caroused just like Dean did, decided to manage Martin himself and paid a few of his bills.

In exchange for signing away these percentages, Dean got paid advances of several thousand dollars, which he would promptly spend on good times instead of paying his creditors. The London Terrace apartment house in Chelsea evicted him and put a lien on his earnings to recover the back rent, but Dean made sure the clubs paid him in cash so he could avoid it. Dean never filed a tax return. Periodically Betty would come back from the suburbs of Philadelphia with the children to see if her marriage could be salvaged, but Dean was always out playing bachelor boy and didn't seem to care if she was in New York or not. When there was no longer an apartment for her and the kids, that was the last straw. Meanwhile Dean moved in with Sonny King, another Italian-American singer and former boxer who already had a roommate but made room for Dino. For months two of the men would take turns sharing the sofa-convertible while the third slept on the floor of the tiny apartment. Life was music, booze, and broads, with no money and lousy sleeping arrangements.

When Dean did get his hands on some dough he had only one thought in mind as to what to do with it. Did he send for his wife and kids? No. Get his own apartment? No. Pay off some of his bills or reimburse all the friends who'd lent him money? No. Pay the IRS? Definitely not. There was only one thing he wanted and that was a nose job.

Lou Costello agreed that the nose nature had given Dean was just too damn big. Lou had been talking about possibly putting Dean into one of the movies he made with partner Bud Abbott, but if he did that nose would have to go. Dean said he was saving up the five hundred bucks it would cost for rhinoplasty—in truth Martin couldn't save five cents—but Costello took pity on him and gave him the money. Dean, of course, spent this on booze and women in short order, so he had to go to other sources for the cash, including "manager" Dick Richards. By this time everyone knew Dino could not be trusted with money, so the plastic surgeon was paid directly or else the Dean Martin the public came to know might have looked quite different.

No one would have known from Dean's financial troubles that he actually had a successful career, and was playing all the top nightspots in Manhattan to generally enthusiastic crowds. Like Sinatra, he came under fire for singing while other American men were fighting for their country, and like Sinatra he got a chip on his shoulder over it. Every now and then he'd be heckled and called a coward and would have to punch somebody out to prove his manhood, but the fact remained that he had the cushy life—financial troubles, mostly his own doing, aside—while others were dying. Dino got a new nose while other men came home sans arms or legs. He had no right being angry, but that didn't stop him. He also had a habit of telling paying customers to shut up if they were talking too loudly while he sang. This did not endear him to management or reviewers.

Of course the situation with his various agents and managers couldn't go on forever, and before long Martin was sued by just about everyone. He owed money to friends, landlords, agencies, *Variety* and other trade papers for ads, restaurants, bars, you name it. Gradually he settled with some of his creditors (later he filed for bankruptcy to get rid of the others), but not before Lou Costello and Lou Perry arranged a buyout of his contract from MCA. Perry didn't mind when Dean moved in with him to save money, but Costello was furious when Martin charged $2000 worth of clothing and other items to his account. Costello decided it was time to let Dino fall by the wayside and allowed Perry to manage him all by his lonesome for a mere 10 percent. Years later when Dean snubbed him in a nightclub, Costello got even by suing him for breach of contract. Lou hadn't a chance; he had dropped Martin himself and everyone knew it, but he accepted a payment of $20,000 from producer Hal Wallis, who owned a piece of Dean at the time.

Dean unveiled his new nose at The Glass Hat nightclub, another popular spot in New York City during the forties. Among the several entertainers with whom he shared the bill was an eighteen-year-old comedian named Jerry Lewis. Jerry, born Joey Levitch, had accompanied his entertainer father on the road and broken into show business by lip-syncing—he called it "practicing"—to phonograph records. His act had advanced, if not by a lot, when he was playing at The Glass Hat. From the very first Jerry looked up to Dean, who was nine years older, and saw him as his big brother and best friend, someone to assuage his loneliness. Although the term was not much in use in the forties, Dean basically saw Jerry as what today we'd call a "geek."

In late 1945 both Jerry and Dino were booked into the Havana-Madrid club on East 51st Street, where they invoked the special magic that would lead to their becoming a team. As each performed, the other would do a little impromptu shtick from the sidelines, proving they could work well together even without a script or preparation. For the special post-midnight show the boys would go out on stage together and do another unscripted duet, just the two of them making with the jokes and clowning around. They established the characters that would serve them for many years to come: Dean the practical, normal lover boy, Jerry as the lovable jerk. They had no plans to team up; they were just having fun. Still, the trade reviews for their duet were sensational. Doing similar stuff at the 500 Club in Atlantic City (although they were each booked as solo acts) had them breaking records for attendance.

By this time, through more byzantine maneuverings, Dean's sole manager, Lou Perry, had been replaced by one Abby Greshler. After that there was no more Dean Martin or

Jerry Lewis, there was only Martin and Lewis. At Loew's State theater in New York in January 1947, they officially opened their new two-man act. Another important person in their lives at this time was George Evans, the same high-powered publicist who almost singlehandedly engineered the success of Frank Sinatra complete with screaming bobby-soxers. One of Evans's stunts was to have Dean allegedly "disappear" just before an opening to stir up some publicity.

Martin and Lewis were a tremendous hit from the first. Fans of the lovable "monkey," Lewis, and fans of the groovy crooner Martin combined to form a formidable force of men, women, and children. Unlike Sinatra, they had never had to depend solely upon teenage girls. By the time they played the Copa—where their act was a little bit more sophisticated (i.e., risque) than at Loew's—they were getting $3000 a week. Dean and Betty had another reconciliation—Betty now certainly had good reason to return to New York—and he put the wife and kiddies up in a huge apartment on Riverside Drive. Dean Martin had arrived and so had the missus, but Dean had no intention of giving up the ladies on the side now that he could really afford them. If he had attracted women pre-fame and pre-nose job, one can only imagine how many offers he got once the bandages came off and the money started rolling in. Jerry Lewis didn't do so badly himself.

Not that Dean charmed all the ladies. On a radio show a snooty soprano named Dorothy Sarnoff commented on the air that Dean sounded just like Bing Crosby, a tacky implication that he was stealing Crosby's sound. On the air Dean merely said that maybe it was Crosby who sounded like Martin, but backstage he called Sarnoff a nasty name. At the Copa, Martin and Lewis were the number-two act after Vivian Blaine, but the pretty headliner fumed when the audience kept begging for more from the stud and the geek. When the Copa management told her that she was getting the number-two spot and Martin and Lewis would be the headliners, she chose a few salty words to express her opinion and then quit in mortification.

When the boys opened at Slapsy Maxie's in Los Angeles, it seemed all of Hollywood had come out to fete them. In the audience was producer Hal Wallis, who had seen them in New York at the Copa and had the idea—as did a half dozen other producers—of putting them in the movies. Abby Greshler had fielded several offers already but turned them all down because the producers demanded exclusivity. Jerry and Dean, who had gotten the cinema lust in their blood, got so frustrated with what they saw as Greshler's interference that they threatened to fire him. Greshler was only trying to protect their interests, but neither of the boys were capable of seeing his side of it. Eventually Greshler worked out a deal with Wallis that seemed to satisfy everyone. Not much later the boys replaced Greshler with MCA's powerhouse agent Lew Wasserman.

But there were problems. Wallis had made the mistake of giving the boys scripted material to do for their screen test and they were awful. It was only when they did the kind of stuff they did in their act that their special byplay and chemistry came forth and convinced Wallis that he had two valuable properties in Martin and Lewis. Shortly afterward, Dean and Jerry began to make their first film at Paramount. Betty was left behind in New York to see to what was now four children who hardly ever saw their father. Jerry kissed his own wife Patti and their son Gary good-bye, and they were off.

Jerry and Dean wasted no time getting girlfriends in Hollywood, both of whom were also married. Jerry somehow managed to get a hold of Gloria De Haven, who was married to handsome hunk John Payne. (Lewis apparently derived a special pleasure in helping to cuckold husbands who, like Dean, were handsomer and more manly than he was.) Dean followed in the footsteps of Peter Lawford and slept with June Allyson, who was married to Dick Powell. Although rather plain by Hollywood standards and with a hoarse, unpleasant speaking voice (and a singing voice that was even worse), Allyson was able to attract some of Tinseltown's most dedicated rovers. Some women slept around—with Jerry, with Dean—just to get even with their philandering hubbies.

George Evans worked overtime trying to keep these two very public adulterous couples from attracting the attention of the press, but he couldn't keep the news from Patti and therefore from Betty. Betty had a fit—"I'll bald that Allyson bitch if I get my hands on her!" she ranted—but eventually she calmed down and forgave Dean. It was not so easy for her to forgive him, however, when he met a twenty-one-year-old beauty queen named Jeanne Biegger while performing down in Miami with Jerry. Jeanne had no idea Dean was married and made up her mind that she was going to make him her own. Even when she found out about Betty she lost none of her determination to land him.

There has always been an epidemic in the entertainment business of men divorcing the wives who stood by them through the bad times and trading them in for a more glamorous model once they hit it big. Now it was Dino's turn. He moved out of the Riverside Drive apartment while Betty ran to her lawyer. At first Betty refused to divorce him, queering his plans to marry his beauty queen, but an increase in alimony finally convinced her to let go. Thirty-two-year-old Dean married Jeanne, who was ten years younger, in 1949. June Allyson cried into her pillow and hid her tears from husband Dick. Dean, of course, continued to see other women even after he was married to Jeanne. The women may have done the initial chasing, but Dean could usually be counted on to be caught.

Of course, Dean left some women cold. He was perhaps more attractive and well-groomed than genuinely handsome, even with a nose job, and there was an oily, vulgar quality about him that many women found repellant.

My Friend Irma (1949), taken from a radio show, was chosen as Martin and Lewis's debut vehicle, although they were only supporting players in the film. Marie Wilson starred as the moronic Irma, whose boyfriend John Lund attempts to turn the characters played by Dean and Jerry into stars while avoiding marriage to Wilson. Irma's roommate (Diana Lynn), meanwhile, has a romance with a wealthy employer. The picture was sporadically amusing and basically amiable, but also rather dull and forgettable.

When Jerry read the script he saw two characters named "Al" and "Seymour." Al was handsome and appealing and intelligent, while Seymour was, like Irma, dopey—and worse—asexual. He went into Wallis's office and demanded that he be cast as Al instead of Seymour. Wallis tried to reason with him, pointing out that the characters in the script were natural extensions of their stage act, but Lewis would have none of it. Wallis finally had to threaten to fire him before he'd shut up and leave and accept the role he'd been offered.

When the picture opened to good box office, most critics observed that Lewis was the best thing in the picture. This time it was Dean's turn to be angry. When they made the sequel, *My Friend Irma Goes West* (1950), he felt that all of the good scenes were being thrown in Jerry's direction, but in actuality Dean was given plenty of screen time and plenty to do in the movie.

In *My Friend Irma Goes West* John Lund meets a producer who wants Lund's only client, Al (Dean Martin), to hop on a train to Hollywood, where he intends to put him into pictures. Unfortunately, Lund is unaware that the "producer" has actually escaped from a mental asylum. He and the gang accompany Al on the train trip where en route they meet a beautiful movie star (Corinne Calvet) who makes a play for Al, inspiring jealousy in Diana Lynn. Although the villain of the piece is a man who represents "a group of men who are opening a casino in Vegas," the film also has a Las Vegas sheriff who talks about how he "runs a clean town," a sop to the mob. Jerry and Dean had already started appearing in mobster-controlled casinos in Las Vegas and it wouldn't do to offend the wrong people. In the film the crooked casino owners were portrayed as atypical rotten apples in a city full of nothing but honest businessmen.

Although Marie Wilson has her moments fighting off a hoodlum who's been told to off her, the film's most priceless bit has Jerry and an adorable chimp chewing gum and blowing smoke rings at each other. Jerry's imitation of Bette Davis at one point is surprisingly bad but that probably makes it funnier. The film was slightly better than the first installment. Pretty French actress Corinne Calvet had no end of trouble with the chimp, who apparently had the hots for her and hadn't the slightest hesitation in making his feelings known. Jerry and Dean may both have found Corinne attractive, but it was producer Hal Wallis who put his hand on her ass, something, unfortunately, that he was known for.

A creditable service comedy, *At War with the Army* (1951), was followed by the odd *That's My Boy* the same year. Screenwriter Cy Howard supposedly based the story on producer Hal Wallis's own life, and the result was neither fish nor fowl. Jerry plays a nice nerd whose football-hero father hires Dean to instruct and befriend his son in the hopes of toughening him up, with predictable complications. Instead of sending the message that all men are different, and not all of them can be football heroes, *That's My Boy* instead offers the dubious thesis that there's a "hero" inside every nerd—all of this accompanied by hardly a laugh and absolutely no development of the dramatic potential. Martin and Lewis's performances were on the beam, however.

The two 1952 offerings from the team were divergent in quality. *Sailor Beware* was a forgettable remake of *The Fleet's In*, rather tiresome stuff with a few mediocre musical numbers. On the other hand, *Jumping Jacks*, in which the boys joined a troupe of parachutists, was one of their best pictures, with a lot of great gags, good performances, and entertaining song numbers. *The Stooge* (1953) was inspired by show business personalities of previous eras, but it certainly seemed partly about Martin and Lewis. In this one Martin is a singer whose career plods along unspectacularly until he hires a stooge, Jerry, to heckle him from the audience and introduce laughs into the act. Martin eventually gets rid of his stooge—a sensitive type—but he can't make it on his own and gratefully takes Jerry back. This was not how it turned out in real life, but their split would be some years in the future. *The Stooge* was even more serious than *That's My Boy*, but it didn't convince anyone the boys were ready for *Hamlet*.

That same year they came out with a remake of *Ghost Breakers* (a Bob Hope starrer) entitled *Scared Stiff*, but even Carmen Miranda couldn't do much to liven up this turkey. Rounding out 1953, *The Caddy* was of interest mostly because this was the picture in which Dino introduced his second-most-famous song, "That's Amore."

Money from Home (1954) was their tenth film and it was pretty awful, a labored "comedy" with the boys involved with hoodlums, horses, pretty ladies, and racetrack shenanigans. A film that's tedious and painful to watch, *Money from Home* is basically one bumbling routine after another. Jerry's spastic act is less palatable than usual, and scenes that could have been hilarious (such as when the inhabitants of his ant farm get loose at a fancy dress party) look inept and overacted. The picture was proof positive that no matter how talented or genial the boys may have been, they needed good scripts and direction, which Hal Kanter and George Marshall were not able to provide, their work being very obvious and heavy-handed.

Lewis was a gifted comedian, but when his shtick wasn't

funny he was merely annoying. And Martin sank or swam in his numbers depending on the songs. Martin had a perfectly acceptable, even strong baritone voice, but his singing could be wretched. Like many a singer before and after he would ruin his natural gift by further debasing the negro jive that had influenced Bing Crosby. There was nothing wrong with rhythm, but Martin's delivery twisted vowels in an unappetizing, unmusical manner and made everything he sang sound alike. (Years later Cher would basically do a distaff take on Martin's song stylings, but both of them certainly had their fans.)

Yet it also has to be said that there were times when Martin did more for one of the team's movies than Lewis, who was generally considered the big draw during all these years. *Money from Home* is a case in point: Lewis is terrible in the picture while Martin and leading lady Pat Crowley come off best.

Of the remaining six Martin and Lewis films, two are worthy of special mention: *Artists and Models* (1955) and *Hollywood or Bust* (1956). The former marked the first time that any Rat Packer worked with their future "mascot," Shirley MacLaine.

The picture took its cue from a rather silly book by Fredric Wertham, *Seduction of the Innocent*, which charged that comic books, particularly of the horror variety, were corrupting the youth of America. Naturally Jerry Lewis plays a comic book enthusiast who is in love with the super-heroine known as the "Bat Lady." Dean was cast as an aspiring comic book artist. Ironically, in real life it was Dean and not Jerry who was an unapologetic comic book lover. Dean would send Jerry to the newsstand to buy the comics, but he would read them right in front of anyone and to hell with them if they objected.

To be fair, the movie has some good points to make about the horror comics of the fifties and (unlike Wertham) makes them without getting too strident about it. The problem was that the picture just wasn't terribly funny. Shirley was cast as Bessie Sparrowbush, a receptionist who models for the Bat Lady. She later noted that the only man in Hollywood who ever tried to put her on a casting couch was the producer of the film, Hal Wallis. Eva Gabor had a supporting part as a spy who masquerades as Jerry's beloved Bat Lady. "Jerry and Dean were darling," she recalled, "but Jerry wasn't always as much fun as I had thought he'd be."

Martin and Lewis had always included what was known as "nance" material in their act, with Jerry typically camping it up with "faggy" mannerisms. This material began making its way into their movies until, especially in *Artists and Models*, they seemed like the gayest heterosexuals in movieland; at one point in the picture they're practically trading kisses. This kind of humor was right up director Frank Tashlin's alley; he also employed it in the films he made with Bob Hope.

But Martin found it embarrassing. Lewis certainly didn't have a crush on him in real life, but it seemed as if he always did in the movies they made together. Martin also was tired of being perceived as merely support for "the monkey." He felt he was being given less to do in their movies, beginning with *Three Ring Circus* in 1956, which was scripted by Sinatra's friend Don McGuire (*Meet Danny Wilson*). Dean noted that Jerry seemed to have placed all of his "people," his friends or those who were primarily loyal to him—McGuire, for instance, and director Joseph Pevney, who helmed both *Circus* and *Meet Danny Wilson*—in key positions. They even had Jerry singing on his records with him, an awful mistake from an artistic point of view if not a financial one. Adding to the frustration was the fact that Dean was beginning to get solo offers, such as the lead role in *The Pajama Game* with Doris Day, and he was loathe to keep turning them down because of yet another Martin and Lewis feature.

Dean was unhappy and wanted out, but he was also afraid of what might happen to his career—a la the character he played in *The Stooge*—after he split with Jerry. Jerry sensed Dean's mixed emotions, and most people who worked with them after the first couple of pictures noted that the two men did not seem to like each other. They made films together, did TV shows together, performed at clubs together—saw too much of each other, in fact—but sometimes weeks would go by when they wouldn't say one word to one another that was not part of the act. Those rare days when they weren't working they simply did not see each other or even communicate. They were friends who were not friends.

Before long the two were openly feuding, trading insults when they were talking at all. When they calmed down, both realized that they could not continue the way they'd been going. Their first step in dissolving the partnership was to renegotiate separate deals with the network presenting their TV show and with producer Wallis. They paid Wallis off so that they would not have to make all of the pictures they were committed to do for him as a team. Their seventeenth film together, *Hollywood or Bust* was their last. Frightened over what would become of him beneath his arrogant, confident veneer, Lewis was so difficult while making the picture that director Frank Tashlin had to order him off the set at one point.

Dean was not only in for a professional separation, but a personal one, too. His life with second wife Jeannie was not exactly wedded bliss, and like Betty before her, she was always taking the children and leaving Dean for good, only to return to find him just as distant as ever. Dean indulged in affairs with pretty co-stars—another sore point with Jeannie—and drank too much because of all the career pressures and his desire to finally be rid of Jerry. It would be years before he was rid of Jeannie, however. It seemed that every time Dino wandered, Jeannie would get pregnant again and home he would come—until the next fight or indiscretion.

The amply endowed Anita Ekberg, who had had a small role in *Artists and Models*, was the centerpiece of *Hollywood or Bust*, making the title an in-joke that had adolescent boys of all ages yukking it up. The first half of the picture is excellent, detailing how the boys share the prize of an automobile won in a contest and ride out to Hollywood where Jerry hopes to meet his crush, Ekberg, who plays herself. Dean tries his best to rid himself of Jerry, but Jerry and his big lovable dog—who drives off in a runaway car in one memorable sequence—are always one step ahead of him. Frank Tashlin keeps the sight gags coming fast and furiously—nothing that hadn't been seen before but better done than usual, including a bit when M & L try desperately to get their car off some railroad tracks before a train can crash into it. The well-edited sequence is actually thrilling. The always reliable Pat Crowley—one of Hollywood's most underrated actresses—meets up with the boys on the road and helps to bolster these early sequences.

Jerry is in top form at a film opening where he salutes movie fans by dressing up as different international movie-goers, and he has a hilarious bit where he drops popcorn onto a lady's head, and, trying to brush out the kernels, completely undoes her hairdo. Unfortunately—considering this was their last movie together—the picture drops in quality quite a bit once the boys get to Hollywood and environs, although chesty Ekberg and a chase through a movie studio help to liven things up. None of this mattered, however. By the time the film was released their fans knew that Martin and Lewis were no longer together and not even speaking to one another. Disillusioned, they stayed away from the picture in droves.

While Jerry started work on his first solo picture, *The Delicate Delinquent*, which had a screenplay and was directed by his and Frank Sinatra's good friend Don McGuire (Darren McGavin took over for Dean in the straight role), Dean had time to mull over the offers coming in and see friends whom previously he had only had time to know casually. Frank Sinatra had met him and Jerry several times over the years—they all performed at the Sands in Vegas, had the same publicist, drank at the same clubs, like Ciro's, dated the same "broads," met at the same parties—but Frank and Dean had never been close. Sinatra's sun had begun to set in the late forties just as Martin and Lewis's star was rising; Dean didn't really want anything to do with some has-been. By the late fifties, however, Frank was back on top and the two crooners could meet on a more or less equal level.

They didn't make "dates" to meet; "men" didn't do that. They'd run into each other at Ciro's or some other place and get loaded, trading dirty jokes and stories about some broad or other. When an interviewer once asked Dean about Sinatra, Dino winked and said, "Frank is my dearest, closest friend. In fact, we slept together last night." It's unclear whether the two were truly capable of having a genuine friendship with anyone. Whatever the case, after the breakup of Martin and Lewis, Frank would naturally gravitate to another cool "wop" like Martin than to a crazy, kvetching, difficult Jew like Lewis, even if Frank and Jerry had many friends and co-workers in common.

As mentioned previously, Dean and Jeannie had been befriended by the Bogarts when they first arrived in Hollywood, but now that they had a marriage in name only, they had drifted away from Bogie and Betty. Jeannie was the one who had accepted and extended invitations; Dean could not have cared less. Every night was a party for him; all he had to do was hop off the stage wherever he was appearing and head for the bar. Besides, Lauren and Jeannie, who had a lot of things in common, had been the close ones, not Dean and Bogart. (Dean was very fond of tough-guy movie actor, George Raft, however.)

Dean passed on *Pajama Game*—he just couldn't stomach the thought of making whoopee, real or otherwise, with freckle-faced Doris Day—and decided to do a spoof on Conrad Hilton, the hotel king, entitled, with typical subtlety, *Ten Thousand Bedrooms*. In this he plays a tycoon who takes over a hotel in Rome, getting involved with three beautiful sisters. The beauty of co-star Anna Maria Alberghetti was some compensation for a weak script that details unfunny romantic complications. It's all just a tease, in any case; none of those ten thousand bedrooms are ever used. Paul Henreid was along for the ride and provided some much-needed professionalism. "The picture was very bad," he said. "I think everyone—including Dean himself—thought his career in pictures was over without Jerry Lewis."

Without Jerry the eternal kid the picture lost its "for the whole family" quality but couldn't compete with sophisticated European fare for adults. While *The Delicate Delinquent* established Jerry Lewis as a movie star on his own, *Ten Thousand Bedrooms*, a box-office failure, did not do the same for Dean. Although he still had highly lucrative Vegas engagements and recording deals, he pretty much figured he was washed up in the picture business.

When Humphrey Bogart died in 1957 Dean didn't call Frank to offer condolences; it would have seemed inappropriate and wasn't his style. Undoubtedly Jeannie called Lauren. Dean had other things on his mind. He didn't know that the film he was to make with the future wife of Sammy Davis Jr. would turn him into a major player again.

Or that he was to become part of a team with Frank Sinatra that would make him even more famous and show-biz-respected than he had ever been with Jerry.

7

Sammy

Dean Martin was an eight-year-old playing in Steubenville and Jerry Lewis not even a twinkle in his father's eye when Sammy Davis Jr. was born in Harlem in 1925. His father was a dancer in a vaudeville troupe headed by a friend named Will Mastin. Sammy's mother had left his father and gone off with another vaudeville group, so his father took him along with him when he went out on the road. When Sammy was three and bookings—and food—became scarce, his grandmother Rose told her son, Sammy's father, that he had better send the boy home to live with her. Sammy Sr. hated the idea of being separated from his son and namesake, so he decided to grit his teeth, leave show biz, and get a normal job, although he was heartbroken at the thought of it.

After a few weeks of looking for show business jobs in New York and finding nothing, Sammy Sr. tried to steel himself to get something similar to what he'd done before becoming a vaudevillian, driving a taxi or washing dishes, but he couldn't bring himself to do it. One afternoon he saw his small son dancing with Grandma Rose—whom Sammy Jr. always called "Mama"—and recognized that the kid had absorbed some of his talent. When Will Mastin asked Sammy

Sr. to come back out on the road with him he eagerly agreed and decided to take his boy along with him. In between gigs they'd go back to Mama Rose.

In New York Rose hid Sammy Jr., who was now five and eligible for school, from the truant officers, but she insisted her son get a tutor for the boy when they were traveling to some misbegotten town or another. Sammy Sr. and Will had included the child in their act: they hired two other dancers and billed the fivesome as "Four and a Half." They were on the bill in a theater in Michigan when a lady do-gooder marched backstage and raised hell with the manager. According to her Sammy Sr. and Will were practically child abusers, forcing such a small boy to dance and pretending he was having fun when he was obviously just being exploited. The result was that the manager let the act go and for several days the boy, his father, and "Uncle Will" went hungry, sleeping in train terminals and making tomato soup out of hot water and catsup. The temperature outside was minus 32 degrees. It wasn't the aforementioned do-gooder who rescued them but another woman who saw their plight, took them home with her, and fed them.

Eventually the group got more bookings and life looked a lot brighter, except for the times when Sammy's father drank too much, ranted at everyone, and created tension. There were also more do-gooders in the guise of the Geary Society, who enforced a law that said no one under the age of sixteen could appear on the stage. Not even disguising little Sammy as "Silent Sam, the Dancing Midget" could keep the Society off their backs. The result of this was that Mama Rose was granted custody of the boy. She would allow her son to take the child with him on the road but only if he followed strict orders. If Sammy Jr. hadn't been so desperate to go— show business was already in his blood—she probably would have forbade it altogether.

When Sammy was seven his father took him out to

Brooklyn, where Warner Bros. maintained a film studio. He auditioned for a singing and dancing role in an Ethel Waters two-reeler, *Rufus Jones for President*, and won the title role. He followed this up with another small role in a picture starring Lita Grey and her son, Charlie Chaplin Jr. Lita wanted to adopt Sammy and take him out to Hollywood with her— she could see that vaudeville was on its last legs—but Mama Rose would have none of it. As far as she was concerned, her grandson was as much her "baby" as his father was.

Will and the two Sammy's continued their theatrical wanderings, only now their official billing was "Will Mastin's Gang, Featuring Little Sammy." The three of them always dressed exactly alike: spats, vest, cane, and so on. In a restaurant in Missouri little Sammy got his first taste of racism when a white waiter at a restaurant counter told the trio that "niggers" had to sit on the other side of the room. People in show business, the white folks they met on the road, had generally been friendly and open-minded. Occasionally, when they'd been refused service or a room in a particular inn, Big Sammy had told his son that it was because they were show people. Now he had to tell his son that as far as some people were concerned, their skin color made them different, something to be feared and even hated. It troubled Sammy Jr. that there were individuals who would dislike him when they didn't even know him.

As the years proceeded, the Will Mastin Gang criss-crossed the country, slipped back and forth across the border into Canada, went hither and fro, piling up bookings, making money, getting somewhere if never quite where they wanted to be. They were stars, but only on a third-rate vaudeville circuit. At least the days they had money outnumbered the days when they were broke, which was different from the way it used to be. No one could deny that having little Sammy in the act was what made all the difference, although there would come a time when his partners would deny all that and more.

Sammy was fifteen and the trio was playing Detroit when there occurred the first, if hardly momentous, meeting between Sammy and future fellow Rat Packer Frank Sinatra. The Will Mastin group was on the same bill as Tommy Dorsey—Dorsey's usual opening act was apparently stranded somewhere or other—and guess who was Dorsey's vocalist? Frank came over to Mastin and his gang backstage and introduced himself. Sammy had heard of Frank—who had yet to make a movie and hadn't quite started to cause feminine hearts to flutter—and had heard him sing on Dorsey's records, but neither of them had any idea that someday they'd become very close friends.

During World War II Sammy was inducted into the Army, where he encountered more prejudice of a particularly vicious kind than he ever had before. The corporal in his unit put him and another black soldier in one corner of the barracks and pushed the cots six feet away from the nearest ones, when all the other cots were only divided by two feet. When the sergeant saw what had been done, he insisted that the "Negro" cots be moved and be made uniform with the others. Then there was one soldier named Jennings who influenced a whole group of his friends to pick on Sammy: pretending to be friendly they handed him a glass of beer which was actually urine, and later tricked him to an isolated barracks where they drenched him with white paint and wrote "coon" on his forehead. They called him "nigger" and "ugly pygmy." Sammy got many a black eye in fights with these charmers whenever he could.

On the other hand, many of the white soldiers had no problem with Sammy and left him alone. The aforementioned sergeant, who was also white, was always friendly and sympathetic to Sammy. He lent him books from his library and encouraged him to read. Learning of his vaudeville background, he convinced him to appear in shows at the Service Club, although Sammy was afraid of how the soldiers might react. "How can you run out and smile at people who despise you?" he asked. An "athletic" heart condition kept him from going overseas, and he had never received any training for something of practical use to the Army. To his amazement and delight his dancing seemed to win over—or at least "neutralize," as he put it—many of the soldiers in the audience. He began to think of his talent as power, a weapon he could use to make sure he was acknowledged. A determination for this "pygmy" to succeed in spite of all the odds, in spite of whatever hatred his enemies could muster, was born in him. It was this determination that turned Sammy into a veritable giant.

Sammy had his second, slightly more momentous meeting with Frank Sinatra when he got out of the Army. By this time Sinatra had become a gigantic star, a singing sensation, the guy who drove all the gals gaga. Sammy, who was back with what was now called the Will Mastin Trio, was doing a gig in Los Angeles when he heard Frank singing live on the radio show "Your Hit Parade." He decided to go to the NBC studios where "Your Hit Parade" originated and sit in the audience. Sammy couldn't stop thinking of how they'd once shared a stage in Detroit when Sinatra was nobody. Now he was a star, and the Will Mastin Trio were still, for all intents and purposes, nobodies.

After the show Sammy went around to the stage door with around five hundred screaming fans and waited for their idol to appear. Finally Sinatra stepped out and the crowd went wild. Considering the influence Frank was to have on the life and career of Sammy Davis Jr., it is interesting to note how Davis describes this moment in his autobiography: "God, he looked like a star. He wasn't much older than a lot of us, but he was so calm, like we were all silly kids and he was a man, sure of himself, completely in control."

When it came Sammy's turn to get an autograph, Frank thought he looked familiar. Sammy reminded him that they had been on the same bill in Detroit about five years previously. Frank recalled that Sammy had done an act with his father and another man. Then he told him he'd leave a ticket for him if he wanted to see another show sometime the following week. Sammy went to the show and got word that Frank wanted to see him in his dressing room, where he found him holding court with a dozen show biz insiders. "He had the aura of a king about him," Sammy remembered. Before he said good-bye, Frank told him he could come around and watch a rehearsal sometime.

Meanwhile, things weren't going so great for the Will Mastin Trio. They were booked for another tour and would be working steadily for several months, but comparing their lot to Frank's, Sammy knew it was another dead end on the third-rate circuit. When this was over, however, the Trio got booked at the El Rancho in the new happening spot of Las Vegas, Nevada. Arriving at the fabulous hotel with its huge band and modern (for the period) technology, Sammy was impressed and felt like his group was finally moving a little closer to the big time. He knew, however, that it was the same old story in certain regards when he found out that they would not be allowed to use rooms in the hotel or enter the casino while they were working there. Instead they were escorted to the impoverished Negro section of town, where they would have to rent rooms. A colored woman—the terms "black" and "African-American" weren't in vogue at this time—charged them twice what it would cost at El Rancho for three rooms in a comparative shack. Sammy's father was disgusted that one of their own would do that to them, but they had no choice but to agree to the terms if they were to keep the gig. It was in Vegas that Sammy began perfecting some of his soon-to-be-famous impersonations of everyone from Stepin Fetchit to Jimmy Cagney.

From then on things began looking up. For one thing,

the Trio moved upward to the infinitely more prestigious RKO circuit, which ensured them bookings at much better places—and at higher fees—than they had been doing previously. Mickey Rooney was putting together a post-war stage show and decided to have the Will Mastin Trio open the bill. Sammy was impressed with Mickey's down-to-earth, gracious attitude when he first met him at the Copley Plaza Hotel in Boston. And their senses of humor were a good match. Looking Sammy over, Mickey said, "Damn, I never find anybody who's shorter than me. Everybody's taller—even you. And you're a midget!"

Mickey was the first Hollywood personality to befriend Sammy and try his best to enhance his career. Rooney tried to get Sammy a role as a fighter in his film *Killer McCoy*, a remake of *The Crowd Roars*, but the studio went with another actor. One Christmas Eve when Mickey's show was playing Cleveland, a gatecrasher came into their post-theatre party shouting about "niggers" and Rooney hauled off and belted him. "It took four of us to pull him off," Sammy said.

Some time later Sammy was watching a show at the Strand Theatre when he noticed something about the negro acts on the bill. They all spoke that certain "colored" dialect (what today we might call "ebonics") on stage even if the performers did not speak that way off-stage. And the performers never directly addressed or really communicated in any way with the audience. It was as if they felt they hadn't any right to, as if they were expected to shuffle and speak bad grammar because they were colored.

Sammy made up his mind that that was not going to be the case with the Will Mastin Trio. Or at least, that was not going to be the case as far as he was concerned. His father and Will were older, set in their ways, too accepting of the colored man's place in the world (or comparative lack of it) to change now, but he was younger, sterner, more determined to have everything white men had, everything Sinatra had. His talent was his power, and his talent was undeniable.

Then a dream came true. Neither Will nor Sammy Sr. had ever imagined the day would come when they'd play one of the first-class circuit theaters in New York City, but through the intervention of another show business figure who had never forgotten Sammy, they were about to become the opening act at the Capitol Theater. Three weeks at $1250 per week, a sum that had been unheard of when the act first began.

Their benefactor? Frank Sinatra.

"Frank took me completely under his wing," Davis wrote in his autobiography. "He didn't just say, 'Well, you're working and that's fine.' He had our names up out front, he was wonderful to my family, and he had me to his dressing room between almost every show. If I was there at dinner time, he'd take me out to eat with him."

Many people have wondered how come Sammy Davis spent so much time seeking Frank Sinatra's approval, emulating him, agonizing whenever Frank got mad at him, loving him, and obsessing over him to such a degree. Why did he—as many of Frank's friends did—put up with so much crap? The answer is that Frank Sinatra was a true friend when Sammy needed one. Frank stuck up for him, went to bat for him, gave his career the boost that it needed to push him into the majors—and in a time period that is very different today, a politically incorrect era when no white man had to go out of his way for a black one.

The head of Loew's Booking, Sidney Piermont, told Sammy that not only did Sinatra insist on having the Trio in the show—Piermont felt they were still comparative unknowns and didn't want to risk it—he demanded the $1250 for them, too. Frank had never let on how big a role he had played in getting them hired.

It was also Sinatra who suggested that Sammy do some singing of his own. He heard Davis do an impression of him, and of several other singers and thought his own voice was good enough to do a straight number or two. Later on Frank thought Sammy might have picked up a little too much by listening to him and suggested he develop his own style.

From New York the Trio traveled to Los Angeles, where they appeared at the famous Slapsy Maxie's nightclub, and then went on to the even more famous Ciro's, the top of the lot. The headliner at Ciro's was supposed to be Janis Paige, but audience reaction to the Trio, especially Sammy, was so strong, that the blonde didn't have a chance. It was in her contract that the opening act only perform for so many minutes and could only take two bows, but the audience kept asking for more. Not only did they take four bows, Sammy gave an encore, his impression of "a colored Jerry Lewis." Janis Paige cooled her heels in the wings, her fury mounting, and shot out looks that could kill as the three men finally vacated the stage. The unexpected feedback got her off her game and she was off-key and rattled throughout the set; everyone in the audience kept talking about the opening act. From then on she decided that she would go on first and the Trio could bring up the rear in what was actually the coveted headliner spot.

It was around this time that Sammy first met Dean Martin's then-partner, Jerry Lewis, who was to become a close friend. Jerry gave Sammy some good advice, too. It was one thing for Sammy not to speak in a so-called colored dialect, but his grammar and speech were impeccable—by any standards. It made him sound "high-falutin'," as if he were condescending to his audience. The average white person didn't speak that well, let alone a black one. Jerry argued that if Sammy wanted to appeal to the widest possible audience, he had to be "a little less grand." Sammy admitted that he did sound "like a colored Laurence Olivier." It was understandable that he had rejected the Negro-speak, but he had gone too far to the other extreme. Worse yet, it sounded phony. Jerry also suggested that he screw up once in a while, that the occasional mishap would only endear him to the audience. Lastly, he said that it came off as if his father and Will were his servants, the way he spoke to them and had them hand him his props on stage. Davis absorbed this excellent critique and made some changes, although throughout most of his career he continued with the somewhat pretentious "with your kind permission I'd now like to sing" patter.

There was something else that troubled Sammy, but that he could do nothing about: his appearance. It wasn't so much his height that bothered him. Mickey Rooney had certainly proven that you didn't need to be tall to make it to the top, and he'd given out enough black eyes in the Army and elsewhere to know size didn't always matter. But one critic, in a positive review of his act, referred to him as "ugly looking." Sammy recalled the time when he was around ten years old or so when a little colored girl drew a picture of him making him appear grotesque and underlined the word "ugly" at the bottom of it.

True, the lower half of Sammy's face did pull to the side when he sang or talked, creating distortion in his face, but aside from that he was rather handsome. He had gotten used to his face. He looked at it in the mirror and decided he'd be so damned busy on that stage that no one would ever notice what he looked like anyhow.

But then something happened that for quite a while took his mind off merely whether he was pretty or not. During an appearance at the New Frontier in Las Vegas in 1954, he was involved in a severe car accident and lost an eye. Although he learned to compensate and discovered he could see more with one good eye than he ever imagined, his equilibrium was affected and while convalescing he entertained fears that he might fall on his face when attempting to dance. Sinatra visited him at the hospital, causing a near-riot among the nurses, and gave him a pep talk. He told him he looked dynamic in his black eyepatch, and for awhile Sammy toyed with the idea of leaving it on for good as a trademark.

One of the major early triumphs for the Will Mastin Trio was being hired to sing and dance for the crowd at the world-famous Copacabana club in New York. Sammy would never forget the night he and drummer Buddy Rich had gone to the Copa to see Frank Sinatra. The minute the doorman saw Sammy's black face, Rich was told his reservation had been "misplaced."

When Sinatra found out about it, he called Sammy personally and invited him to his show. He laid down the law with the management and the reservations clerk and told them all how very unhappy he would be if his friend wasn't admitted. Sammy was understandably apprehensive but on the chosen night he was admitted without incident. Furthermore, he discovered that Frank had invited several of his friends to sit with Sammy at his table so he wouldn't feel isolated in the audience. Now he and Will and his father were headliners at the same club that had once refused to seat him.

That was why Sammy was devastated when one night at the height of his glory he saw Frank Sinatra walking dejectedly down Broadway, virtually unrecognized by passersby who'd once screamed at the sight of him. This was at the point when Sinatra's career had hit the toilet. Sammy ran after him and tried to get his attention, but got the feeling that his friend would rather not be seen by anyone, that he'd rather not know anyone had witnessed his humiliation: Frank Sinatra, once the idol of millions, walking down Broadway unmolested. . . .

While Sinatra plummeted, Sammy went higher and higher. First he tackled television, becoming a frequent guest star on Eddie Cantor's show. After his first appearance, his representatives at the William Morris office were flooded with hate mail. In a panic the sponsors told Cantor that they might pull him off the air if anything like it happened again. Cantor's response was to tell his sponsors to go to hell and let him deal with the public. He hired Sammy for all three of the remaining shows of the season. Not for the first time Sammy realized that many people of the Jewish faith, who'd been persecuted themselves, refused to go along with other whites who discriminated against black people.

Sammy and the rest of the Trio had done vaudeville, the greatest nightclubs, radio, television, and Sammy had even been in films. The only field left to conquer was the Great White Way. It was only a matter of time before Sammy was signed to do a Broadway show. The show was *Mr. Wonderful*.

In its original concept, the musical would have been ahead of its time. Sammy was to play an entertainer much like himself, only he goes to Paris where he figures there will be less racial prejudice to deal with. The conflict comes when he meets up with an old friend who urges him to come back to New York, to try and make it in his own country no matter how much more difficult the odds.

But in out-of-town tryouts the critics responded well to everything but the message of racial equality, or at least to the fact that they felt the message was delivered with little subtlety. Sammy felt it was important for the musical to say something; the backers argued that what good would having a message do if there was no audience to deliver it to? The public was coming chiefly to be entertained and that was it.

By the time *Mr. Wonderful* got to Broadway most of the juice had been taken out of it. Sammy's character had never gone to Paris; instead he was a big shot in a small pond, a small town somewhere in the good ol' U.S.A. The conflict was still supposed to be whether or not he would leave the small success he had in Nowheresburg and try to make it in New

York City, only Sammy argued that there really wasn't any "conflict" anymore. Why wouldn't the fellow want to try for major success in the Big Apple? "Instead of a story about a sophisticated, sensitive guy who doesn't want to live with prejudice," he said, "Charley Welch has become a schnook who doesn't have the guts to try for success."

In spite of this—or perhaps because of it—*Mr. Wonderful* became a big hit. One would imagine that by now Sammy had moved on to become a solo, but the Will Mastin Trio was still part of the billing, even appearing on the marquee of the musical. (Will and Sammy Sr. had small parts in the show.) The producers argued that if Sammy truly wanted to go legit, he couldn't just recreate his nightclub act on the Broadway stage; it was time to jettison his father and Will. Underneath Sammy knew that they were right. He was the draw of the act and always had been—but he couldn't be disloyal to the two men who'd helped him enter show biz and who'd meant so much to him over the years. Afraid that they'd eventually be shunted to the side, Sammy Sr. and Will (especially the latter) got Sammy to agree to a contract that everything would be split three ways in virtual perpetuity even if only Sammy were hired for a particular gig. This deplorable situation continued even after the two older men retired.

Each evening after the show, Sammy would have parties at his apartment. Attendance was mandatory. No matter how tired they were or even if they had dates or other things to do, fellow cast members such as Chita Rivera were told to be there; Sammy wouldn't take no for an answer. A night owl, Sammy would want to stay up until dawn and insisted everyone else keep him company. If someone left before the sun came up, citing fatigue or an early appointment, he would sulk and whine. He turned the *Mr. Wonderful* cast and hangers-on into an entourage who had to do what he wanted them to do: play Monopoly (a passion of Sammy's), quote Shakespeare, trade gossip, drink. Years later Sammy would admit that he'd turned these people into virtual prisoners.

Another favorite pastime of his was to hit the clubs, often dragging along with him Chita and the others whether they wanted to go or not. He'd found that not every chic Manhattan nightspot had a color barrier, and if they did, he often was the first to break it. He palled around with the owner of Danny's Hideaway, who wanted him to think of the place as his second home. He ate cheesecake at Lindy's with Milton Berle, another Jew who was all for blacks getting their piece of the pie. He debated whether or not to go ahead with his plans and meet some friends at Longchamps, expecting that certain look from the maitre'd, but when he screwed up his courage and walked inside his friends took him to their table and there was no problem. When he requested that he and a buddy move to another booth—there were chorus girls at their table and he, after all, was a star—he was only half-joking.

Sammy had been instrumental in getting the casinos to change their policies about barring admittance to blacks. He would not perform anywhere where blacks were banned, so casinos or clubs that discriminated never got his services no matter how much money they offered him. As he became a bigger and bigger draw, the recalcitrant markets recognized that it just wasn't good business to keep blacks out if it meant Sammy Davis Jr. wouldn't perform for them. It was largely because of his efforts, his refusing to accept the status quo, that blacks were eventually admitted into casinos and into many of the tony downtown clubs.

Still, there were holdouts. One of these was the famous El Morocco, perhaps the snootiest Manhattan nightclub of all. One night at his apartment where he was, as usual, holding court, his friends begged him to let them all go out on the town somewhere. El Morocco was suggested. But when one person phoned the club and asked for a reservation for Sammy, there was hemming and hawing until they were bluntly told that Sammy and his party had better go elsewhere. Ironically, music from *Mr. Wonderful* was being played that very moment by the orchestra in the background. Yet the star of the show himself would not be permitted to enter the establishment.

From then on El Morocco became a symbol to Sammy, a symbol that he had come this far but not far enough. In truth it had as much to do with ego—how dare they think that a Broadway star wasn't good enough for them?—as with Sammy's constant drive for racial equality. It didn't occur to him that he was seeking the approval of people who judged others by their clothing and pedigree, how much money they made, which block they lived on, snobs who treated other, "lesser" white people like dirt—did he really expect equal treatment for a black man from such as these? Still, his star status had gained him entree into many a place and situation that the average black (and many whites) would not have been privy to, and he was determined that El Morocco would acknowledge his place in the world or else.

While many of Sammy's friends understood his obsession with the club, others, white and black, were tired of the way Sammy always made an issue of his race, tired of the way he would always foist himself—and them—upon Upper East Side people and places where, instead of being able to relax and have some fun, they had to brace themselves for a slight or insult and Sammy's outraged reaction to same. To them, Sammy was courting the favor of frivolous, bigoted, shallow people—people to whom appearance was everything—when he could just as easily have gone bar-hopping in Greenwich Village, where the bohemians didn't care if you were white or black or even what sex you slept with after the bars closed. It became less and less about equality and more and more about living his stereotypical definition of La Dolce

Vita. Just as Sammy had never considered if it would really be so great to allow blacks into—let's face it—crooked casinos where they could have their hard-earned money ripped off along with white folk, he never wondered if acceptance at El Morocco should be his true criteria for success.

None of this, of course, changes the fact that El Morocco's policy was outrageous, and one can't help admiring the bantamweight Sammy for taking on this snooty Goliath as he did—if the whole business hadn't backfired. On the night *Mr. Wonderful* finally closed and a cast party was held, he left the soiree before it had hardly begun and insisted that a white couple he was good friends with go with him to El Morocco. As the couple had been to the club on many previous occasions, they were admitted—with Sammy in tow—but they were given a table in what is known in the restaurant business as "Siberia": the declasse section of the club reserved for tourists and other commoners. So instead of partying with his friends, fellow cast members, and other well-wishers at an establishment that welcomed his patronage, instead of celebrating the long run of his hit Broadway show and saying good-bye to people he'd worked with for months, he sat and stewed at El Morocco until he could take the deliberate slight no more and insisted he and the couple leave.

One Wednesday morning this man with an understandable if occasionally self-destructive chip on his shoulder picked up a newspaper and read the headline HUMPHREY BOGART DIES.

Sammy had been very fond of and grateful to Bogart. He liked his wife, Lauren Bacall. His first thought was to call Frank. He knew how much Frank idolized Bogie. But Frank Sinatra wasn't taking any calls. He was too distraught—and more—to talk.

8

Brother-in-Lawford

Peter Lawford's mother, Lady May, had never wanted a child, and when she had one, in September of 1923, would have preferred a girl to a boy. She not only dressed young Peter in girls' clothing until he was five, which was typical during the period, but continued the practice in private until he was nearly eleven. Lady May was working on her second marriage—her chief reason for marrying the distinguished Sir Sydney Lawford was to gain a title—and neither she nor the aged nobleman had much use for a little boy.

Peter's early years were spent in France, where the Lawfords had fled from the scandal that resulted from their affair—both were married to others when Peter was born. Their respective spouses sued for divorce, understandably, providing fodder for gossip for years to come. Peter had celebrated his first birthday before the couple was able to marry. For years May's cuckolded first husband would tell anyone who listened that he was Peter's real father. He wasn't.

May got the idea that her son could be the English version of Jackie Cooper when he had a bit part in a movie made at the famous Elstree Studios. For his part, Peter had already made it clear that he had no interest in following in his father's footsteps and becoming a soldier. His appearance in several films made in England and in France cemented his desire to become an actor. His youthful beauty at ten attracted the attention not only of casting agents, but certain heinous individuals who had a thing for pretty children. A famous war correspondent tried to molest him in a hotel corridor, and a German governess succeeded in having her way with him when she took him on a picnic.

When he was fourteen Peter accidentally smashed into a glass panel and severely damaged his right arm, slashing an artery and nearly bleeding to death. Throughout his lifetime he would be self-conscious about his "withered" arm, but he compensated by using his left, and few people even knew he had a problem. His lower right arm and hand would never have any feeling in them, however, and this caused him a great deal of emotional distress. In addition, there were painful sensations in his upper arm and shoulder. A doctor suggested the climate of Southern California would be more comfortable for Peter—the damp weather where Peter lived was no help at all—and his mother figured this would be the perfect opportunity for her boy to take Hollywood by storm.

Arriving in Los Angeles weeks later, Lady May wasted no time calling on Hollywood agents, announcing that her son, who had been "big in pictures" in England, was now available for work in America. No one had ever heard of him, of course, and they couldn't have cared less, but a lady agent who had once met May years ago took pity on her and took Peter on as a client. By February of 1938, Peter had been cast in his first American film, a nice supporting part in *Lord Jeff* starring Mickey Rooney. Peter was thrilled to be part of the MGM universe. He and Mickey took to each other right off the bat, and Peter was equally enchanted with Judy Garland, who was to become another good friend—and lover—in later years.

If circumstances had been different, Peter could have

built upon his success in *Lord Jeff*, but the fates were conspiring against him. The family coffers were running dry, and his salary wasn't enough, nor were further assignments coming quickly enough, to do much good. His father wanted to go back to England, but Lady May would have none of it. The old scandals about her and Sydney had resurfaced in the papers, and she would not live in a world where people gossiped about her and stared at her with that look that branded her declasse. To make matters worse, by 1939 the war meant that no money could leave England: the Lawfords' bank accounts back home had been frozen. There was no choice but to move temporarily to Long Island—far away from Hollywood, all the way on the other side of the country—so they could throw themselves on the mercy of relatives, who were undoubtedly thrilled at their arrival. When they wore out their welcome in Manhasset, the Lord and Lady, along with Peter, borrowed enough to get to Palm Beach, where a friend of Sydney's allowed them to use his villa with his compliments. Because of their titles, the Lawfords were eagerly embraced by Palm Beach society—until they were told they must vacate the villa and had nowhere else to move to. Again Sydney suggested they go back to England, where they would have access to his bank accounts, but ever mindful of scandal, and enjoying the admiration of America's upper register, May positively refused.

This, of course, put them in a difficult situation, but Lady Lawford managed to borrow some money (undoubtedly from someone on a lower rung of the social ladder than her newfound friends), and they soon moved into new quarters, the best they could do on such limited funds: a veritable hovel near the railroad tracks. Somehow Lady Lawford survived this mortification, although it wasn't easy. Their money was still frozen, and Lady Lawford would sooner die than go to work, so to pay the rent on their shabby shack-on-the-tracks, Peter was told to seek employment. For the next few months he parked cars and pumped gas, anything to keep his mother happy, which wasn't easy. Horrified at the debased circumstances in which she found herself, still dreaming of the life Peter's success in Hollywood could bring her, she spent her time moaning in her bed under a cold compress, berating her husband's inadequacies, and snatching away Peter's paycheck as soon as he had cashed it. Finally they had saved up enough money to make their way back to L.A. in 1942.

Peter soon discovered that Hollywood had a short memory. He had no trouble getting a new agent, but she had a lot of trouble finding him parts. Lady May was getting impatient, and Sydney was just getting older. Things got so bad that Peter had to take a job as an usher at a movie theater. One evening they held the premiere of Mickey Rooney's new movie, and Peter stood there thinking, "I was in a picture with Mickey and now I'm showing people to their seats!" It was a very disheartening period for him, to say the least.

A bit in *Mrs. Miniver*—he played a young flier who rushes past Greer Garson's car and has all of one line—led to a much more substantial part in *A Yank at Eton*, again with Mickey Rooney. After that it was back to being an extra in such films as Garson's *Random Harvest* and Joan Crawford's *Above Suspicion*. But it was a brief, silent shot of him at the opening of *Pilot # 5* starring Franchot Tone that led to an MGM contract. A closeup of Peter shows him watching Tone take off on a suicide mission; the implication is that the young boy played by Peter is saddened by what he knows will happen to Tone and afraid that death will be his own fate as well. His handsome, evocative features in the shot so impressed the powers-that-be at MGM that a contract for him was drafted.

Peter was thrilled to be signed up by the biggest movie

studio in the world, but at first all he got were more bit parts. He was excited to find he'd be working with Humphrey Bogart in *Sahara* (1943), but he was just one of a large group of soldiers and never really got to know the actor. Bogart, at that point, could hardly have taken Peter seriously; he was just another pretty boy out of a lot of pretty boys that MGM had in their stable. For his part, Peter couldn't have dreamed that some day he would be as famous as Bogie, that he'd be part of the offshoot of a group that Bogart himself would start.

Peter's first important picture was *The White Cliffs of Dover* (1944). In this Irene Dunne plays a young American lady who travels to London for a vacation with her father, but stays to marry a handsome baronet (Alan Marshall) who later dies in World War I. Years later she wants to take her son to America so he might avoid going to war as his father did, but he, too, winds up dying, in World War II. Roddy McDowall played the son as a boy; Peter took over when the boy reached manhood. Lawford got very good notices for this picture, but he was nearly overlooked among such powerhouse supporting players as Frank Morgan, C. Aubrey Smith, and Gladys Cooper, not to mention a very young Elizabeth Taylor (whose scenes were with McDowall). Although well-made, with many charming and moving sequences, *The White Cliffs of Dover* was clearly meant to put American audiences of the time in a mood of starry-eyed sacrifice; scenes that should have been tragic—such as Peter's death scene—are staged in too unreal and theatrical a manner. Characters make propagandistic speeches instead of crying. Because of this the picture is very dated, but it did give Peter's career a boost.

Peter was always a trifle humiliated by his appearing in pictures while other men his age were dying overseas during the war. The injury to his arm had disqualified him from service. He also was the sole support of his parents. "I keep telling myself I could have just bluffed my way in, somehow, someway," he said years later.

Peter found most of his role in *Mrs. Parkington* left on the cutting room floor and was disappointed when the title role in *The Picture of Dorian Gray*, which had been promised to him, went to the mask-like Hurd Hatfield and he got only the consolation prize of a supporting part. But by far the worst thing that happened to him was when his mother took it upon herself to pay a call on his boss, Louis B. Mayer.

May's dreams for her son were coming true, but not the dreams for herself. She had hoped not only to live vicariously through her son—and to live off his money—but that his connections in Hollywood might start her off on a film or related career of her own. She tried to get on the payroll of the studio under any auspices she could think of—Peter's companion or gofer, an "advisor" on films that took place in Britain—but she was, at first, repeatedly turned down. There was no true purpose she could serve. Not only was Peter getting all the glory, but he was the one being feted and fussed over as she had once been in Palm Springs. In Hollywood she was nobody.

Worse, Peter would stay out all night and keep company with women who were no better than whores, as far as May was concerned. Peter saw the bright lights while she stayed home with a man who was nearly eighty and who was no consolation to her at all. Peter had dared to tell his mother that he felt she was neglecting and mistreating his father. Peter was showing independence, getting big for his britches now that he was a star. She had made all this possible— or so she told herself—and she would not be cut out; she would not be shunted aside when she was on the very verge of having everything she'd ever wanted. Now Peter was associating with that dreadful Lana Turner—all boobs and no brain, as far as May was concerned—and worse, some of his male companions, the actors he buddied around with, she swore were homosexuals.

That was it! That was how she would get revenge on Peter and teach him to mind his mother. She was still the boss and it was time that he knew it.

So she went to see Mayer and told him that she was deeply concerned that Peter was, as she put it, queer, and asked if the studio would pay for hormonal shots, psychiatric counseling, or what was especially popular in those days in "treating" homosexuality, electroshock therapy. Mayer replied that he would speak to Peter first. Peter came in and was "thunderstruck"—as he put it—when Mayer told him what his mother had said. He assured Mayer that he had no homosexual leanings (in truth he was bisexual and was to have many affairs with his own gender), but Mayer didn't seem convinced. Disgusted with his mother, horrified at her actions, feeling queasy and desperate and heartsick inside— not to mention terrified at what this might do to his life and career—Peter phoned Lana afterward and begged her to tell Mayer about their affair. After initial reservations, Lana agreed to give Mayer a call, whereupon she proceeded to tell the studio head that there was no way that a man who had proved himself such a great lover could possibly be queer.

After Lana, Peter was involved with June Allyson, many years before fellow Rat Packer Dean Martin got his hands on her. They met while they were making *Two Sisters from Boston*. June was married to Dick Powell at the time, but she found the charms of Peter too strong to fend off. Peter would also dally with Ava Gardner some time after her marriage to Mickey Rooney and before her marriage to Frank Sinatra. His relationship with her would cause a big blowup with Frank many years later.

In between all this romantic activity, his film career was proceeding nicely. *Son of Lassie* (1945) provided him with his first bona fide starring role. Again he played the grown-up version of Roddy McDowall, who had played the same character in the first Lassie film. Young girls in particular reacted to the smooth good looks and continental charm of Peter Lawford. He went to openings, squired pretty starlets to nightclubs, and had the occasional back alley dalliance with a handsome male extra or even a gay star, while his mother sat home and fumed and berated his father for his son's ingratitude.

His affair with Allyson had ended by the time they appeared together in *Good News* (1947), a college musical that was set in the 1920s. Not only was it hard to believe the two of them as college kids, but neither of them could sing, making their casting rather ludicrous. (Allyson's singing voice—let alone her speaking voice—had always been one of the prime horrors of Hollywood.) A harmless bit of fluff, the film boasts some funny sequences and several great old songs such as "The Best Things in Life Are Free."

Shortly before he began making this picture, Peter had his first encounter with Frank Sinatra at a party at Louis B. Mayer's house. The dinner party was held in honor of Henry Ford. Sinatra was at the height of his career at this point and probably attracted even more female admirers among the dinner guests than Peter did, although Lawford certainly held his own. Sinatra met Peter through the former's date, actress Marilyn Maxwell, and the trio sat together commenting bitchily on the other ossified diners, lap dogs, and toadies that Mayer had assembled at his court. They discovered that they found amusement in many of the same things, and both found the other much more genial and down-to-earth than their stardom might indicate. The two became casual friends, going bar-hopping on occasion or playing cards with other young men around Hollywood. (Peter became so well known for rarely picking up a check that when he and Frank appeared in a restaurant sketch in a private revue for guests at a New Year's Eve party at Frank's house, Frank played a waiter who drops a whole tray of dishes when he overhears Lawford ask for the bill.)

Thus it was no surprise that Frank pulled a few strings and got Peter cast in his third picture for MGM, a musical called *It Happened in Brooklyn* (1947). Things were rather tense on the set. Sinatra had asked his wife Nancy for a divorce because he wanted to marry Maxwell (who was herself divorcing actor John Conte), but she had flatly refused. Lawford was also in a state of tension because it was one thing to sing in a movie with hoarse-throated June Allyson and quite another to sing in a movie with the one and only Frank Sinatra. Peter managed to compensate for his mediocre warbling by dancing a jitterbug that had his fans in a lather.

Peter was also delighted with the on-set antics of Jimmy Durante, who gave the film most of its humor. Years later the two would put together a nightclub act. Gloria Grahame wasn't crazy that most of her footage never made it into the picture, and Kathryn Grayson had an unrequited crush on Peter. The movie itself was a typical study of young show biz types hoping to make it into the big time, but it varied the formula a little by withholding the cherished stardom from its characters even in the final reel. Another surprise was that Grayson winds up with Lawford instead of Sinatra. The saving grace of the picture was such songs as "Time After Time."

Peter, unfortunately, wound up doing a number of forgettable musicals, such as *On an Island with You*, which had the same director as *Brooklyn*, Richard Thorpe. In this Peter was a Navy man who courts Esther Williams, playing—what else?—a movie star filming a tropical epic. Her boyfriend Ricardo Montalban stews in the background, and once again Durante was on hand to supply the film's fitful supply of laughter. Not even the adorable chihuahua that shows up at inopportune moments could save this dog. Peter was technically Esther's co-star, but what with Montalban and Durante—and even Cyd Charisse and Xavier Cugat, not to mention dogs—along for the ride it's no wonder he felt that his career was backsliding badly.

When Peter did *Easter Parade* (1948) with Judy Garland, he discovered that the sweet girl he had known when he'd first come to Hollywood—he'd been an extra in *Girl Crazy* with Garland and Mickey Rooney—was now a very screwed up and highly neurotic woman whose difficulties with pills Peter would sadly emulate later in his life. At this time her marriage to Vincente Minnelli wasn't going so well, and she had come back home after being "away"—a forties euphemism for entering a sanitarium—for several weeks. To console her, to give her some life-affirming attention when she was feeling unloved and worthless, Peter went to bed with her. Their affair lasted awhile but didn't really go anywhere romantically.

Things got even more serious when he worked with Elizabeth Taylor on *Julia Misbehaves* (1948), even though—or perhaps because—she was only sixteen at the time. It seems Liz's mother thought Peter would make a good husband for her daughter. Not only did Peter not want to marry Liz, he didn't want to go to bed with her, not only because of her tender age but because Louis B. Mayer had let it be known that whoever screwed Liz—literally or figuratively—would have to answer to him. Liz was devastated as only a sixteen-year-old girl can be when Peter told her they had no future.

There were two women Peter nearly got serious about who weren't in the picture business: Sharman Douglas and Jean Macdonald. The former was a jet-setting socialite who set her sights on Peter and pursued him from coast to coast—and country to country—even after he had broken off their engagement. The latter was a society reporter for a Honolulu newspaper. He became engaged to her after he convinced her to move to Los Angeles, where the two would double date with Frank Sinatra and Ava Gardner. But he also backed out of this marriage, although the two remained friends for many years. Peter also carried on a torrid affair with Dorothy Dandridge, but they never reached the engagement stage, let alone marriage. That daring Peter wasn't.

In 1950 Lady May threw a big party during which she announced her big news: after years of beating on MGM's doors, she had finally—against all odds—been granted a contract, both as actress and an "adviser" for movies that took place in England. She managed to get small roles in such films as *Mr. Peabody and the Mermaid*, but her "career" never amounted to much. She was desperately trying to beat Peter at his own game; it was a competition he had no interest in taking part in. His mother's later mistreatment of Jean Macdonald during their engagement period so enraged him that he cut off as much contact with her as he possibly could. If it hadn't been for his ailing father, he would probably never have seen her again. It was bad enough that she'd tried to destroy him by going to Mayer—he'd never forgive her for that—but when she attacked his friends, women he cared about, that was too much.

The year 1952 was Lawford's last at MGM. One of his films released that year was *Just This Once*, in which he was teamed with fringe Rat Packer Janet Leigh. Not much later his contract was dropped. His pictures just weren't making very much money. One can imagine the mixed emotions mother May had when she learned the news: a smirking satisfaction coupled with the alarm that her meal ticket could no longer deliver (she was hardly making much of a splash in Tinseltown; years later she would write her autobiography and entitle it, appropriately enough, *Bitch*).

May was even more upset when she learned that Peter

had to sell his house, the house she'd lived in since he'd started earning real money. He pocketed the profit of the sale, then shunted May off to a small apartment in Westwood.

Salvation of sorts came in the form of a new manager who promptly got Peter into *It Should Happen to You* (1954) with Judy Holliday and film newcomer Jack Lemmon. Judy fell madly in love with Peter and he was only too willing to bed her, whereupon the usual pattern asserted itself. As soon as the woman—in this case, Holliday—got too serious, Peter would have to break it off. At least he was no longer getting engaged to every woman he slept with.

Peter couldn't have known what was in his future with the Rat Pack when Judy suggested they put together a nightclub act. It was a way for her to continue working and being with him once filming on *It Should Happen* wrapped. Peter was interested enough in the idea to go with her to meet with writers Betty Comden and Adolph Green, whom she hoped would write material for them. Judy was so excited she contacted the Sands in Vegas and told them to make room for her and Peter in the fall. When Peter realized what was really behind this he quickly told her that he didn't really think a nightclub act was the best way to make use of his talents. Judy then suggested that they appear in a play together somewhere, maybe even do dinner theater. Peter nixed that, too. "I haven't a theatrical background, honey," he told her with a shrug. It wasn't long before he stopped returning her phone calls.

It Should Happen to You was successful at the box office, but it failed to revive Peter's film career. This time he sought salvation on television—a TV series called *Dear Phoebe* and later the *Thin Man* knockoff with Phyllis Kirk— and in the arms of Patricia Kennedy, one of Joe Kennedy's daughters. By 1954, Peter and Pat were married, and as one of the Kennedys he became more famous than ever.

When he read of Humphrey Bogart's death in 1957, Peter would have given a call to his former buddy Frank Sinatra, but ever since the Ava Gardner business Frank had refused to speak to him.

It wasn't until Peter's brother-in-law decided to run for president that Frank would find a use for him.

9

The Bishop

He was born in the Bronx, the man who would become known as Sinatra's sidekick, the comedian Joey Bishop. Becoming friends with Frank catapulted Bishop from the ranks of moderately successful standup comics to a superstar, but none of this happened overnight.

He came into the world on February 3, 1918, under the moniker Joseph Abraham Gottlieb, the son of an immigrant machinist, Jacob, and his wife Anna, who already had four children. When Joey was three months old the family moved to South Philadelphia, where his father managed a bicycle shop. Jacob played the ocarina and Joey's older brother Morris had a banjo-mandolin, and Joey pestered them until he was fairly proficient—for a child—with both instruments. His father also taught him a few Yiddish songs while Morris showed him how to tap dance. But Joey's on-the-money impressions of visiting friends and neighbors were the delight of his family. Little Joey loved entertainers, and when he got older he would hang around the stage door of Philadelphia's Earle Theatre hoping to catch a glimpse of some vaudevillian like Ted Lewis.

Although Joey did well in junior high, he never finished high school, not only because his academic level had plummeted out of basic disinterest but because the family needed him to go to work. He got a job at a luncheonette, but his impressions of the customers got on their nerves and he was eventually asked to leave. That same year, at nineteen, he entered a variety show and won three dollars doing impersonations of everyone from Jimmy Durante to Katharine Hepburn. Convinced that he could have a highly successful career in show business, he took off for New York City to take the town by storm. He had a fortune of thirty dollars in his pocket and two suits for all occasions.

He moved in with relatives on the Lower East Side of Manhattan and got a job at a Chinese restaurant as "master of ceremonies." The owner of the restaurant paid him thirteen dollars a week but refused to feed him, so he had to bring sandwiches to work. He wore a rented tux while he told a few jokes and introduced singers and piano players to the diners. To feel more like a true entertainer, he wore makeup and kept it on during the subway ride home so everyone would realize that he must be in "the business."

Unfortunately he wasn't in the business very long, as the gig at the restaurant only lasted two weeks. Only a few months after he'd left South Philly, he was back in town, working at the bicycle shop his father ran. It was a depressing period for him, and although his family did their best to convince him he needed a steady trade and steady job to keep food on the table, Joey never stopped believing in himself. As he followed his father's edicts in the bicycle shop, his mind was working, working, thinking up ways of getting away from the grease and oil and back into the business that he loved.

Salvation, of sorts, came in the form of two friends of his who agreed to form an act with him. Mel Farber was one of the two boys and he became a lifelong friend of Joey's, although their careers took very divergent paths. Joey, Mel, and "Rummy" Spector decided they might be more of a novelty if they pretended they were brothers, so the Bishop Brothers comedy trio was born. The name Bishop came from Glenn Bishop, a black friend of theirs who drove the three to engagements in Pennsylvania and New Jersey. These occasional gigs helped Joey feel he was in the business again, but by any name the Bishop Brothers were broke more often than not. The biggest city they got to was Chicago—mostly they played the burlesque circuit and did the Catskills—but their circumstances there were so reduced that they were forced to eat a half-spoiled salami from home and got food poisoning.

Spector dropped out of the act and Mel and Joey, both of whom retained the name Bishop (sporadically for Mel) for the rest of their lives, became a duo. They hadn't much more success than they'd had as a threesome, part of the problem being that "Rummy had supplied the punch lines," as Bishop put it, and he and Mel were straight men. That situation had to change, and Joey was willing to oblige, but by 1940 Mel dropped out and Joey was on his own. Joey had extremely mixed emotions about doing a solo: on one hand he liked having the spotlight all to himself, but on the other hand, he was nervous at the thought of facing a possibly hostile or indifferent audience on his lonesome. Part of Bishop deeply resented Mel's quitting on him while the other part was glad to see him go.

Joey's first job as a solo act was in a club actually named El Dumpo in Cleveland, Ohio, in 1940. Frank Sinatra had yet to become a superstar but was already a successful vocalist at this time. Dean Martin was anxiously awaiting his first look at his new nose, and Peter Lawford was an extra in Hollywood. Sammy Davis Jr., all of fifteen, had met Sinatra in Detroit when the Will Mastin Trio was on the same bill as Tommy Dorsey.

Bishop was twenty-two years old and anxious to make good. He had a long engagement at El Dumpo, but also did other clubs along the East Coast. He was working in Miami Beach when in-between shows a young lady named Sylvia Ruzga said, "I haven't seen you do anything funny." Something must have clicked in spite of this because Joey and Sylvia walked down the aisle on January 14, 1941, less than two months after meeting.

In April 1942 Bishop was drafted. Like Sammy Davis Jr., he was not a big enough star at the time to avoid it; also like Sammy, he never went overseas. Assigned to Special Services, he became a sergeant and was eventually made the Director of Recreation at Fort Sam Houston in Texas. Discharged in 1945, Joey remained with Sylvia in Texas, where he tried to revive his stand-up career in clubs in San Antonio. Entertainment contacts he'd made in the Army led him to sign up with the William Morris Agency, who called him one afternoon to let him know that a dream of his had come true: They'd managed to book him into the Greenwich Village Inn in New York City. This time, he told himself, he wouldn't leave New York in defeat as he had years earlier.

While the Greenwich Village Inn was hardly the Copa, it was a step up from the Chinese eatery and provided Bishop a place where he could hone his act before a more sophisticated audience. Gradually news of him began to travel through word of mouth and small bits in columns. More and more people went downtown to catch his act until he began developing a following. He stayed at the Inn for some months before his agents told him it was time to move on to bigger fish in both New York and Chicago. One successful club engagement led to another, but it was seven long years before he hit the top markets, such as New York's famed Latin Quarter, where he earned $1000 a week.

It was while he was at the Latin Quarter that Frank Sinatra first saw him perform and liked what he saw. Sinatra went backstage and advised him not to change a thing about his act. Whatever his flaws, Sinatra had always admired talented people and did his best to help them when he could. He told Bishop that he wanted him to open for him when he, Sinatra, appeared at the Riviera nightclub in Fort Lee, New Jersey. Bishop was happy to do so, although being on the same bill as Frank Sinatra was not as prestigious in 1952 as it was in the forties or would be after Frank's comeback. Luckily, Bishop took the gig, and from thereafter was seen by Sinatra as a friend. A friend who went big places after Blue Eyes found himself back on top again.

Of Frank, Bishop was to say, "Frank is a friend indeed. If he doesn't like something he barks, sure. But often he has real justification, or at least thinks he does. I think basically that he's fair." Frank said of Bishop: "The guy's always good for a laugh, fun to be with. Somebody who can bring you up if you need it. He never fails me on that score." Friends noted, however, that Bishop was never really Frank's toady, unlike certain other members of the Rat Pack.

During these early years Bishop developed a philosophy that was a significant part of his success. It didn't matter how funny you were, he figured, if the audience didn't like you—if they didn't think you were a nice person offstage, no amount of humor could save you. Some comics, in his opinion, depended too much upon jokes. "If you've got a joke in your routine that'll cause an audience to walk out talking about the joke instead of you, take it out." He added: "Everything I do is within the framework of a certain attitude." The attitude he projected was casual, friendly, likable, and definitely—if not defiantly—uncontroversial. He wanted to appeal to the largest possible audience and that wouldn't work if you turned off half of it with something too tactless, risque, or political. (It took Frank Sinatra to make Bishop embrace a particular political candidate years later, something he would probably have been loathe to do on his own.)

Bishop was so determined to be liked by the audience that he refused to do jokes that deprecated another comedian even if the comedian himself suggested such jokes. Appearing with Jack Benny, Bishop was supposed to make comments making fun of Benny's stinginess and other aspects of his put-upon persona, but he refused to do so, reasoning that it might turn the audience, Benny's—and hopefully someday, Bishop's—fans, against him. One writer characterized Bishop's work as "homogenized" and added that "his jokes have been worked over so sedulously that they no longer require any frame of reference more special than English, a realization that New York is not the United States and a knowledge of the difference between the sexes."

Bishop's career was certainly successful in his pre-Sinatra days, but he wasn't quite "big" yet, certainly not big enough to be invited to Holmby Hills on a regular basis. Bishop was never a member of Bogie's Rat Pack, but that would change once Sinatra took over.

In 1957, when Bogart died, Bishop was ready, willing, and able to take advantage of every opportunity that came his way, not the least of which was the chance to become a member of Sinatra's famous Rat Pack and all that came with it.

Bogart was dead. The players were all in place. And Betty Bacall, the grieving widow, needed a shoulder to lean on.

It was time for Sinatra to take over.

PART TWO

The Golden Years

1957–1970

10

Sinatra Takes Over

Now that Bogie was dead there was the question of who would deliver the eulogy for this beloved man. Lauren first asked Spencer Tracy if he would do it, but Tracy told her that he had been too close to her late husband and he would get too emotional; he'd never be able to get through it. "Forgive me, but please ask someone else," Tracy told her.

Considering their feelings toward one another, Bacall knew that Frank Sinatra would not be the appropriate person to deliver the eulogy no matter how much he had idolized her late husband. She decided to ask director John Huston, who accepted.

Frank was in New York when Bogie died, appearing at the Copa. After he heard the news he told the Copa management not to expect him to perform that night; he was too upset to go on. He called Lauren and expressed his sincere condolences—among more personal sentiments—and told her he would fly to California for the funeral.

Out in Holmby Hills, Lauren and her children were surrounded by the other members of the Rat Pack: the Nivens, Romanoffs, Lufts, etc., but Frank was conspicuous in his absence. Bogie's death had, of course, awakened the thought of his own mortality. Frank's idol had died of a disease that chose its victims carelessly, indiscriminately, unfairly. He was also haunted by his strong feelings for the woman whose husband had just died and hers for him. He canceled several more shows at the Copa and wondered what the future held and exactly how he should proceed with Lauren, if at all.

Frank did not show up for Bogie's funeral. Afterward, everyone went back to the house in Holmby Hills for a "party" or impromptu wake that Bogart would have enjoyed and appreciated. Mike Romanoff had catered the affair with food from his famous restaurant served by a host of busy, starstruck waiters. The usual suspects were there, in addition to such luminaries and their spouses as the Gregory Pecks, the Ira Gershwins, the William Wylers, as well as Spencer and Kate, Marlene Dietrich, Danny Kaye, and many, many others paying homage to Bogie.

In the midst of this Sinatra called Lauren and told her he was sorry he'd not been able to make it; he was nursing a sudden onslaught of laryngitis. He told her she should go to his house in Palm Springs with her kids and get away from it all for a couple of weeks. She agreed, and told him she'd let him know when they were leaving. Frank was the only one of her close friends not to be at her side and, ironically, the one she would turn to increasingly as the weeks after Bogie's death went by.

Lauren also derived great comfort from David Niven, whose first wife had died years before at an early age. Niven knew what it was like to lose your soulmate, and whatever Betty and Bogie may have lacked in the romantic and sensual arena, they were definitely soulmates. Niven told Lauren that every day the pain would lessen a little until "one day you can put it in a different perspective." He told her that one day she would be able to put Bogie in a "different place" in her life, although she would never forget him.

Of course, it's much easier to recover from the loss of a spouse if one is still at a relatively young (and attractive) age and can start over again. Had Lauren been fifty-seven, as Bogie had been at the time of his death, she may have found it much more difficult to deal with her grief and go on with her life with someone new. That someone, at least for a while, was Frank Sinatra.

In Palm Springs, Lauren entertained the Nivens and Cary Grant and other famous friends who came to visit her. These friends, of course, included Sinatra, in whose house she was staying. They did not go out publicly as a couple for quite some time, however. The closest thing to a public appearance was a small dinner party Frank arranged for Lauren before she was to leave for New York to do publicity for her film *Designing Woman*. Also at this party were Spencer Tracy and Kate Hepburn, who had never gone anywhere as a couple except to Bogart's house as he was dying and after his funeral. Lauren was touched that they had bothered to come. "Katie even wore a dress!" she remembered years later.

In New York Lauren made the rounds of bars and parties with close friends in the business such as Betty Comden and Adolph Green (who co-wrote the *On the Town* screenplay), Arlene Francis, and Sydney Chaplin. Knowing it would be in the worst possible taste to go out with Bogie's widow so soon after the man's death, Frank limited his interest in Lauren to frequent phone calls. In her own words, Lauren began to "depend" on those phone calls. For one thing, every other man in her social circle except Swifty Lazar—who was not terribly attractive—was married. Swifty was a good shoulder to lean on, someone to talk to, but he couldn't fulfill a basic human need she had. Frank Sinatra represented at that time her only chance for future romance.

It was four months after Bogart had been buried that Lauren and Frank went out on a nominal "date." Frank had gotten the idea that if they went out with a whole group it wouldn't be seen as if the two of them together were a couple. The battle for the middleweight boxing championship between Sugar Ray Robinson and Gene Fullmer provided the perfect opportunity for Frank to put his plan into action. As the fight was shown on closed-circuit television in certain theaters, Frank bought an entire row of seats and invited Lauren—along with nearly a dozen other people—to watch the action with him. Having set her sights on him quite a while before, Lauren wasted no time telling Frank that she'd be delighted to come.

At the theater there was a bit of comedy as Frank's guests played musical chairs so that Frank could wind up sitting next to Lauren. (Nobody wanted to sit next to Frank and face his ire over the fact that it wasn't Lauren sitting next to him.) He had planned it that way, but somebody didn't stick to the seating arrangement and after a few significant glares from Frank and much hasty chair-hopping, the desired seating plan was finally arrived at. Frank and Lauren held hands as they watched the fight.

But the battle really began when the twosome emerged from the theater still basking in the afterglow of spending so much time in the dark together. News had leaked about Sinatra being in the theater, and as soon as he and his group emerged, the photographers started snapping. By this time, Lauren and Frank weren't bothering to hide the fact that she was his date, and they walked out of the lobby as an obvious couple. Shots of the two of them wound up in virtually every paper from coast to coast and overseas. Captions hinted that there was a romance between the two without actually coming out and saying it.

Lauren had begun to rely on Frank long before Bogie's death. During his lengthy illness when it seemed she was constantly surrounded by medicines and sick smells and encroaching decay, Frank represented youth and vitality.

It was inevitable the two would become a very public couple after Bogart's demise. There had been something magnetic between them from the very start. Frank had every bit of Bogie's charisma, but on top of it he was—to Lauren—a lot sexier.

Before long they were an item; people expected to see them together, invited them to the same parties, sat them next to each other at the dinner table, talked of them always as "Betty and Frank, Frank and Betty." Lauren saw marriage in the cards, and their female friends with a yen for the crooner grew catty and jealous. Other friends told Lauren to take it easy; if she pushed she'd lose him but if she let things run their natural course she might become the third Mrs. Sinatra—to her possible regret. But nothing ever runs smoothly where love is involved, and before long there were disturbing incidents to mar the surface of Lauren's dream of perfect love and her image of Frank as Prince Charming-to-the-rescue.

First, Frank stopped calling her for more than a week. Previously he had either seen Lauren every day or called her if he was out of town or otherwise unable to drop by. Lauren became hysterical, imagining all sorts of dire reasons for his silence, the worst of which being that he had decided to dump her. Just when she had nearly convinced herself that it must be over, Frank called with no explanation or apology and told her what their next week's itinerary would be, the places he'd be taking her to. Frank always liked to plan their evenings; she could "suggest" things, as he put it, but never, ever did he want her "telling" him anything.

This sort of thing kept repeating itself. Frank would make big plans for a weekend together or some holiday celebration, but days before the event he'd completely withdraw—no phone calls, no explanations—leaving Lauren wondering if the plans he'd made were on or off. When he did call again, to tell her what time he'd be picking her up, for instance, it was as if the intervening days or weeks of silence had never existed, as if he was taking up the tail end of a conversation he had started and never finished the last time they spoke.

Lauren knew better than to ask him what he'd been up to or why he didn't call—he would never have told her and would have hated being asked—but she was left completely unsettled by his on-again, off-again attitude. Were they a couple or weren't they? Lovers were supposed to spend all their time together, weren't they? She never knew what to tell her friends; she couldn't make any concrete plans with others. What sort of "fine romance" was this?

Frank's moodiness continually left Lauren nonplussed, such as the time Frank just took over as the host-with-the-most at a Halloween party Lauren threw at her home. He was utterly lovely to her and the children most of the evening, but grew sullen and difficult later and stalked out with hardly a word. His heavy drinking would occasionally exacerbate the problem.

The relationship nearly came to a finish one weekend in Palm Springs. On New Year's Eve Frank threw a party at the new edition of Mike Romanoff's restaurant, but, since he wouldn't be able to arrive until later, asked Lauren to act as hostess. When he arrived he greeted her with real affection and the two went on to have a marvelous evening with their friends. But the very next morning Frank told Lauren that it would be better if she went home—no explanations, he just wanted her gone.

Lauren refused to leave, but when the gang came over to Frank's place in the evening, Frank completely shut her out. He consumed drink after drink at the bar while Lauren tried to put a brave face on it for their friends, who sensed something was up. By now everyone in the crowd—the old Rat Pack on its way to becoming a new Rat Pack without either Bogie or Betty—would study the couple's faces as they arrived to see what sort of mood Frank was in and whether or not he and Lauren had been fighting. Frank's moods could create, as Lauren (and many others) put it, a "volcanic atmosphere." They weren't exactly the "Battling Bogarts" (Bogie and Mayo) or "Battling Sinatras" (Frank and Ava), but their arrival at an affair often created immediate tension until everyone could see that Frank and Lauren were smiling and all was well. Sometimes it didn't work out that way. One night at the Beachcomber Jule Styne's date told Frank he'd be lucky to have Lauren for a wife, and he shut her and Jule out for the rest of the evening.

Lauren didn't understand that she was putting on too much pressure—and on the wrong man at that. Lauren had always been taken care of, first by her mother, then by Bogart, and she was looking not just for a lover but someone who could take her under his wing and deal with each and every one of her problems, fears, concerns; she was a child as well as a woman, and it was the child part that especially bothered Sinatra. Like a little girl she clung to him, she smothered him. He ran out of parties and asked her to leave his house when she began acting too much like a girl-bride. Bad enough she came on like a wife, a potential ball and chain, at times, but he couldn't deal with that wounded, vulnerable, puppyish quality she exuded; it was just too overbearing.

Frank liked broads—broads who knew their place but could take care of themselves, who cut their men some slack. He knew that Lauren would not be able to handle his need for other women. She herself came to realize that he was a restless, unsettled individual who wanted a family life on one hand, and freedom—freedom from responsibility, freedom to pursue—on the other. Frank liked barrooms, easy women, the whole smoky, boozy atmosphere of late nights out on the town, and there were times he just didn't want a woman—certainly not "the" woman—along for the ride.

They were not a good match. Still, their relationship continued—after the New Year's debacle Frank called her when she was in New York and they had dinner together—until Frank finally popped the question when she returned to California. He admitted that he had felt trapped, but now he told her he had built up his courage and was ready for the plunge. Delirious with joy, Lauren told him she'd marry him without hesitation. The two were so excited they wanted to share the news. They made the mistake of calling their friend, Swifty Lazar, and asked him to have a celebratory drink with them at a Japanese restaurant not far from the Garden of Allah, where Bogie had lived before marrying Lauren.

Swifty was incredulous at first, but finally realized the two weren't joking when they started making plans for the wedding right in front of him. The following day Frank left for work in Miami, and Swifty took Lauren to see a play starring Emlyn Williams. Sitting in the audience was gossip maven Louella Parsons, who cornered Lauren and Swifty during intermission. She asked Lauren if it were true that she was engaged to Frank Sinatra, but Lauren ducked the question and went back to her seat. Swifty, however, remained with Louella for several minutes. The next day Louella's column broke the story: "Sinatra to Marry Bacall." Lauren was in shock.

Swifty seemed to think he had done nothing wrong in blabbing to Louella, but Lauren knew that Frank would be furious, which he was. Swifty agreed to give Frank the bad news, but severely downplayed his role in it. Frank took out his anger on Lauren and—again—stopped calling her for several days. If his withdrawals had been bad before, this time it was a real killer. When he finally broke his silence from Miami, he berated Lauren again and told her that now that the cat was out of the bag he was so besieged by the press that he couldn't even leave his hotel room. He told her it would be better if they not see each other for awhile. A long while, his tone of voice implied.

That was the last time that Lauren ever got a phone call from Frank Sinatra, but things got even more brutal. When Frank got back to Los Angeles, he went out to dinner with Swifty—the one he should really have been mad at—and never went to see Lauren to talk things over as he had said he would. After that, Lauren found herself cut out of the Hollywood loop, as friends she had made through Frank completely shunned her. She rarely got invited to the same parties he did anymore, but when it happened, even if he was seated nearby, he would look right past her and not say a word. It was as if she no longer existed.

Six years later Lauren and Frank were both invited to a party given by the notorious Swifty, who was hoping for fireworks but got more than he bargained for when Frank, inebriated, tore off the tablecloth, threw drinks around, and screeched at him that he was to blame for what happened between him and Bacall.

Lauren always assumed that Frank had finally accepted that night that it was Swifty who had leaked the news of their engagement to Parsons, and not her, but there are strong reasons to believe that he was referring to Swifty's general sabotaging of the Betty/Frank romance. An ugly little man addicted to power plays and the beautiful people he resented—as a top literary agent years later he held famous Oscar-night parties in Hollywood up until his death—Swifty was fully capable of viciously turning people against one another if it suited his purposes. Swifty was furious that pretty Lauren treated him like a shoulder-to-cry-on while she saved her kisses for Frank. Whether Swifty actually wanted Lauren for himself or not is irrelevant; he was jealous of Frank's chemistry and sex appeal, qualities he was totally lacking (although he had plenty of chutzpah).

He was also angry at Lauren for berating him, "turning

on him," when he had his little chat with Louella. For Bogie's
sake Swifty had done a lot to help Lauren after her husband's
death, but he was suspicious of—and morally outraged by—
how long before Bogart's passing she may have been carrying
a torch for Frank.

"Swifty could charm the pants off a serial killer," a long-
time associate of his has said, "but he had no true concept of
'friendship.' Lauren was too young and naive, too sheltered
by Bogie's basic goodness, to understand Swifty's type of personality. He loved having power over people's lives. He was a
truly putrid person. No matter how well you got to know him,
how nicely he seemed to treat you, you had to watch your
back—or else."

Suffering from cold feet, Sinatra saw an out for himself
when he heard about Louella Parsons' column. Although it
was true that he had always valued his privacy, his reaction
to the leak of their engagement was overplayed, to say the
least. Sinatra has always claimed that there's another side to
the story of his break up with Lauren—that he is not the villain she has portrayed him as—and that is true as far as it
goes. But his behavior was still abominable and cowardly
and nothing to crow about. But he was not the main villain
in this mess.

According to reliable sources, Sinatra had fully intended to follow up his last phone call to Lauren with a personal
visit when he was back in Los Angeles, but it was Swifty who
headed him off. During their dinner together Swifty did a
number on Frank's head, warning him of how needy and pos-
sessive Lauren was and how much she needed a new Bogart
in her life. Angry at Lauren and jealous of Frank (and envious of their much more successful positions in life), Swifty
probably told himself he was doing the both of them a favor
by breaking them up for good. Recognizing that twice-
divorced Sinatra had mixed emotions about getting hitched
again, Lazar played on those emotions by feeding every pri-

vate paranoid feeling Frank had ever had about Lauren and women in general. First wife Nancy had been too much of a whiny drag on him; Ava had cuckolded and deserted him. Now Swifty told him that Lauren was only out to use him, that without Bogie she was washed up in Hollywood and needed Frank to go to bat for her the way Bogie had. Before the dinner—and much drinking—was over, Swifty had his willing victim convinced that Lauren was a conniver and opportunist out to use him and that she had never really loved him; he ought to get rid of her. He also strongly implied that Lauren hadn't done all she could have to help him win Ava back—just the opposite, in fact—because she had made up her mind to land Frank for herself. That was all Sinatra needed to hear.

Frank wanted to believe all of this; that way he was off the hook with Lauren. He wouldn't even have to go and see her, the bitch, and tell her they were through, their engagement a mistake, something he had not been looking forward to. He owed her nothing. When he told Ava Gardner, who called him when she heard the news of their engagement, that he'd never intended to marry "that pushy broad," Ava thought the whole thing hilarious, which she told Frank— and that Lauren, despite her tears, was well rid of him, which she did not.

Frank was home free.

Six years later Swifty invited Lauren and Frank to the same party—another power play on his part—hoping to see them squirm or possibly have a to-do, but to his surprise it was Swifty himself that Frank turned on. Feeling a bit sentimental and six years wiser, Frank had begun to realize what Swifty may have done to him—and especially Lauren—but he also felt guilt over believing Swifty's lies so quickly out of his own needs.

Of that period he once said, "Betty had a tough row to hoe after Bogie's death. I tried to help. Maybe things got out of hand, but I have no regrets." Peter Lawford defended Sinatra, sort of, by saying, "I think the publicity overkill was too much for Frank. Things got too hurried for him. If they had been able to take their time they might have made it. But the press got in the way."

Bogie was dead and Bacall was out of the picture, torn from his life, ostracized by his friends. Betty's friends all thought that Frank had treated her abominably and wanted nothing to do with him. Lauren had moved from Holmby Hills by now, but when she got together with the old Rat Pack—the Nivens, the Romanoffs, the Lufts, even Swifty, whose duplicity she was largely unaware of—Sinatra was never invited.

But it didn't matter. There really was no Rat Pack now that Bogart was dead. And Frank had bigger fish to fry. And his own, more pliable friends for a Rat Pack of his own.

11

The Benevolent Monster

Amidst all the love struggles with Ava and Lauren, the newspaper scandals, the death of Bogie, and the problems with the Rat Pack, Sinatra's career kept flourishing. His records may not have sold as well as they had before, but they were climbing up the charts again; he was having hits. And his movies were making money at the box office.

Throughout the fifties Frank had been busy in Hollywood since his triumph in *From Here to Eternity*, although some projects were more successful than others. One particular film would come back to haunt him years later. In *Suddenly*, which was released in 1954, Frank played the leader of a gang of hit men who are planning to bump off the President when he disembarks at the train station in the small town of Suddenly. Frank's character plans to fire at the platform from the window of a house where resides an old retired Secret Service man and his widowed daughter-in-law, who's the girlfriend of the town's sheriff (Sterling Hayden). While the theme of the film—that violence is justified in self-defense and the defense of loved ones (Sterling's girlfriend, who hates war and guns, saves the day by shooting Frank)—

was admirable, the picture was too indifferently directed by Lewis Allen to have much impact. Stagy, talky, and badly acted by Frank and company, the film only gets interesting at the suspenseful climax. *Suddenly* would have been suddenly forgotten had it not been for the assassination of JFK years later. Sinatra immediately had the film taken out of circulation and it wasn't seen for decades, creating a mystique around it that it never deserved.

Young at Heart (1954) teamed Frank with Doris Day in a soap opera detailing the romantic entanglements of several daughters in a large family and was notable for two reasons: Frank worked with director Gordon Douglas (who would later direct *Robin and the 7 Hoods*, among others) for the first time; and the scene in which Frank tries to commit suicide in a car. Sinatra summoned up all his hurt, humiliated feelings over Ava and the years when he was a has-been, the memories of his own suicide attempts, to make it work and was almost frighteningly convincing in this scene. Douglas's direction made the most of the sequence. Two hours of unrequited love, attempted suicides, and tons of depression were whitewashed into a ludicrously "happy" ending wherein Doris Day and Sinatra have a baby and all is suddenly right with the world.

Not as a Stranger (1955) was really Robert Mitchum's picture, but Frank was determined not to lose any momentum in Hollywood now that he was again in demand, and he figured this adaptation of a bestseller would be a "big picture"—like *From Here to Eternity*—that he would want to be a part of. Unfortunately, he wound up virtually the comedy relief in the minor supporting role of Mitchum's buddy. While this story of a determined young doctor who marries a woman for her money was better than a soap, it wasn't substantial enough in script or treatment to amount to much more.

The Tender Trap (1955) was a trifle with Debbie

Reynolds, while *Guys and Dolls* brought him into contact—and conflict—with Marlon Brando. Sinatra had coveted the role in *On the Waterfront* that went to Brando and thereafter began bad-mouthing the actor whenever he could. News of this got back to Brando, so things were pretty tense on the set when they finally began to work together. The two men never liked one another. Sinatra thought Brando was a phony, playing at being a tough dockworker (in *On the Waterfront*) and other gritty types when he, Sinatra, was (in his view) the real thing. Another problem was that Brando was no singer but insisted on doing his own rather lamentable warbling in *Guys and Dolls*.

Earlier Frank had started filming *Carousel* but walked off when he learned two versions (in different "scopes" or film sizes) were being filmed and he was only being paid for one. While his voice was not appropriate for Rodgers and Hammerstein's soaring, near-operatic score in *Carousel*, it was just right for Frank Loesser's bouncy, jazzier songs in *Guys and Dolls*. Sinatra already thought, as many did, that Brando was hopelessly overrated as an actor, but when he heard Brando butchering some great tunes he nearly gagged. He consoled himself with the thought of how much better he would sound than Brando did when the film came out. Except for unrealistic Brando apologists, every critic felt that Sinatra put Brando in the shade as both actor and singer in the film. The light touch required by material like *Guys and Dolls* was much more up Frank's alley than Brando's.

The Man with the Golden Arm (1955) earned him an Oscar nomination for Best Actor and teamed him with Kim Novak for the first time. Novak would have professional and personal encounters with most of the members of the Rat Pack at one time or another. *The Man with the Golden Arm*, in which he played a tormented heroine addict, was to become Frank's favorite out of all of his movies. *Johnny Concho* (1956) was another project Frank did with buddy

Don (*Meet Danny Wilson*) McGuire; this time McGuire directed as well as co-wrote the screenplay. The western did little at the box office. *High Society* (1956) teamed Sinatra with Bing Crosby for the first time; as this was before a certain misunderstanding developed between the two singers, there were no major incidents while making the film. Then Frank and Shirley MacLaine both had cameos in the massive production of *Around the World in 80 Days* (1956).

Sinatra worked with Sophia Loren and Cary Grant in *The Pride and the Passion* (1957), but the cannon everyone was fighting over got most of the closeups. Then he reteamed with Kim Novak—and Rita Hayworth—in Rodgers and Hart's musical *Pal Joey*, for which he was perfect. In *Kings Go Forth* (1958) he got former girlfriend Natalie Wood a juicy role as the center of a love triangle whose corners consisted of Frank and fringe Rat Packer Tony Curtis. Sinatra was also able to work in some of his beloved social commentary when the Wood character was made part black. Sinatra's next film was to be the first real Rat Pack movie, *Some Came Running*, with Dean and Shirley MacLaine.

Interspersed with all these films—he was one of the busiest Hollywood actors of all during this period before and right after Bogie's death—Frank's personal life was as chaotic and fraught with controversy as ever. Although Sinatra would eternally blame the press for blowing things out of proportion (actually he did not want them reporting on anything but his professional projects), the trouble always lay with Frank himself.

Back in the forties in the days of the Varsity he had been given the nickname "the Monster" by Jimmy Van Heusen, which he and others used strictly behind Frank's back. Many people Frank mistreated put up with it because their professional or personal lives owed a lot to Sinatra; in Van Heusen's case, Frank recorded his songs, and the tremendous sales gave Van Heusen huge royalties. Other friends were genuinely grateful for the sincere kindnesses Frank could bestow when he felt like it, although often his acts of generosity were a form of apology for some "monstrous" act he had earlier committed against the person in question.

For instance, there was the time Frank got into a fight with Desi Arnaz because the latter was producing *The Untouchables*, the television program in which Elliot Ness weekly combated a host of hoods with vowels at the end of their names. Frank's mob friends didn't like the show, but claimed it was only because it was insulting to Italians, and they pressured Frank to do something about Desi. "What do you want me to do," Desi asked Frank when the latter told him his objections, "make all the gangsters Jewish?" Van Heusen and his date were with Frank when he confronted Desi at the Indian Wells Country Club. When the argument got heated, Desi hollered at Frank and told him to stop making a big deal out of nothing. Frank had threatened to beat the crap out of Desi, but Desi, hearing of Frank's angry intentions, had taken the precaution of travelling with two hefty bodyguards. Frank walked away from the fight, saying he didn't clobber Desi only because Desi and then-wife Lucille Ball had been friends of his for so long.

But this left Frank with pent-up violence that had to be expressed somehow. When he went back to Van Heusen's place for a drink, he took out his anger on one of Jimmy's most prized possessions, a Norman Rockwell portrait that the famed artist had done of Van Heusen as a special favor. Sinatra took a knife to the irreplaceable, once-in-a-lifetime painting and slashed it to ribbons, pretending it was Arnaz, who had, in Frank's skewered view, "humiliated" him. When Van Heusen began to scream in protest—"Frank! Why destroy my portrait?"—Frank bellowed at him, "You're bought and paid for, Chester! Just shut up or next time I'll take down the wall instead of a fucking painting!"

Within a week Frank sent Van Heusen a very expensive

Japanese print as an apology (no note, no "I'm sorry"), but of course it couldn't really replace the Rockwell painting no matter how much it cost. Frank would often take out his anger on men who he felt owed him something, and on women who became surrogates for the taunting, tempestuous Ava. As for Van Heusen, a musician friend once said of him, "He really was Frank's dog and slave, except for that one time he told Frank he had to go see a shrink. Van Heusen should have let it drop there and never gone back to him. Being friends with Frank may have been good for his career, but a man has to have some pride and dignity or he's just a lackey and nothing's worth that."

Frank could also be vicious with strangers, particularly if they were members of the press or even innocent bystanders. One night he and some friends, including Judy Garland, were coming out of the Crescendo Club on Sunset Boulevard after hearing Mel Torme. Torme's publicist made the mistake of asking Frank the names of his other guests so he could plant an item about Frank and friends coming to see his client. Thinking the man was a reporter, Frank started hitting the man in the face and only stopped when the startled man began to hit back, bloodying Frank's nose. This was only one of literally dozens of documented incidents when Frank got physically violent with reporters and those whose opinions he didn't agree with (though usually only in the presence of several of his friends or mob backup; Frank would rarely take on anyone alone). One time at a party in Palm Springs at an executive's house, he punched out the bartender for not making his martini dry enough.

There were incidents that were even more sinister, usually fueled by generous amounts of alcohol. Peter Lawford, who had been accepted back into Frank's circle when the two "made up" (or rather Frank "forgave" Peter for the Ava incident) at a dinner party at the Gary Coopers', never forgot the time Frank shoved a young woman through a plate glass window because she got him mad over something at a more-raucous-than-usual drinking party. "It was horrifying," Lawford said. "The worst I've ever seen Frank and I've seen him pretty bad. The girl's arm was nearly cut off! Judy Garland was at the party and I had to hold her up, she was fainting from all the blood. For once I think the drugs and the liquor helped because it made everything seem so unreal. It was just a horror show." According to Peter, Jimmy Van Heusen, still cleaning up after Frank, took the girl to the hospital. Like many another of Sinatra's victims, the girl was paid off and kept silent.

By far the most infamous account of Sinatra's belligerence had to do with a deputy sheriff named Richard E. Anderson. Anderson's wife had once been involved with Sinatra, but now she was working as a cocktail waitress at a casino Sinatra co-owned in Lake Tahoe. When Anderson came to pick up his wife one night at the casino, he and Sinatra got into an argument and came to blows. Without any of his hired muscle or mob buddies to back him up, Sinatra came out the loser and was so injured he couldn't do his stage show for several days. Members of the casino staff heard Sinatra screaming at Anderson that he'd get even with him no matter what it took. He contacted the sheriff's office and got Anderson suspended.

About two weeks later Anderson was killed in a suspicious automobile accident, run off the road by a convertible that sped off after the accident. Anderson's wife, who was in the car with him, survived and told police as much as she could, but, although there were strong suspicions from law enforcement officials and Anderson's parents that Anderson had died due to foul play, nothing was ever proven. Nevertheless, because of his legendary temper, mob connections, and very public animosity toward Anderson, Sinatra came under suspicion at the time. According to Ed Olsen, then-chairman of the Nevada Gaming Commission (who would have his own problems with Frank), "The matter was ultimately dismissed."

One of the biggest things that contributed to Frank's dark image was his association and friendship with numerous known mobsters going back to the very beginning of his career. Frank worshipped the power they held and represented, and he wanted—sadly, for such a gifted artist—to be more like them. He palled around with some of the worst people on the planet because he liked their style. He met these heinous individuals because they both owned and hung out in the clubs and casinos that Sinatra worked in. Having drinks with these common fellows who, like Sinatra, loved booze and broads and silly horseplay made him feel like one of the gang, a real man, and the liquor helped him forget he was in the company of killers.

There was Bugsy Siegel, West Coast chief of Murder, Inc., who built the Flamingo Hotel and virtually created Las Vegas, and Mickey Cohen, who took over after Siegel was snuffed. Not to mention Albert "The Executioner" Anastasia. Then there were the Fischetti brothers, killers and cousins of Al Capone, who invited Frank to come with them when they paid homage to exiled syndicate leader Lucky Luciano in Havana. Frank brought an attache case to Lucky and got a gold cigarette case in return. This got Frank an invitation to answer questions for the famous Kefauver hearings on the Mafia, but he was dismissed from giving public testimony when a private pre-interview with committee lawyer Joseph Nellis made it clear that Sinatra, who was characterized as being "cagey," wouldn't admit to knowing anything. It was reasoned that having Frank testify in public would serve only to sensationalize the hearings.

Frank was given nearly 10 percent ownership of the Sands hotel and casino in Vegas because the mob owners realized what a great draw he would be and that if he owned a big enough percentage he would have no reason to perform anywhere else in Vegas. Frank later went into "business" with the notorious Sam Giancana when Sam used Sinatra as the front man for the Cal-Neva Lodge in Lake Tahoe. Giancana's presence at the lodge—his girlfriend was the trampy Phyllis McGuire of the singing McGuire Sisters; their association with Sinatra gave the mediocre group a brief run—attracted the attention of the aforementioned Ed Olsen of the Nevada Gaming Commission. Sam wanted Frank to handle Olsen with extreme delicacy, but as usual Sinatra behaved like a pit bull and Giancana lost the club. That was the end of his friendship with Frank.

Frank's Mafia buddies also got him to invest in a magazine entitled *Hollywood Night Life*, a rag similar to *Confidential* magazine with its nasty exposes of celebrities. Although Sinatra later implied that he had only invested in the magazine to prevent publication of a nasty article about him, he was actually more interested in ensuring good, controlled coverage of his activities. *Hollywood Night Life* went one step further than *Confidential* in that it would shake down the subjects of its upcoming exposes. Given his hatred of the press and love of privacy, it was hypocritical of Sinatra, to say the least, to have any part of a publication that treated other celebrities the way he himself hated to be treated.

But there was another side to Frank Sinatra, a side that could be kind and generous to people he required nothing of and hadn't necessarily treated badly. He had never even met Bela Lugosi, but when the former Dracula had to be committed to a hospital because of his drug dependencies, Sinatra was the only Hollywood star to send him a note of good wishes with a fruit basket. He not only put perky, perennial starlet Joi Lansing into his movies (as he did many gal pals) and got her on friends' TV shows, such as *I Love Lucy*, when she developed leukemia he paid all of her medical bills. He did the same for Lee J. Cobb when the actor had a massive coronary and his career was in the doldrums. Although they were only acquaintances at the time (Cobb had had a small role in Sinatra's film *Miracle of the Bells*), Sinatra took Cobb under his wing, making sure he had the best medical care and a nice place to live in while he convalesced. For awhile Sinatra even insisted Cobb share Frank's own house in Palm Springs. "When I was sick, Frank was wonderful," said Cobb. "That's a side of him people ought to know more about." There were also many widows and down-and-outers who received life-saving checks from Sinatra, probably enough to fill pages if Sinatra had talked to the press about these acts of generosity.

Sinatra was never stingy when it came to helping other singers' and actors' careers. He was instrumental in bringing Mario Lanza to Hollywood and making sure the right people heard his magnificent voice. When one considers that Lanza had, as Arturo Toscanini put it, "the most beautiful voice of the twentieth century," it was certainly not self-serving for Sinatra to help the tenor. Yes, Sinatra knew that he and Lanza were different kinds of singers with very different material, but a lesser man would have balked at the idea of promoting such a monumental figure. It was not well-known that Sinatra had always been a fan of classical music. (Of course, there were those who cursed Sinatra for helping Lanza "go Hollywood" when he should have been a great star of the legitimate opera.)

Right or wrong, Sinatra was always willing to buck all opposition if he felt strongly about someone or something, such as the time he decided that he wanted to use blacklisted "Hollywood Ten" writer Albert Maltz to write the screenplay for the proposed film *The Execution of Private Slovik* (about a U.S. Army deserter). When news of this hit the papers, Sinatra was supported by some but excoriated by most. Sinatra felt Maltz was the best person to write the screenplay, and was convinced that he would have an "affirmative, pro-American approach." One editorial countered that Maltz was "not a free thinker but a hard revolutionist who has never done anything to remove himself from the Communist camp." Maltz himself felt that Frank was following in the footsteps of Otto Preminger and Kirk Douglas, men who'd hired Dalton Trumbo to write screenplays for, respectively, *Exodus* and *Spartacus*. "He wanted to break the blacklist," Maltz said. Sinatra could empathize with anyone who was down and out and unable to get a job no matter what the reason.

By the time all the criticism came in, including acid comments from John Wayne and William Holden, it was less Sinatra's social conscience (such as it was) at work than his desire to tell anyone who dared tell him what to do to go fuck themselves. He refused to back down until Joe Kennedy himself told him it might hurt his son's chances for the presidency (this was in the Jack Pack era) if he didn't fire Maltz. Sinatra did as Joe told him, but he paid Maltz in full.

Of this brouhaha Bill Holden said in 1970, "That was Frank wanting to be a do-gooder without thinking through all the consequences. Why didn't Maltz answer HUAC's questions? He brought it all on himself. In all the hysteria and witch-hunting of that period, everyone forgets that there were legitimate communists who did not have America's best interests in mind. Frank is a talented man, but all his years of hanging out with the dregs of society didn't exactly make him the best judge of character."

Sinatra did have a sincere commitment to civil rights that was probably not shared by the Mafiosi he hung out with. This led him to appear in the mid-forties in a short entitled *The House I Live In* (written by the aforementioned Maltz), in which he preached racial and religious tolerance to a group of children. One could argue that he did this only to counteract all the bad publicity he was getting during the wartime period, but given the racial situation in the country at the time, he knew he would lose as many fans as he would gain. He later gave speeches for tolerance at high schools across the country and tried to intervene when the white students at a school in Gary, Indiana, went on strike because the principal allowed black kids to sit in the same classrooms with them. The girls were thrilled to see "their Frankie," but he didn't change their bigoted minds one bit, despite a heartfelt and convincing speech.

Frank Sinatra had learned long before that no matter what he did some would love him and some would hate him, and that was just fine with him.

Before their final falling out, Peter Lawford said of Frank, "He can be a real Jekyll and Hyde, but generally his bark is worse than his bite—though I know there are people who wouldn't agree with me. Frank has been hurt by a lot of people, so a lot of what he does that's bad is more defensive than offensive, if you know what I mean. Frank gets hurt and angry—he's had a lot to be hurt and angry about—and he bears with it as well as he can until suddenly he snaps. He doesn't suffer fools easily."

On another occasion Peter said, "Frank can be wonderful if you have a problem. He helps you get to the bottom of it and is there to help you through it." Later, of course, he would revise his opinion of Frank and classify him, squarely, as "that prick."

Shirley MacLaine, who was to become a part of Sinatra's Rat Pack in a big way during *Some Came Running*, once said of Frank, "He's a wonderful friend, but he does have an ego. He did wonderful things for me over the years. I wouldn't want to be an enemy of his, though.

"I wouldn't want to know that side of him."

12

Shirley Comes Running

Just as Sinatra had bounced back from his worrisome slump and became a major movie star again, now it was Dean Martin's turn to revive his Hollywood career after his split with Jerry Lewis and the disastrous *Ten Thousand Bedrooms*. His agents at MCA figured the only chance he had was to break entirely away from the old persona he'd had in the Martin and Lewis films and take a stab at a dramatic part.

They enjoined director Edward Dmytryk to cast Dean in his production of *The Young Lions* instead of Tony Randall, who was nearly signed. Dmytryk thought it had to be a joke: Dean Martin appearing with the likes of Marlon Brando (a conflicted Nazi officer) and Montgomery Clift (a scrappy American G.I.)? Frank Sinatra had already worked with both of them but he was already more or less a proven dramatic actor at the time (*Miracle of the Bells*; *Meet Danny Wilson*), but Martin was best-known as that "monkey's" ex-partner. Dmytryk finally went ahead and cast Martin only after Clift said he thought the crooner would work out better in the part than Randall would. Dmytryk only agreed because he figured Monty could do for Martin what he had done for Sinatra in

From Here to Eternity—coach him on how to play the part, read the lines, create the character from the inside out—as the two had a number of long scenes together.

When the film came out the irony was that in playing the character of Michael Whittaker, Martin was essentially just playing himself. Whittaker is a womanizing, boozing singer who will do anything to stay out of the draft as the war approaches. (Martin got the hernia that classified him 4-F fixed years after World War II, when there was no more danger of him being drafted.) When the doctor at the draft board asks Whittaker how he stays in such good health, Martin wisecracks, "Clean liquor." The only major difference between Martin and Whittaker was that Martin had never been a big Broadway star.

With Sinatra, Clift had helped to bring out some of the vulnerability and insecurity beneath the surface, but all he and Dmytryk could do with Dean was fit the character to the actor instead of the other way around. There was no way to change the basic Dino persona in any concrete fashion. Still, his performance isn't bad except when strong emotion is required, such as in the final scenes at the concentration camp. No G.I. who helped liberate the camps could have remained untouched, but Martin just stands there as if he's waiting for Dmytryk to yell "cut" so he can go grab a martini.

As for Montgomery Clift, he still seemed to be under the influence of Frank Sinatra, as his Noah Akerman has many of the qualities of Sinatra's Maggio. Like Maggio, Akerman seems to have a masochistic streak, fighting four guys who have stolen his money until he is practically beaten to a pulp. Like *From Here to Eternity*, *The Young Lions* has too many scenes that simply don't ring true, and despite some of the best cinematography of any film of the fifties, the movie doesn't exploit its situations fully and is not the moving document of its events it should have been. Brando, complete with a very convincing German accent, gave one of his better performances, however.

Also in the cast of *The Young Lions* was a pretty Swedish starlet named Mai Britt, who is rather good playing the superficial woman who cuckolds her German officer husband (played superbly by Maximillian Schell) by sleeping with one of his men, Brando. Within two years she was to marry Sammy Davis Jr., but at this time he and Dean were barely acquainted, and Sammy would not meet Mai until after she appeared in the remake of *The Blue Angel* the year after doing *The Young Lions*. Meanwhile Sammy was off making his film debut in *Anna Lucasta*, in which he played the boyfriend of prostitute Eartha Kitt. He would play Sportin' Life in Otto Preminger's production of George Gershwin's opera *Porgy and Bess* the following year. Sinatra was one of several people who went to bat for Sammy and convinced Samuel Goldwyn to give him the part.

Frank was also instrumental in getting Joey Bishop film roles around this time. Bishop wound up as comedy relief in two World War II films back to back: *The Deep Six* had him lightening up the tension between Alan Ladd and William Bendix as they sailed on a dangerous mission; and *The Naked and the Dead*, an adaptation of Norman Mailer's novel, cast him as the "comic jew" among a group of soldiers fighting in the Pacific. At least in *Onionhead* he was in a genuine comedy, but he was only support for the shenanigans of Andy Griffith in the Coast Guard.

Shirley MacLaine had had a brief fling with Frank, as had many women, and she wound up being cast in *Some Came Running*, which was released in 1958. Frank was also instrumental in getting Dean Martin cast, the first role in which he did absolutely no singing, not even offhandedly in a party scene as in *The Young Lions*. Frank always liked to be surrounded by his friends, people he was simpatico with, when he was doing a picture. Although it must be said that

Martin and MacLaine stood a good chance of getting the roles even without Sinatra's endorsement. (On the other hand, if Sinatra had objected to either one of them, new actors would have been found post-haste.)

Sinatra was the obvious choice—by Hollywood's way of thinking—for the lead role in *Some Came Running*, which was based on a novel by James Jones, the man who'd penned *From Here to Eternity*. It was about a World War II veteran coming back to the town he hasn't seen in many years and has avoided since leaving the Army; it holds too many painful memories. Presumably the title refers to the fact that many soldiers were eager to go to war, "came running," in fact, just to get away from a stifling, negative home environment. (Although Sinatra's character had left home long before the war.)

The film was directed by Vincente Minnelli, who had long since divorced the difficult Judy Garland. Sol C. Siegel had taken over the MGM studios as production boss and this was the first big production under his auspices. When one of Siegel's associates suggested that perhaps Minnelli could get ex-wife Judy Garland for one of the two major female roles—both of which she would have been all wrong for—he was stared down and vetoed vehemently. For one thing, at that point Frank would have had no interest in working with Garland: neurotic women were not his cup of tea.

Frank plays David Hirsch, a character Jones based loosely on himself. Hirsch has tried to make it as a writer since the war ended; his books have gotten great reviews but made little money. It's hard to take Sinatra seriously in the role; he doesn't look like someone who reads books, let alone writes them. The scene in which he unpacks in his hotel room and pulls copies of Faulkner, Steinbeck, Thomas Wolfe, etc. out of his suitcase is therefore unintentionally hilarious.

Hirsch grew up in Parkman, Indiana, whose sole claim

to fame is a brassiere factory. He hasn't been to Parkman in sixteen years because there's no love lost between him and his brother, Frank (Arthur Kennedy). The Hirsch brothers' parents died young, and when older brother Frank got married, he put younger brother David, who was twelve, in a home. David has never forgiven Frank for this; Frank thinks David is only looking at things from his point of view. "We were just married!" he tells him. "What did you expect me to do?"

During a night of drinking before leaving for Parkman, David encounters Ginny Moorehead (Shirley MacLaine), whom he invites along with him while under the influence. When the bus arrives in Parkman, he apologizes, says it was a mistake and gives her bus fare home. Smitten with David, Ginny decides to stay and gets a job working at the brassiere factory. David winds up moving in with a gambler and gadabout he meets in the local tavern, a man named Bama Dillert (Dean Martin). Ignoring Ginny, who has been fending off the advances of a jealous suitor, Raymond, who followed her from the city, David falls for a repressed schoolteacher ironically named Gwen French (Martha Hyer). But when things don't work out for them, David asks Ginny to marry him. He tells an astonished Bama, who thinks Ginny is a "pig," that he's "tired of being lonely" and he knows that Ginny adores him. Unfortunately, at the country fair that evening where Ginny and David have come to celebrate their quickie wedding, Raymond darts out of the shadows and shoots at David. Poor Ginny throws herself in front of him to save him and winds up taking the fatal bullet herself. Although the final scene—Ginny's funeral—hints that David and Gwen may finally get together, this isn't likely. For one thing, David went off and married another woman, and her murder is just another sordid incident for prim and proper Gwen to be scandalized by.

Sinatra is okay as David Hirsch, but he seems to have no true understanding of the rather underwritten character. His laid-back approach—in contrast to his performance as Maggio in the film's predecessor—lacks energy. Instead of coming off as confused and troubled and defeated, he merely seems blase, such as when he barely reacts when Gwen tells him a short story of his that she submitted to *The Atlantic* has been accepted. Sinatra seems about as sensitive as a rock; in fact, Dean Martin comes off as more sensitive and likable.

Dean thought his part was "a snap. I just played cards and talked Southern," which was no problem for him as he'd always had a kind of southern drawl in spite of the fact he was born in Ohio. His oddball character of Bama Dillert never takes his hat off and punches out anyone who tries to remove it. As a gambling, boozing, love-'em-and-leave-'em type, Dino hardly had to act, just show up and do a variation on himself. The picture's second biggest unintentional laugh comes when Bama learns he has diabetes mellitus and his doctor tells him he has to give up booze. Another whopper occurs when Sinatra leaves a bar with Dino and Shirley in tow and leaves a whole bottle of scotch that he just paid for on the table.

Shirley MacLaine plays the dumbest but nicest person in the movie, Ginny, who sacrifices herself saving the man that she loves. A nightclub scene in which she approaches the mike in a drunken dither and sings off-key for a few minutes until the bandleader insists Sinatra subdue her is interesting in that MacLaine had to suppress her natural instincts to belt out a song with vigor and rhythm. MacLaine is touching and pathetic as she confesses her love for David to her rival, Gwen, and especially in the scene when she tells David how much she loves him after he's proposed to her. Floozie Ginny is like a dog desperate for affection from her master;

she goes to work cleaning up David and Bama's messy bachelor pad and seems grateful for the opportunity to do so.

At the time of filming Shirley said of Frank, "He's wonderful to work with; a true professional. And he always builds up other people in a scene. He's very generous that way." A highlight of the film is the scene in which David tries to get stupid Ginny to explain exactly what it is she likes about his story in *The Atlantic*, which is sort of like asking Pamela Lee to describe the brilliance of Beethoven's symphonies.

As the creative writing teacher Miss French, Martha Hyer confirms that she will never be a great actress, but she does play with passion, no doubt inspired by the "generosity" of Sinatra. Arthur Kennedy as Frank Hirsch offers his usual standout performance. Although much better than Sinatra, he was gracious at the time of shooting: "Frank is a pleasure to work with because he keeps you on your toes— unexpected sallies and original twists. That characterizes his style. And it's fun to play against." Nancy Gates was also excellent in a supporting part.

It's a shame that for all the effort on a part of a few, *Some Came Running* isn't very good. Most of the problem is the meandering, highly superficial script, but Vincente Minnelli's direction isn't of much help. Screen composer Elmer Bernstein came up with some nice ersatz Chopin for the love theme for David and Gwen (in fact the scene in which David awakens the schoolteacher's passion after she reads his manuscript in her cabin is one of the better ones in the picture), as well as some nice background themes for Ginny, but his dynamic opening credit music is the most memorable.

The best scene in the picture is the moving conclusion showing Ginny's sacrifice (when all else fails, bring in the psycho with a gun), but according to Shirley MacLaine this was not the way the picture was supposed to end. One afternoon Frank had decided he didn't feel like working anymore and invited Shirley to his trailer for a couple of martinis. The assistant director came in, frantic, and complained that they had to get back to work because the picture was two weeks behind schedule. Sinatra's response was to pick up the script, tear out about twenty pages of material that had not yet been shot, and say to the A.D., "Well, we're back on schedule now."

Unfortunately, among the pages he'd arbitrarily excised was one of Ginny's big scenes. While the writers tried to come up with an ending that would still make sense after all the "cuts" Frank had made, Sinatra went to producer Sol Siegel and suggested a new wind-up. Ginny would get shot throwing herself in front of David when jealous Raymond shoots at him. (Apparently David was to get killed in the original script.) This would give Shirley a chance to have another big scene. Ironically, it's the only part of the movie that has any real impact, and to her delight MacLaine was rewarded with her first Academy Award nomination.

Dean and Frank had been casual friends up until the making of *Some Came Running*, but working together on the film really gave them a chance to get to know one another. "He's fun to be with," said Frank. "We understand each other. We don't always agree with each other but we click anyway. Isn't that the definition of a friend?" During the filming in Madison, Indiana, Shirley and the supporting players were put up in a hotel, but Frank and Dean rented a house nearby (just as their characters lived together in the movie) so they could have wild all-night parties virtually every day after shooting. Jimmy Van Heusen came around to play the piano and generally oversee things. Sam Giancana, Frank's mobster friend, was also a frequent visitor, telling everyone he was "hiding out" from authorities in Chicago. He dragged along many of his equally sinister underlings. The boys would sit around with Frank and Dean and other fellows—Shirley was one of the few women admitted to the house who wasn't a hooker or one of Giancana's party girls—playing endless rounds of poker, telling dirty jokes, boozing it up until the wee hours. Sinatra had known that the racket level would have been too high for a hotel room, so the separate house was essential. The parties would usually go on until five in the morning. An hour later Frank and Dean were supposed to report to start preparations for the day's shooting. Needless to say, the two fellows were rarely on time. It didn't matter what Minnelli, the various assistant directors, or even Sol Siegel said; everyone knew that Sinatra was the boss.

The house was constantly surrounded by women of all ages who knew that Sinatra was inside. A full crew of security men had been hired to keep the women out of the building, although several of them found their way inside once Frank or Dean got a look at them. The security men were bribed with money, food, kisses, even the promise of sex, if only they'd let the gals inside just to get a peek at the Hoboken Casanova. One evening Frank was patiently teaching Shirley how to play gin rummy when one of the adoring women outside somehow "got past" security and made her way into the building. Spotting Frank, she literally dived at him and started covering him with smooches, smearing lipstick all over his face and neck. A moment later she got a good grip on his shirt and began tearing it right off his back.

Frank was not amused. If Shirley hadn't been a witness he might have hauled off and belted the woman. As far as Frank was concerned, he was supposed to chase the broads and not the other way around. Women were sex objects—but only in their place, only when he wanted it. Another man might have found the whole situation amusing or sexy or at least somewhat flattering, but Frank only hated the way the woman had taken control and left him helpless in the face of her onslaught. From then on the guards—the ones who weren't fired—resisted any and all bribes from the anxious women storming the barricades at Castle Frank, Indiana. In the meantime, Frank washed off the woman's kisses in the shower as if her lipstick had carried the plague.

Frank and Dean had plenty of women, of course, but women of their own choosing and at the right time and place. Shirley was married at the time, but that didn't stop each of them from paying separate visits to her hotel room where she later claimed she politely rebuffed them. MacLaine was carrying on an admitted open marriage with husband Steve, who spent most of his time at this point in Japan on business. Shirley accepted that this long-distance relationship would entitle both of them to have their little flings. Eventually Shirley would set her sights on Dean Martin, but that was to come a bit later.

One evening Shirley was at the house playing cards when she realized that Sam Giancana was reading her hand off the reflection in her sunglasses. When she went to put a food delivery in the refrigerator, she found that someone had put a water pistol on the shelf. Not really realizing exactly who Giancana was, she grabbed the pistol and marched into the room pointing it at the underworld boss. Giancana jumped up and pulled a real gun out of his pocket. Who knows what might have happened if Dean and Frank hadn't walked in at that point.

Once the wide-eyed Shirley understood exactly who she was dealing with, she was appalled at how the Rat Pack had done so much to help glamorize the Mafia. (Years later, of course, Francis Ford Coppola's *Godfather* movies would do the same, only worse.) She was amused the way Frank and Dean would really spruce up before they took her out to a club. (When she wasn't hanging out at the house waiting for

Minnelli's summons, she and Frank and Dean would take the occasional side trip to Cincinnati to explore the gambling dens there.) They would keep her waiting as they perfumed and pomaded and fussed over which was the right suit to wear, as they chose the freshest underwear and cleanest socks of the bunch. "Why was it that they who consorted with gangster types . . . insisted on being perceived as so impeccably clean?" Shirley wondered in her memoirs.

Vincente Minnelli did not have an easy time filming *Some Came Running*. First, the set was overrun with screaming girls and scary-looking mobsters. Second, when he didn't have to contend with producer Siegel, he had Frank to deal with. Sometimes Frank would just decide he wasn't going to show up to shoot a scene, and an entire evening's work would go down the drain. A basic problem was that Frank—and Dean Martin—had taken a dislike to Minnelli, whom they both found a bit on the prissy, vaguely effeminate side. He had an irritating way of pursing his lips that wasn't manly enough for Frankie Boy's standards. He also found the director to be too artsy fartsy, such as when they filmed the next-to-last scene with the shooting of Ginny at the carnival. Minnelli wanted the Ferris wheel in the background to occupy just the right space in the shot, but he couldn't seem to get it just so no matter what angle he tried. Finally, he told the camera crew that the only thing to do would be to move the enormous Ferris wheel to another location in the carnival.

When Frank heard this—he'd been sitting around for hours—he flipped his lid and stormed off the set. The next thing everyone knew he and Dean were back in Los Angeles refusing to finish the picture. Sol Siegel had to track down Frank, talk to him when he was in an accessible, sober mood and not with some broad or at a club, and get him to listen to reason. It took nearly a week for Siegel to get

Frank—and Dean, who knew there was no point returning if Frank wasn't there—to report back to Madison and Minnelli.

At the time Minnelli was careful with his statements to filmland reporters. "People think Frank blows his top very easily, but I've seen him infinitely patient with other actors. He can be very understanding."

Minnelli later said, "If I could survive marriage to Judy Garland, I could survive the Rat Pack. But barely."

13

Fewer by One

Thanks to Frank Sinatra and others, Sammy Davis had gotten the part of Sportin' Life in *Porgy and Bess* that he so coveted. Unlike *Anna Lucasta*, this was to be a major production directed by no less than Otto Preminger. The one thing *Porgy and Bess* did have in common with Sammy's first film was that it, too, featured an all-black cast. (The first film version of *Anna Lucasta*, made in 1949 with Paulette Goddard, had changed all the Negroes into whites.)

Sportin' Life was essentially a pimp and drug dealer, but Sammy later claimed he was so naive at the time that he had no idea the "happy dust" Sportin' Life kept talking about was actually cocaine. Years later he would, unfortunately, become all too well acquainted with not only that "recreational" drug, but many others.

Before Preminger somehow took over, Robert Breen, who had produced *Porgy and Bess* on the stage, was scheduled to direct the film. Sammy was grateful that even after he was replaced, Breen stayed on to help him shape the role. "Bobby spent an awful lot of time with me," Davis said, "helping me bring Sportin' Life to life. He helped me understand where the character was coming from. I was nothing like Sportin' Life and he was nothing like me." Although his role was actually a small one, Davis's performance, particularly his singing of "It Ain't Necessarily So," became one of the highlights of the picture. Samuel Goldwyn wanted him to be a contender for an Academy Award, but knew the part was too small for Sammy to win for Best Actor and it was too late to change the billing. (Sammy was billed as a lead when he really just had a supporting role; as Best Supporting Actor he might have won.)

Sammy enjoyed making the picture, particularly as how the ever-upbeat Pearl Bailey was part of the cast. He also became friends with the much more serious Sidney Poitier. He found Dorothy Dandridge to be rather remote, however; not so much rude or unfriendly but "out on another plane somewhere," as he put it. Once when the cinematographer, Leon Shamroy, got so upset over some aspect of the filming that he began cursing like a sailor, Dorothy reacted as if he were yelling at her personally and ran off the set in tears. She couldn't be coaxed back until the perplexed Shamroy (that was how he always spoke) apologized.

In the meantime, *The Young Lions* and *Some Came Running* had turned Dean Martin into a Hollywood player—the latter film also did it for Shirley—and the two of them were busy making important films (or at least films that seemed important at the time). Dean dallied with sultry Angie Dickinson while filming *Rio Bravo* (directed by Bogie's old-time co-worker and post-Bacall nemesis, Howard Hawks), but had passed her on to Frank by the time of *Ocean's 11*. In that way she became another leading lady in the Rat Pack roster. Dino was teamed with Tony Curtis and Janet Leigh in the comedy *Who Was That Lady?* and the still-married couple became fringe members of Sinatra's group as they had been of Bogie's.

Of these two, Martin once said, "I always felt Tony and

Janet would be married for keeps. It was a complete surprise to me when they split up." Sinatra said, "When they first hitched up they were like two high school kids in love. But sometimes I think nothing really good ever lasts."

Then Dino was reunited with Shirley for *Career*, but this turned out to be Tony Franciosa's finest hour as an actor who goes through hell and humiliation to finally get his chance above the footlights. Shirley also appeared with original Rat Packer David Niven in the dated, unfunny sex comedy *Ask Any Girl*. In this Shirley is "saving herself" for Gig Young, and she asks his brother (Niven) to help mold her into the type of woman Young would most desire. Frankly, Shirley didn't seem a chaste twenty-one in this, and there were those who thought Niven and Young were a bit long in the tooth to still be playing swinging bachelors.

As for Sinatra, his next film project after *Some Came Running* was *A Hole in the Head* (1959), directed by Frank Capra, who hadn't made a film in eight years. (His last "big" film had been *State of the Union* ten years earlier.) Many stories have circulated about this collaboration of the two Franks—some have it that the two constantly butted heads, others that Capra was so grateful to Frank to be working again that he practically let Sinatra direct the picture—but the truth is the two men, torn somewhat from similar cloth, had respect for each other's talent and got along well. Undoubtedly Sinatra had pulled strings to get the once-powerful director the assignment, but Frank always liked to work with the best, and Capra had proven how good he could be many times over.

That said, it is also true that *A Hole in the Head* is not on the level of Capra's greatest works (*It's a Wonderful Life*, among them), but by no means is it a bad picture. Sinatra plays a Miami hotel owner with a small son who must turn to his more conventional older brother (Edward G. Robinson) for financial aid. In addition to the fine performances from all involved, the movie contains some good material on the price one pays to live an unconventional life, the deadliness of middle-class values (oh, how Frank had hated to go home to Nancy and the kids in those old days), and that old bugaboo, the work ethic. Also admirable were the film's avoidance of the cliched happy ending and an easy resolution of Sinatra's many problems. Capra, who was ailing, directed only one more picture, *Pocketful of Miracles*, whose star, Bette Davis, he found much more of a trial than Sinatra.

Frank's next project, *Never So Few* (1959), took place in the Kachin Hills of North Burma, where it was 40,000 Japanese versus American troops and the Kachins. But the real drama was taking place behind the scenes before the picture was even made. Sinatra had not only decided that he wanted Italian bombshell Gina Lollobrigida in the picture as his love interest, but he had to have fellow Rat Packers Peter Lawford and Sammy Davis Jr. in the film, too.

Peter Lawford's career fortunes had slipped by the late fifties, if not earlier, and he was anxious to play the part in what he was sure would be a major motion picture. "If Frank's in it, it's going to be big," he kept saying. The part of Captain Gray Travis wasn't a very substantial one, but he thought a lot of people would see him in the movie, and he hoped it might lead to better things. So Peter wanted the part and his agents wanted him to get as much money for playing it as possible.

When Peter's agent demanded $75,000 for what would amount to barely three weeks' work, MGM executives told him he was crazy. One suggested that it was a small, nothing role and couldn't understand why Peter even wanted it. The budget wouldn't allow for a hefty paycheck in any case. "Frank wants Peter to be in this movie," the agent told the executives. The executives muttered amongst themselves and made a counter offer of $25,000. "Frank wants Peter to get $75,000," the agent said. When the executives raised their eyebrows at that, the agent added, "Frank wants Peter to be in this movie, and Peter won't be in this movie unless he gets $75,000—even if it's just for three weeks' work." The studio paid Peter his $75,000.

No matter how much he was paid, the film did nothing for Peter's career. Captain Gray Travis was truly a zero part. Although Peter received third billing, he hadn't a single big scene and in fact had hardly anything to do in the movie but stand around behind Frank in a few sequences, occasionally speaking a line or two. Still, Frank liked having him around. "He knows how to let his hair down," Frank said of Peter. "He's no snobby Brit. He tries to be one of the guys." Then Sinatra laughed. "Okay, sometimes he tries too hard. Then I rein him in." Lawford was certainly "reined in" by the script of *Never So Few*.

Sammy Davis Jr. fared even worse; he wasn't in the movie at all. Frank Sinatra had absolutely insisted that he be given a part even though there were those who argued there was no justifiable way a Negro character could be introduced into the picture. Actually, there was no reason why his role— of a jeep driver who joins up with Sinatra—couldn't have been played by a black, although dialogue changes might have been necessary. There is a Navajo character in the film named Danforth (Charles Bronson) who is irritated at the way some fellow soldiers keep making references to his being an "Injun," but when he himself refers to the Kachins as "gooks," Sinatra calls him on it. Undoubtedly the addition of Davis to the mix would have created further potentially interesting racial encounters to go with the politically correct conversation. In any case, the execs at MGM had no wish to go against Sinatra, so a contract was drafted for Davis.

Sammy was anxious to do the picture with Frank even though his role was hardly bigger than Lawford's (in fact, it was insultingly tiny). He signed the contract with a flourish; he was to get the same $75,000 that Lawford was getting. But then came the notorious Chicago radio incident.

Before he'd become a star Sammy had loved to listen to Jack Eigen's famous radio show—which at one time had been broadcast from the Copa in New York—and had always dreamed of the day he himself would be interviewed by Eigen. When that day came, shortly after his signing to do *Never So Few*, he was so caught up in conversation with his hypnotic host that he said things as if he'd forgotten the words were going out over the air to millions of listeners.

At one point Frank Sinatra came up in the conversation, as he always did. Eigen suggested that of course Sinatra was a great talent but perhaps he did not always behave as he should have; there had been stories—hadn't he done this and said that? Without thinking Sammy replied, "I love Frank and he was the kindest man in the world to me when I lost my eye in an auto accident and wanted to kill myself. But there are many things he does that there are no excuses for. Talent is not an excuse for bad manners . . . it does not give you the right to step on people and treat them rotten. This is what he does occasionally."

That would have been bad enough, but Davis compounded his faux pas by telling Eigen that it was he and not Sinatra who was the "number-one singer" in the country. "You think you're bigger than Frank?" Eigen asked, leading him on. "Yes," Davis replied.

Why would Davis act in so suicidal a fashion? Not only had Frank been kind to him over the years, he had been responsible for giving him the biggest boost of his career. The answer wasn't just that Frank could be mean-spirited and rude—to Sammy and all of his friends—from time to time, but that Sinatra could also be terribly patronizing. Without meaning to (or perhaps on some subconscious level it was deliberate), Frank often made Sammy feel like the mascot, the house Negro. Dean Martin could make (mostly) affectionate fun of him, but Sammy didn't expect so much of Dean, he wasn't as close to him. On the other hand, he felt that he and Frank were like brothers, and he was tired of feeling as if he owed everything to Frank. For one thing, Sinatra never seemed to acknowledge the fact that Sammy was a genius in his own right, a brilliant performer, every bit as talented as Frank if not more so. When he told Eigen that he was "number one" it was not just ego, it was honest pride in his abilities, which he felt some Rat Packers overlooked. He hadn't been called "America's Greatest Entertainer" time and again in the press for nothing. He didn't pack 'em in the clubs because he was a second-rater.

Another factor was that whenever someone feels they owe a large debt to another person, an inevitable resentment sets in, which was the case with Sammy. Frank may not have constantly reminded Sammy of how much he'd done for him, but Sammy may have felt it was tacit in their whole relationship, its very underpinning.

And of course there was the whole business with *Never So Few*. Whether Sammy should have been grateful that Frank had gotten a part for him or insulted that the part was practically a bit, was a conundrum to challenge the mystery of the chicken or the egg.

It wasn't long before news of the interview and of what Sammy had said reached Sinatra. Not only had Davis dared to criticize him on the airwaves, but he had done it in Sinatra's town, Chicago, where all of his mobster friends could hear exactly how much "respect" he got from people who owed him. He was so enraged at this "betrayal" that he called Sammy a "dirty nigger" to everyone within earshot. (Frank had not suddenly become a racist. He used this ugly word out of hurt and fury, just as he might call a Jew a "kike" or an Irishman a "mick"—and indeed an Italian a "wop"—because he was angry at them and wanted to lash out in the most expedient way he knew how. At the same time, while Frank would have been equally furious if a white friend had done this to him, the fact that Sammy was black undoubtedly affected his pride in front of his probably racist gangster buddies.) He called MGM and told them that he wanted Davis out of *Never So Few*. He was told that the contracts had already been signed. Practically foaming at the mouth Sinatra screamed, "I don't give a shit about contracts!" and slammed the phone down. If Sammy had sued MGM—which he could have done—it would have been like suing Sinatra. Frank knew Davis wouldn't dare. Sammy never did get the $75,000.

When Sammy got wind of Frank's reaction, he was desolate. Not only because he wanted to do the movie, but because he honestly did cherish Frank's friendship (not to mention the entree into certain circles that came with it). He called Sinatra a hundred times, but Frank would never take his calls. He called the other Rat Packers and their friends and associates and asked them to intercede on his behalf, but only Peter Lawford went to bat for him; the others felt Frank would be implacable. (And wondered what Sammy might say about them on the air; there were those who felt Frank's actions were totally justified.)

Davis went backstage at the Copa where Peter was doing an act with Jimmy Durante and asked him how his talk with Frank had gone. Peter had to tell Sammy that he had argued with Frank for over an hour but he wanted nothing more to do with Davis.

In truth, Frank would not even let Peter bring up the subject. "I wanted to defend Sammy," Peter said in his dressing room on another occasion, "he was indiscreet but not cruel or dishonest; he probably had a couple of drinks before talking to Eigen and that must have loosened him up a bit—but I knew Frank would bite my head off. I just mentioned his name and Frank started cursing. There was really nothing I could do; he was that mad." Peter also wanted to hold on to his part in *Never So Few*. "I love Sammy, but really—what was he thinking of? We all know what Frank can be like. I've been on the end of one of his tirades myself, and it isn't much fun. But friends don't talk about it on the air." He took a swig of his drink and added, "Poor Sammy." Peter was happy to be back in Frank's good graces after their own misunderstanding, and he hoped things would also work out for Sammy. But Sammy had really brought it on himself, he felt, and he, Peter, had not.

According to Joey Bishop, "Sammy went too far with what he said about Frank [that] one time. Frank needs loyalty all the way. I don't think Sammy realized he had hurt him so badly. Sammy probably thought he was being funny."

Not much later Sammy was booked into the Eden Roc in Florida, while Frank was doing his own show nearby at the Fontainebleau. Sammy was sure Frank would break down and be buddies again once they were out of Chicago and the worst moments were over, but Frank never came to see his act, and he left word that Sammy was not even to be admitted to his show at the Fontainebleau. If he got past the doorman, Sinatra intended to immediately stop performing and walk off the stage—and he would have done it. Sammy was *out* and that was that.

Finally the banishment ended a few weeks later when Sammy made a public apology to Sinatra on another interview program. Sinatra found out about it and decided to accept Sammy's call, wherein Sammy offered a more private apology. It is highly unlikely that they ever really talked about the reasons for the controversial radio remarks in the first place. Instead they concentrated on the good memories and mushier sentiments. Whatever tensions or resentments were between them were washed away in a tidal pool of sentiment and whiskey. For now.

Still, Sammy was out of *Never So Few*. The part had been rewritten and recast. Now Steve McQueen would play the part of Bill Ringa, the driver. This was long before McQueen's stardom and his part amounted to little more than a cameo. Although everyone knew the real reason why McQueen had replaced Davis, Sammy came up with an "official" explanation: he and Frank had "entirely different concepts" of how Sammy's part should be played. Sammy had had enough experience in movies by that time to know what would work for him in the role and what wouldn't. Neither would bend on it and since Frank had the final say he "pulled me out of the deal." Sammy was happy that the film had helped make Steve McQueen a superstar. (Actually, the picture didn't do a heck of a lot for McQueen's career or anyone else's; it was a financial bomb.) With consummate understatement, Davis added that because of the disagreement over the role he and Sinatra "parted company for awhile."

In the meantime Lawford gratefully reported to the set, but it wasn't long before he realized how peripheral his part was. He understood as no other member of the Rat Pack did, besides Sammy, the grudging resentment one could feel toward one who kept throwing you crumbs. Peter was to have this feeling often over the years—toward Frank, toward the Rat Pack, toward the Kennedys, toward the entertainment industry in general. Much of Peter's footage wound up on the cutting room floor through no fault of Sinatra's—Peter's character wasn't really very important to the storyline—but there hadn't been that much to begin with. The only sequence he was handed that had any meat in it at all was when Lawford's idealist disagrees with Sinatra's realist over the latter's shooting of some Kachin traitors. But it's handled more in look and attitude than in juicy dialogue.

The title of *Never So Few* comes from the Winston Churchill quote, "Never in the field of human conflict was so much owed by so many to so few." Sinatra plays Army Captain Tom Reynolds, who needs a doctor for the war zone in the Kachin Hills and shanghais an objecting Lawford for the position during a period of R-and-R away from the fighting. At the same time he meets and romances Gina Lollobrigida, who is being kept by the wealthy Nico (Paul Henreid). Gina isn't much impressed with Frank when she first meets him; she sees him as a warmonger and has contempt for him. "Go back and play with your popguns," she says with saucy insolence. Yet she's also intrigued with him as a man (or undoubtedly Sinatra would never have done the picture).

Frank and Gina play cat-and-mouse games under the eyes of Nico, and manage to fall in love. But then it's back to the Kachin Hills for Frank, who discovers there are added complications from Chinese troops. When he learns that some Chinese bandits under the command of a warlord named Chung King have killed thirty-four American soldiers—only their wallets and dogtags are left—he angrily orders their execution after they've been captured. This does not sit well with his superiors who, wishing to avoid an incident, have directed Frank to return their arms to the bandits and let them go! Frank is nearly court-martialed over this, but sanity rules in the end.

Sinatra is somewhat more energetic in this than he was in *Some Came Running*—particularly in various confrontation scenes—but his performance is still second-rate. He sports a goatee that doesn't flatter him in the slightest, nor does it add much to his characterization. That unfortunate, languid approach of his really helps sink a few scenes that could have been powerful had he given them the proper intensity, such as when he has to shoot a fatally wounded Asian in order to relieve him of "sixteen hours of pain." A scene that should have been devastating has no real impact at all.

Gina Lollobrigida, although her part was mostly window dressing, is a bit more spirited as Nico's mistress. Gina was one of the screen's great beauties, and the cinematographer made sure she was seen to full advantage in the movie. Although her scenes don't do much to move the plot along, you can't wait for the camera to get back to her. While her character warms up a bit later on, she initially exhibits a very sexy and alluring condescension. Paul Henreid offers a touch of class as her lover Nico. "How's the Englishman?" he asks her. "He'll live." "How's the American?" "He'll live, too." "And how are you?" To which Gina replies, "I'll live forever."

Henreid had worked with Dean Martin two years earlier in *Ten Thousand Bedrooms*. Now it was time for a filmic encounter with Frank Sinatra. "Let's just say we have very different approaches to filmmaking," Henreid said years later of his stint with Ol' Blue Eyes. "I can see why he and Dean are friends," he added.

Henreid, a self-styled ladies' man, was no match for Frank, who wooed Gina relentlessly on and off the set. Gina's attitude toward Frank was much the way her character's was toward Captain Reynolds when they first meet in a nightclub. Lollobrigida was no screaming American bobbysoxer who would slip out of her panties if Sinatra merely winked at her. Frank had his hands full trying to get her to warm up off-screen as much as she does on-screen. At the time she was very diplomatic in her statements about him. "That Frank— he is the best. Always a laugh while we're working. He helps me feel at ease. He teases me all the time, but in a nice way."

As one of the superior officers who confronts Frank over his actions with the Chinese bandits, Brian Donlevy, always an underrated actor, radiates that note of command and authority that Sinatra, surprisingly, completely lacks (even taking into account that Sinatra's character is sort of an anti-authority maverick). This scene fairly crackles; Sinatra, inspired by Donlevy, follows through in the next scene when he tells off the Chinese officer who has come to represent and defend the aforementioned warlord. Sinatra is also better when he deals with some hospital bureaucrats who are not treating or feeding their injured Kachin soldiers as well as the American patients. (The film is PC to a fault but, in this case, correctly so.)

British actor Richard Johnson, who was briefly married to sex kitten Kim Novak, also had a supporting part in the film and enjoyed Frank's onstage and offstage antics mightily. Johnson has a good scene where he tells Frank how fond he is of him just before being shot and dying. In a nightclub scene early in the picture, he and Frank ad-libbed a lot of their risque dialogue, such as the business with Johnson's omnipresent monocle. "I have such trouble getting it out," he tells Frank's date. Steve McQueen had so little to do in the movie that he hardly mentioned it years later, and would in fact pretend he had never even been in it if anyone asked him about it.

Never So Few could have been a memorable picture, but Sinatra's weary playing and John Sturges's workmanlike but uninspired direction do little to lift Millard Kaufman's screenplay above the routine. At least Hugo Friedhofer contributed some powerful and evocative opening theme music. The romance between Gina and Frank is never very convincing, especially in one love scene when Frank tells her dreamily that his greatest desire is to see her at the stove cooking pasta! The whole conflict over whether or not to execute, first, the Kachin traitors, and later, the Chinese bandits, seems cooked up only to create some suspect drama. The former's actions allowed a sneak attack by Japanese that led to many deaths, and the latter murdered dozens of innocent

American soldiers. Considering the stakes involved—in wartime no less—it's hard to see anyone in the Army really objecting to their demise.

While Frank and Peter made *Never So Few*, Dean and Shirley were making *Career* with Anthony Franciosa. It wouldn't be long before the four of them were reunited to work on the first major Rat Pack movie deluxe.

14

Ocean's 11

Shirley MacLaine found that she had fallen pretty hard for Sinatra by the time they worked together on *Can-Can* (1960), a rather indifferent film adaptation of Cole Porter's musical. But it was too late. Frank had had his fling with her, had put her in the movies with him more than once, but that was that. Shirley was wise enough not to push, as Lauren Bacall had, or he would have cut her completely out of his life. Instead, they remained friends and frequent co-workers. But Shirley never quite forgave Frank for dumping her and would get even with him in a very public way years later. During the filming of *Can-Can*, Sinatra concentrated on the leggy supporting player Juliet Prowse while Shirley hid her feelings and did her numbers. Sinatra played a solicitor who defended the right of MacLaine to dance the shocking new can-can in her nightclub.

Before long, Frank and Juliet Prowse had become an item. Juliet spoke glowingly of the joy of working with Frank to the press. "Frank can play wonderfully with people of different styles and backgrounds," she said, "like Louis Jourdan or Maurice Chevalier (who were also in the film). He adjusts

to their pace and humors their moods. That's a true artist."
On another occasion she vowed, "Frank is a very sweet and
tender person. People always think of him as a tough guy, but
they don't listen to his love songs attentively enough. If they
did they'd be reminded of what a really sweet man he is."
Frank confided to Shirley that not only was he in love with
Juliet, but he thought of her as a friend as well as a lover.
Eventually Frank asked Juliet to marry him and she agreed.
The engagement lasted all of forty-three days.

The official story of the breakup was that Juliet had
refused to give up her career to become his wife plain and
simple, and Frank refused to ever again go through what he
had gone through with Ava. Since it was unlikely that
Prowse's career would ever have eclipsed Frank's the way
that sensational Ava's did, this excuse was rather specious.
Juliet told Shirley that her mistake had been in asking him to
accompany her on a trip home to South Africa to see her parents. Sinatra was mortally offended that he would have to
"pass muster" with anybody. Even when Juliet agreed to give
up her career for him it was too late. He cut her totally out of
his life just as he had expunged Betty Bacall.

In the meantime, Sammy Davis Jr. was coming off a
depression after being told that an episode he wanted to do
for Rod Serling's *Twilight Zone*—in which a white bigot, to be
played by Sammy, wakes up permanently black one morning
in a hospital after an accident and is treated with the same
mixture of hostility and indifference he always held toward
Negroes—had been nixed as too controversial by the network. That same day Sinatra visited him in his dressing room
after his show and told him he wanted him to be in the new
movie he was making, a heist caper called *Ocean's 11*. Right
away, Sammy's spirits were lifted. He told Sammy he would
make sure he got 125,000 smackers for doing the movie.

In his memoirs Sammy writes that he was touched that
Sinatra didn't expect him to do a screen test when "he didn't

know if I could say hello on film and make it sound convincing." But Davis's memory was failing, because he had forgotten that he had already appeared in the film version of *Porgy and Bess* a year earlier and Sinatra would have had some idea of what he was capable of achieving on celluloid. True, this time Sammy would have lines of spoken dialogue, whereas as Sportin' Life he only sang, but he had had plenty of lines to say in *Anna Lucasta*, and Frank would have recognized his undeniable screen presence in any case and been perfectly satisfied. Why ask a man who had already appeared in two pictures, and was nearly nominated for an Oscar for his second one, to do a screen test, particularly for such a small part?

The idea to make *Ocean's 11* had actually originated with Peter Lawford, who bought a five-year-old screenplay with his wife Pat's money. ("Why not?" he said. "She could afford it.") He suggested it to Sinatra, who thought it would be the perfect vehicle for him and his buddies. Studio head Jack Warner read the story and suggested it would be better to pull off the job in the script than to film the damn thing, but he knew it would fly since Sinatra was involved and therefore gave the go-ahead.

Now there was the problem of what to do with Peter Lawford. Sinatra had managed to get MGM to put him into *Never So Few*, but Jack Warner was another cookie altogether. Warner had bought the script from Peter and assumed that would be that. Luckily Warner allowed Frank's agent Burt Allenberg to put together the whole deal, although at first neither Allenberg nor Sinatra were interested in Lawford's participation. If Lawford hadn't married into the political Kennedy family, whose friendship Sinatra coveted, he probably would have gotten bupkiss; instead he got 17 percent of the profits and a part in the movie. He also got to join the act—literally—when Frank and the guys took over the stage of the Sands in Vegas while filming. As all of the action of *Ocean's 11* took place in Las Vegas, Sinatra reasoned they might as well make the movie by day and perform at the Sands by night. (By this time Dean Martin also owned a piece of the Sands.) Who needed sleep?

"We're not setting out to make *Hamlet* or *Gone with the Wind*," Frank told Sammy. "The idea is to hang out together, find fun with the broads, and have a great time. We gotta make pictures that people enjoy. Entertainment, period. We gotta have laughs." During this time Eisenhower, De Gaulle, and Khrushchev were planning to have their famous summit conference in Paris. Sinatra decided he and his friends would have a "summit conference of cool." When the newspapers got wind of this they were full of stories about the "Rat Pack Summit." Sinatra had taken the term from Bogie's old group and applied it to himself and his friends.

Virtually every hotel room in Las Vegas was sold out after Sinatra announced his summit. The Sands was packed solid and there was standing room only in the Copa Room where they performed. Eight security guards were hired to watch over Sinatra alone. Each night the boys would do two shows in the Copa Room, then sit in the lounge as the movie crew came in and set up for the early morning shooting. Nobody got any sleep. The day's shooting had to be over by four or five—unusual in the motion picture business—so that the boys could have dinner and get ready for their show again. On some days none of the five would report for filming before noon, just too exhausted to go to work. The Rat Packers would meet in the steam room at six after it was closed to the other guests. Henry Silva, who appeared in the film, said, "There was no sleeping—there was fun time. You were in Vegas and you're young and there's all these girls. It was an electric excitement that permeated the town. Frank was the engine; he was the guy."

During one show Sinatra noticed that Sammy was wearing his usual outré outfit while the rest of them were in tuxedos and began chewing him out, telling him he was all grown up now and had to wear a tux like the rest of them. "Go on now! Go and change and don't come back till you do!" For a panic-stricken moment Sammy wasn't sure if Frank was joking or not; the truth was Sinatra had taken his genuine feelings about Sammy's silly getups and, fueled by liquor from the rolling bar right up on the stage, decided to make an issue of it and get some comic mileage out of it at one and the same time. In other words, Frank was joking—but he was serious. He had assumed the audience would go right along with him but he didn't reckon with Sammy's fans, who loved his colorful costumes, every ring, spangle, and pair of super-tight, basket-hugging jeans. (That night he had on a pair of grey flannels with a silk ascot and blue blazer for accompaniment.) Sammy resisted the temptation to slink off the stage and instead stood up to Sinatra: "Nobody tells me what to do!" Like Sinatra, he was joking—but he was serious. The audience loved the way the underdog stood up to the Chairman of the Board and cheered the whole gag for as long as the two could milk it.

One day Peter Lawford came across a newspaper article which in part read, "The quintet of Sinatra, Martin, Davis, Lawford and Bishop moved into Las Vegas in the form of an attack force with Sinatra as the nominal leader of their clan." This term—"the clan"—stuck, and for awhile the Rat Pack was simply known as the Clan, but Sammy, understandably, objected to the appellation. Frank insisted (not too strenuously) that he did not wish to be the leader of the group, but it looked like he was stuck with it. And Lawford could forget for awhile that he was not really an integral part of the group of which he was supposed to be a primary member; he had never been a "showman" or entertainer like the others. After a while, everyone started calling them The Rat Pack again and that was that.

Sinatra liked the idea of putting all these guys who alone

had considerable drawing power together into one picture—just like the "all star casts" in the movies of yesteryear—and said it would be a good idea if they did several more of these Rat Pack movies. His "five-year plan," as he called it, would have them doing one movie a year for the next five years, which is not exactly the way it turned out, life and the movies being what they were.

In 1960, Frank and the Rat Pack were the epitome of cool. Men wanted to be like them, live like them, make love like them; they wanted to stay out all night like they did, bed a different broad whenever they felt like it, and never fear any consequences. They wanted to smoke and drink until it made them sick, throw money around like it was meaningless, and feel like irresponsible, irrepressible college boys again. In some ways the Rat Packers were the ultimate symbols of arrested development; in others they were the ultimate party boys. Their message: life was to be enjoyed and only a square would say "neigh."

To their fans, in fact to the entire public at large, Frank and his boys led the kind of lives other people only dreamt about. They got paid big bucks for doing what they loved instead of just having a "job" that merely paid the bills. They were adored and admired by millions of people, not just everyday folks but politicos and royalty and other movie and musical stars. They got instant attention, instant respect. They made hard work—filming all day, the show all night— look like fun. It was fun, and people loved them for the joy they brought into their lives. When they went to see Frank and company they were transported from a humdrum ordinary world into one that was rich with talent, good-natured ribbing, unabashed sexiness, and undeniable glamour.

To increase that feeling of specialness, the idea that they belonged to an exclusive club only the cool could belong to, Frank and the others came up with their own special

Who would have guessed that Sinatra would make it big? People who knew him in the early days thought he wasn't very special.

"I found him very intense, but pleasant," said Mary Wickes (left), who worked with Sinatra (as well as Jack Haley and Michele Morgan) in *Higher and Higher* (1943).

Sinatra preached racial and religious tolerance to a group of children in the forties short *The House I Live In*.

Shelley Winters (center) hated working with Sinatra (pictured here with Raymond Burr and Alex Nicol) on the autobiographical *Meet Danny Wilson* (1952). She only went back to the set after Frank's wife Nancy begged her to—Nancy wanted to seize Frank's salary.

Sinatra was essentially washed up in both the recording and film industries until his comeback in *From Here to Eternity* (1953).

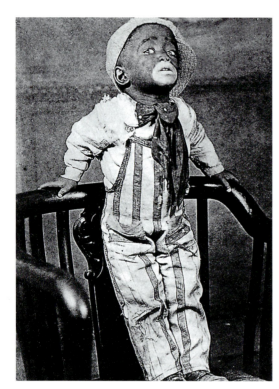

Sammy Davis Jr. as a child entertainer. On the road with his father and "uncle" he was billed as the "half" in Four and a Half, as "Little Sammy," and even as a dancing midget.

Davis in the seventies. He was arguably the most talented member of the Rat Pack.

Sterling Hayden, Nancy Gates, and Sinatra—who wants to kill the president—in *Suddenly* (1954). Sinatra had the film taken out of circulation after JFK's assassination.

Frank got Sammy Davis Jr. thrown out of the cast of *Never So Few* (1959); during filming Sinatra wooed Gina Lollobrigida relentlessly.

Frank and Dean Martin appeared with Judy Garland on her TV show. Judy wanted to marry Frank, but he would have none of it.

"It was more like a party than a film set," said Akim Tamiroff (holding billiard ball) of working with the Rat Pack in *Ocean's 11*.

The cast of *Ocean's 11*: Frank, Dean, Sammy, Peter, and Angie, who said, "Frank understands women as well as any guy I ever knew."

Filming a casino sequence in *Ocean's 11*. Director Lewis Milestone is in the dark suit with his arm resting on his knee. "He won't take crap from people," he said of Sinatra.

Left to right, Lawford, Sinatra, Martin, Davis, and Bishop on stage at the Sands Hotel and Casino's famous Copa Room. They filmed *Ocean's 11* by day and entertained at the Sands by night.

Dean Martin and Peter Lawford during the filming of *Ocean's 11*. "I wish Peter would relax more," Dean said of Lawford, whom he didn't especially like.

The ultimate party boys: the Rat Pack in the sixties.

Martin, Sinatra, Lawford, and Ruta Lee in *Sergeants 3* (1962). One critic called it "a $4 million home movie."

While filming Sergeants 3, Peter Lawford had no idea a monumental "quarrel" over JFK would lead to Frank permanently ousting him from the Rat Pack.

Frank and Dino appeared with the voluptuous duo Anita Ekberg (left) and Ursula Andress (right) in *4 For Texas* (1963), but it was the Three Stooges who stole the picture.

Sammy, Frank, and Dino in *Robin and the 7 Hoods* (1964).

Bing Crosby (seated) replaced Peter Lawford in *Robin and the 7 Hoods*. Dean Martin had modeled his singing style on Bing's but added a certain vocal leer.

f

Dean appeared as superspy Matt Helm in several campy James Bond spoofs; here he and Stella Stevens take direction in *The Silencers* (1966).

Not to be outdone by Dean, Sinatra appeared in his own action series, though there were only two films made about detective Tony Rome. This shot is from the 1968 sequel *Lady In Cement*, which co-starred Raquel Welch. Frank's marriage to Mia Farrow was disintegrating and he took it out on the cast.

Sammy Davis Jr. and Peter Lawford teamed for *Salt and Pepper* in 1968, hoping to recreate some Rat Pack magic.

Jerry Lewis (center) directed Lawford and Davis in *One More Time* (1970), the unsolicited sequel to *Salt and Pepper*. Sammy loved Jerry's cut but Peter thought it was awful and didn't protest when the studio recut it. This put a serious damper on his friendship with Sammy.

Peter Lawford in 1970. The years ahead would be grim ones full of financial troubles, marital mayhem, and a crippling professional slump not helped by his fall from the grace of Sinatra.

Sammy and Dino appeared in both *The Cannonball Run* (1981) and (pictured here) the 1984 sequel *Cannonball Run II*. Sinatra and Shirley MacLaine also appeared in the sequel, director Hal Needham's attempt to make a new Rat Pack out of himself and stars Burt Reynolds and Dom DeLuise. The attempt was a dismal failure. "It was a disgrace," said MacLaine.

Even though his daughter Tina produced it, Sinatra was enraged by the 1992 miniseries *Sinatra*, which was a little too "frank" for his comfort. Marcia Gay Harden and Philip Casnoff were cast as Ava Gardner and Frank Sinatra.

language, sort of the way *Captain Midnight* fans had had their decoder rings and membership badges. To wit:

> The Big Casino = Death.
> The Big G = God.
> A little hey-hey = a good time or a sexual experience.
> Bird = penis.
> "How's your bird?" = "How are ya?"
> Dullsville, Ohio = any dull place or situation; i.e. not Vegas.
> I think it's going to rain = I'm bored; let's go someplace else.
> Clyde = a geek, a jerk, a loser, or just a dude, depending upon whom it was applied to; the term wasn't always disparaging.

During filming the Rat Packers were all, as Sammy put it, "One-Take Charlies." This wasn't just out of necessity; Sinatra still feared that if he did take after take he would lose all freshness and spontaneity. Hanging around the set for hours bored him, and when he was bored he lost the feel for the work, for what he needed to feel to do the scene. Judging from his acting in *Ocean's 11*, Frank was probably bored a lot. Drinking, carousing, performing at the Sands, and making love to the broads all interested him a lot more than making the movie, and it shows.

Despite his two previous films, Sammy was still a neophyte compared to Frank—whose advice he found very helpful—but on certain occasions he wouldn't listen to Sinatra and insisted on doing things his own way. As he was having trouble figuring out what to do with his hands in some scenes, Sammy decided he would light up a cigarette; it would help make up for the absence of the mike he always used in his act. Sinatra warned him it wouldn't fly, but Sammy was a real clyde and insisted on smoking. This was one of the rare scenes that required several takes, and things slowed to a crawl as Sammy realized his cigarette had to match in each shot. "We spent most of the day burning cigarettes down to the same size," he said. By the time the day was over, a fuming Sinatra could have handed Sammy his bird.

Joey Bishop once said, "Sammy was always a little—no, a lot—insecure. Frank understood that. He always made Sammy feel included." Of Frank and the Rat Pack, he said, "If you reach stardom you've got to be true to yourself. Frank is honest—that's for sure. He and the boys do things not for their effect on people but because they believe in them all the way. Am I a full-fledged member? No, I'm more of a mascot, but even the mascot gets to carry the ball, too."

The one member of the pack who wasn't quite carrying the ball was Peter Lawford, who participated in the stage shows on most nights even though he couldn't sing, dance, or do imitations à la Sammy. The others tried to dream up bits of business for him to do, put him in sketches, that sort of thing, but Peter knew that he was the odd man out, the fifth wheel. Yet he wanted to be part of the action, part of the fun, feel like somebody again. Dean Martin said, "I wish Peter would relax more. I wish he wouldn't, I don't know, kowtow so much. He thinks he doesn't really belong with us, so he tries too hard to please Frank and the pack."

Dean was never one to kowtow to Frank, their mob buddies, or anyone else on the planet. In his own way he was tougher than Frank. He was also the one Rat Pack member who didn't need him. Joey and Sammy practically owed their careers to Sinatra—Lawford was also beholden to the Chairman of the Board, as he was called—but although Frank's friendship with Dean had certainly not hurt his movie career, at this point in time he was not so dependent as the others. Sammy, Joey, and Peter needed an *Ocean's 11*; Dean didn't. He had other fish to fry. Frank could boss the others around but not Dino.

To direct this unruly group in the picture they were supposed to be making was the well-known Lewis Milestone. In his early years Milestone had directed such fine films as *All Quiet on the Western Front* (1930), *The Front Page* (1931), *Of Mice and Men* (1940), *A Walk in the Sun* (1946) and *The Red Pony* (1949), but in 1960 he was three years from retiring, in failing health, and lately had done too many routine pictures to be a real player anymore. He was a solid professional, however, and Sinatra counted on him to somehow craft a well-made movie around the busy antics of the Rat Pack. Sinatra was sure the aging Milestone would be putty in his hands, and in truth Sinatra was such a ball of energy there was little the director could do to reign him in even if he had wanted to. Still, Milestone had a certain respect for Sinatra.

"Some people think Frank is arrogant and overbearing and something of a bully," he said in 1962. "Well, he isn't really; he just won't take crap from people. But with people [who have been] put upon, he is the kindest guy I know, [he] sides automatically with them. 'People think I'm on top of it,' he told me, 'but I've been an underdog, too—more times than I want to remember—I know just how it feels.'"

The story of *Ocean's 11* revolves around several men who were once paratroopers in the 82nd Airborne. Fifteen years have gone by and most of them are in pretty sorry circumstances. Danny Ocean (Sinatra) has come up with a brazen scheme to improve their lot in life: rip off all five casinos in Las Vegas—the Sands, the Sahara, the Flamingo, the Riviera, and the Desert Inn—all on the same night. The take will be at least one million a piece. The plan is to cause a short circuit that will black out all the lights on the Vegas strip. During the blackout, the wires that control the cages that hold the money will be doctored in such a way that they will automatically open when the lights go back on, allowing easy access to the cash. The scheme is successful, but the boys make the mistake of hiding the money in the coffin of one of their number (Richard Conte) who had a fatal heart attack during the robbery. Sitting in the funeral parlor, they are dismayed to learn that their buddy is being cremated along with all of the loot.

First-billed Sinatra as Danny Ocean has such a slight build that he looks like a ninety-pound weakling. His acting style in *Ocean's 11* can best be described as an intramural, laid-back, condescending, and to-hell-with-it-all approach. He doesn't so much act as inhabit the film between singing engagements. The only time he really exhibits any energy is when he affects an Irish brogue over the phone to play a trick on someone he owes money to.

Second-billed Dean Martin (as Sam Herman, an entertainer at The Sahara), thinks Danny's plan is crap and doesn't mind telling him so. In front of Sammy he talks about how much fun it would be to make women slaves. "I don't like Foster much," he says in reference to Lawford's character, which is interesting because in real life Dino never did care much for Peter.

Third-billed Sammy plays Josh Howard, who wanted to be a ballplayer but now drives a sanitation truck. "Imagine how I'd work out," he says, "a one-eyed outfielder in Mobile." Sammy was afraid his glass eye would be obvious to the camera (it isn't) so he ad-libbed references to it whenever he could. It's Josh who drives off with the loot in his garbage truck right after the robbery. When a cop tells him to "move it!" Sammy/Josh starts talking like a dumb "colored" guy to placate the officer. Fourth-billed Peter Lawford is Jimmy Foster, who desperately needs money so he won't have to depend on his wealthy mother and can cut her apron strings. (With this bit the picture was spoofing—and reversing—his relationship with Lady May.) Lawford looks almost as old as his mother's one-time suitor, Cesar Romero.

Showing where he stood with the rest of the Rat Pack,

Bishop (as "Musky" O'Connor) is billed third down in the supporting cast. He has very little to do and only two or three lines of dialogue. Sneaking around dressed as a janitor, O'Connor sprays the doorknobs in the casinos so his compatriots can know where to go once the lights are out.

Two lady Rat Packers were given small parts in the film. Shirley MacLaine has a cameo as a drunken lady on the sidewalk outside one of the casinos who dallies with Dino. Angie Dickinson, still one of the most sensual women in Hollywood, was cast as Bea, Danny's estranged wife, and offers her usual smooth, sexy performance (although there's precious little of it, unfortunately). She objects to her ex-husband's love of danger, but still has a thing for Danny. Angie herself once said, "Frank understands women as well as any guy I ever knew. He's a jump ahead of you all the time—knows what you're thinking, especially what you're feeling—a minute before you do." Not that every woman that Frank has known would necessarily agree with her.

When the picture came out *The New York Times* objected to the way the audience was put into the position of rooting for crooks. Were the hard-luck stories (the interesting character vignettes that make up the early sections of the film) meant to excuse the actions of Danny and his men, or simply provide the motivation? The film never makes it clear. The leisurely pacing of the movie—as laid back as the Rat Pack themselves—works against it during the crucial robbery scene, which takes all of five screen minutes and is completely devoid of any suspense or tension. An odd mix of comedy and drama, the picture emerges as alternately interesting and boring and is primarily remembered today because of the ending with the money being cremated. The only trouble is that considering all they've been through, all the hours of planning and rehearsing—and all that they're losing!—the men's reactions to it aren't nearly strong enough. (And would they have really all gathered together in the funeral parlor?) In his heyday, Milestone would never have let them get away with such indifferent thesping. One thing is for certain: the boys' plan to rob the casinos would never have worked in real life. Frank and Dean would have been risking their lives to provide a blueprint for ripping off the mob.

Of the Rat Pack members, Sammy and Dino come off the best (at least Sammy exudes some energy), but all of them are out-acted by old pros Ilka Chase (as Lawford's mother) and Akim Tamiroff as questionable Spherous, to whom Sinatra owes money.

Tamiroff had the last word on the picture. "Ah, that movie! I waited and waited and waited for them to show up to do one little scene (he was actually in two or three scenes) and Milestone keeps telling me, 'Be patient, be patient, they're coming, they're coming.' I said, 'When will we shoot the scene, at two in the morning?' When they finally show up it's more like a party than a film set. I've never worked like that.

"To tell the truth," he added, "it was sort of fun."

That, of course, had been the goal all along. Which was all well and good for the Rat Pack, but not so great for movie-goers.

And that was only the beginning.

15

The Jack Pack

When Elvis Presley had first appeared on the scene a few years earlier, Frank Sinatra and Dean Martin had thought very little of him; he was the ultimate "clyde." They found his gyrations distasteful, and they disliked the sexual innuendo his voice and smirk seemed to add to all the lyrics. The irony was that Dean Martin had been adding a certain leer to the lyrics for many years, and Presley's hip-swinging movements were not that far removed from Sammy's. In fact it could be argued that Sammy—or at least the whole "Negro" approach to rhythm and dance—influenced Elvis more than the other way around.

Frank was also a bit jealous of Elvis. Presley was getting the kind of attention from the youth of America—particularly the females—that he had once gotten. It was Presley's pictures being covered with lip prints now, not Sinatra's. Sinatra was afraid of being supplanted by Presley as the King of Cool. Furthermore he thought Presley's onstage movements and lip-curlings bordered on the epicene—too sensual for a real man to make—and found his hairstyle too fluffed up and feminized (especially compared to Sinatra's thinning locks). He made no secret of his utter distaste for his younger rival. (Frank would save his real ire for the Beatles, however.)

In truth, Elvis was no rival of Sinatra's. They appealed to different segments of the population. Sinatra's fans loved his way with old standards, swingers, and sleepy ballads. Presley's younger fans wanted him to rock and shimmy. Although Elvis wasn't a bad singer and had an acceptable enough voice, he was never in any way, shape, or form as good as Sinatra. Sinatra had a way with a song—the perfect phrasing, the effortless style, the cool expressiveness—that few singers could match. As an actor, Elvis was better than people ever gave him credit for, and might have developed at least as well as Sinatra did if his manager hadn't forced him to make one insipid musical after another after the early years of more interesting, challenging pictures.

In spite of his distaste for the singer, Sinatra wasn't about to come off as an old fogie—a jealous one at that—to the public at large, so after filming *Ocean's 11* he did a TV special (the fourth in a series he did for Timex) that was, in part, meant as a tribute to Elvis after he came out of the Army. The other members of the Rat Pack—except for Dino—were also on hand as Elvis took a bow and did a couple of numbers (a total of six minutes) dressed first in his army uniform and then in a tux. In a 1997 retrospective on "Elvis TV Specials," *TV Guide* seemed to see this as "the passing of the hunk torch." The writer, clearly an Elvis aficionado, then went on to say that Elvis's "slinky dance moves and finger-snapping put a stiff Sinatra to shame. . . . Sinatra makes 'Love Me Tender' schmaltzy while Presley finds all sorts of sexy shadings in 'Witchcraft.'" Sinatra, of course, did not need finger-snapping or slinky moves to get his message across, and his recording of "Witchcraft" is a classic that puts Presley's rendition in the shade. Indeed, nowadays it is Presley who seems dated, while Sinatra never really goes out of style.

Even if Dino had not been making a film he would probably not have participated in the "tribute to Elvis" that Frank had concocted; he thought the boy wonder was a freak. (Ironically, Martin was one of Presley's idols and models, and many of his songs owe a clear debt to Dino.) He and Shirley MacLaine worked with producer Hal Wallis on another sex comedy, *All in a Night's Work* (1961). In this Shirley is a sweet working girl who's suspected of spending the night with a now-dead publishing magnate. The dead man's nephew (Martin) assumes Shirley plans to blackmail the company, which all leads to somewhat amusing but definitely forgettable complications.

By this time Shirley had transferred her affections from Frank to Dino, not only because Sinatra was through with her, but because after making several pictures together Martin had finally noticed that—barrel of laughs that she was—she was not exactly one of the boys. Before long Shirley had convinced herself that she was madly and desperately in love with Martin. It didn't matter to her that Dean was married; she had to have him. One night after filming, she decided to go to his home to talk to him about it. Dean was still married to Jeanne and the household was filled with seven children from two marriages. Jeanne answered the door when Shirley arrived and was perfectly cordial. She told Shirley to wait in the living room for Dean while she finished making supper for the kids.

When Dean came downstairs he was surprised to see Shirley but greeted her warmly. He was used to young women becoming infatuated with him, with that whole image he projected, but even if he had wanted to make a move it was hardly the time or place. As Dean looked expectantly at Shirley, she could think of nothing to say but how much she was enjoying doing the picture with him. Dean told her he felt the same. After a few awkward moments, Shirley said good night. So much for the love affair. Because Dean had never actually dumped her the way Frank had, Shirley was always kinder to Dino in her assorted memoirs—relatively speaking—than she was to Frank. At the time of *All in a Night's Work* she said of Martin: "He can be very genial and I guess you would call it expansive—and kind, very kind, if he's in the mood."

Meanwhile, Frank was in the mood to stump for his pal Peter Lawford's brother-in-law, Jack Kennedy, who had decided to run for president. To that end he rechristened his gang the "Jack Pack" and induced every member—major and minor—to go to bat for JFK. Kennedy had gone to see the Rat Pack perform at the Sands while they were filming *Ocean's 11*, where Frank introduced the senator to the audience. "What did you say his name was?" Dino asked. This was perhaps the first time that Dino and Sammy did what was to become one of their classic jokes. Dean would pick the diminutive Davis up in his arms and say, "I'd like to thank the NAACP for this award."

JFK was fascinated by Frank Sinatra. The future president loved the film world, loved movie stars, loved good gossip (especially about movie stars' sex lives), and particularly enjoyed the beautiful women attracted to the film capital by the hopes of attaining stardom. It has already become legend how Lawford would pimp for John and Robert Kennedy and their relationships with Marilyn Monroe. Like his father Joe before him, Jack Kennedy was irresistibly attracted to the allure, power, passion, and sexiness of Hollywood. He was a frequent visitor to Puccini's, the Beverly Hills restaurant of which Frank and Peter were co-owners. (Despite the name, you were more likely to hear Sinatra's records in the background than *Madame Butterfly*, however.)

Sinatra was as big a pimp for JFK as Lawford was, and would make sure that whenever the senator stopped by the Sands, his suite would be well-stocked with hot and cold running showgirls. Frank also introduced him to Judith Campbell Exner, who years later would claim that she was lovers to both JFK and mobster Sam Giancana, and she squired messages to them when Sam and the CIA, incredibly, planned a joint hit on Fidel Castro (Operation Mongoose).

Frank took "High Hopes," Jimmy Van Heusen's song from *A Hole in the Head*, and turned it into JFK's official campaign song. He called up virtually everyone he knew or worked with and got them to campaign for Kennedy. "He called," said Janet Leigh, "and you went." Sinatra convinced Leigh to hold a "Key Women for Kennedy Tea," which he attended. Edward G. Robinson from *A Hole in the Head* was even drafted, and he was not even a fringe member of the Pack—Rat or Jack.

Sinatra had always been in awe of people with "class," and to him the Kennedy family had it in spades. From old Joe on down, the Kennedys were actually vulgarians of the first order—many thought Joe, who consorted with certain mobsters, was no better than a mobster himself—but to Sinatra's debased viewpoint they were the epitome of gentility and breeding. What made it even better was that Jack Kennedy, although infinitely more sophisticated, liked Frank and could relate to him on his level—booze and broads and Hollywood. Sinatra wanted to be JFK's best friend; he wanted JFK to be president. That way his best buddy could be the most powerful man on the planet.

Sinatra was also being delicately pressured by his mobster friends, who had their own uses for a president who was best buddies with Frank. The Mafia, however, wasn't too crazy about JFK's brother, Robert Francis Kennedy, who later would become determined to wage war on organized crime in America. (Many conspiracy theorists would in fact suggest that the Mafia was secretly behind the assassinations of both brothers.) This would later cause trouble for Sinatra.

At July's Democratic National Convention Frank and his Jack Pack turned out in full force—MacLaine, Angie Dickinson, Leigh and Curtis, even Judy Garland, plus Milton

Berle and Mort Sahl in addition to the others—but the tri-
umphant occasion was marred by two episodes that infuriated Sinatra. When Mort Sahl addressed the convention he
made as many jokes about the Democrats and JFK as he did
about Nixon and the Republicans: "Nixon wants to sell the
country, and Kennedy wants to buy it," Sahl quipped. Sinatra
was not amused.

An uglier episode occurred right after the Rat Pack sang
"The Star-Spangled Banner." Some delegates from the state
of Mississippi not only booed Sammy Davis Jr. but called him
"nigger" and "freak." It wasn't just his color alone that
brought on this barrage, but the fact that he was engaged to
the Swedish, very Nordic actress Mai Britt. Sammy was so
angry and humiliated that he walked out of the convention
hall barely holding back tears. He didn't know that the worst
was yet to come.

Sammy had importuned actress friend Barbara Luna to
introduce him to Mai when he saw her at the 20th Century-
Fox commissary. It took the more reserved Mai a while to
warm up to the outgoing Sammy, but after a bit the two were
dating and making plans for the future. Mai detested it when
Sammy treated her like a sex object instead of a full person,
like when he chided her for wearing a one-piece bathing suit
instead of a bikini on a yachting party. Unlike Frank, he was
happy to fly to Sweden to meet his girlfriend's parents, who
took to him immediately. When Mai told him she wanted to
have his "little brown babies," he asked her to marry him and
she accepted. David Niven, who had known Sammy since the
days of Bogie's Rat Pack, sent the first congratulatory tele-
gram: "So happy you've found a Swedish girl." Niven's wife
was also Swedish. (Sammy had already been married once
before to a black girl named Loray that he had proposed to
while inebriated. Once sober, Sammy went through with the
wedding but paid the girl off and basically discarded her in
true Sinatra fashion.)

Mai and Sammy had gone to London immediately after the announcement for one of Sammy's club engagements. Except for some picketers outside the nightclub, the British reaction was basically benign. Not so back home in the United States, where Sammy received hate mail and columnists seemed 50/50 in favor of or against the upcoming union. One argument often brought up against the marriage was that it wouldn't be fair to the children. Sammy wisely countered by saying that even if he were to marry a black woman and his children were fully black instead of half black with a white mother, they would probably still encounter discrimination, so what was the big deal?

Sammy was concerned, however, with the spot he was putting Frank Sinatra in. Sinatra was so identified with the JFK-for-President campaign that there were those who thought it would hurt Kennedy's chances for election if Sinatra went to Sammy's wedding. Sammy called Frank and told him he was postponing the wedding until after the election but said it was because of scheduling problems. Sinatra saw through the ruse and said he would attend the wedding no matter when it was, but Sammy insisted the postponement was for the best.

Peter Lawford was with Frank at the time and remembered what a touching and powerful moment it had been. "Frank always cared about Sammy and his commitment to civil rights was always sincere. He thought the whole thing sucked, but he was under such pressure from people inside the campaign. He thought Sammy was the best for doing what he did. So did I. It was friendship, pure and simple."

JFK won the election, of course, but the humiliation was not over for Sammy, who received a phone call from the president's personal secretary, Evelyn Lincoln, a couple of days before the inauguration. She told him, "The President has asked me to tell you that he does not want you to be present at his inauguration."

The situation was a volatile one. This was before inter-racial romances became fairly commonplace (if still not entirely accepted), and JFK was nothing if he was not a politician. The ironically named Lincoln oh so delicately explained to Sammy that his appearance might jeopardize the goals JFK had in mind in regards to racial equality in the country and so on, and she was sure that Sammy would understand. . . . Sammy took it meekly, but inside he was boiling.

JFK's act was cowardly and unconscionable. It was as if he were saying that it was okay for Sammy to campaign and bring in the black vote, but now that he had won, the "house nigger" wasn't about to join in the celebration with everyone else. "If the president could do this to me, someone he knows, what hope do the millions of invisible people have?" Sammy wrote about this incident years later.

Peter Lawford later told Sammy that Bobby Kennedy had argued vehemently for Sammy's inclusion and had walked out of the room in a rage when he was out-voted. The truth is JFK was less interested in helping blacks or anyone else for that matter than he was in finding good-looking women. Bobby was always more of a social activist than his brother.

Sinatra presided over the gala showbiz tribute to JFK the night before the inauguration. A Who's Who of Hollywood gathered together to salute the new chief of the free world, but two of the Rat Packers were conspicuously absent. Sammy had decided if he wasn't good enough for the inauguration, he certainly wasn't going to perform for the President he had lost all faith in. (Such black entertainers as Sidney Poitier, Ella Fitzgerald, Nat King Cole, and Harry Belafonte, probably unaware of the situation, did appear.) The other no-show was Dean Martin, who never would fol-low Frank's orders just because everyone else did. Shirley MacLaine flew all the way in from Japan (where her husband lived) just to appear for a few minutes, but Dean was making a movie and he was damned if he'd inconvenience himself for one night for Frank, JFK, or anybody. Throughout their friendship, Sinatra would find Dean the one Rat Packer he couldn't control.

Dino had first met JFK back when Martin and Lewis were appearing at the Chez Paree in Chicago in 1948. The team was staying at the same hotel where Kennedy was holed up rehearsing a speech for the Executives Club. Although Jerry Lewis had liked Jack, Dino was completely unimpressed. Just because the guy had been elected President didn't change the situation. He couldn't have cared less about JFK.

The show was a great deal of work, a logistical nightmare, and there were so many egos to deal with that Sinatra lost his patience and temper on more than one occasion. He had a few too many drinks to help him deal with all the demands of putting the gala together. He was annoyed by people who didn't come, particularly those who cancelled at the last minute, and took out his anger primarily on Peter Lawford.

By this time Lawford was estranged from his wife Pat Kennedy Lawford and Sinatra was mad as hell about it. He was afraid that if Jack got angry at his brother-in-law for making his sister Pat miserable, it might affect his, Frank's, relationship with the President; Peter was also Frank's friend and a member of his Rat Pack, after all. At one point Sinatra screamed at Peter, "Get your act together or you'll blow it for all of us!" It wasn't enough that Sinatra was a world-famous singer and actor. He wanted to travel in the highest possible circles, and who could be higher than the President and his fabulous First Lady?

There was one problem, however, and that was Jackie, who did not exactly have the same feelings toward Frank that her husband did. JFK got a kick out of Sinatra's raw edges, the two could be boys together cruisin' the chicks, but there was no such identification between Jackie and Sinatra. She also suspected that many of her husband's extracurricular activities were aided and abetted by Frank as well as Peter. She related to Peter as another Kennedy spouse and outsider—he was also British and well-mannered, a gentleman—but Sinatra was just dead common as far as she was concerned.

And in spite of his hard work for the campaign, the feeling that Frank had basically won JFK the election, Sammy Davis Jr. could have told him that there was no such thing as loyalty in the Kennedy camp.

Before long it would all boil over, scalding at least two members of the Rat Pack.

16

The Sergeant Loses
His Stripes

Joey Bishop had always felt like the most minor of the Rat Packers and the one who owed the most to Frank Sinatra. In the days B.F.—Before Frank—he had avoided controversy like the plague and been loathe to take sides, but when Sinatra insisted everyone stump for Kennedy there was no way he could not become, in part, a "political" comedian. While this opened doors for him, it closed just as many, such as the time Nixon's secretary called from the White House in 1960 and asked if he could perform at the Republican convention. "I thanked the secretary and the Vice President for thinking of me, but I said I was too busy to go. After all, should Nixon lose, I'd be out politically, out professionally." As one columnist noted, "Especially professionally! As a member in good standing of Frank Sinatra's 'The Clan,' Bishop would no more be seen in Nixon's camp than at a fire sale in men's wear."

Newspaper stories filed on Nixon's invitation and Bishop's refusal all centered on everything that Bishop owed to buddy Frank. "Frankly," said one insider, "it made him

seem like Sinatra's lapdog." Bishop countered as best he
could with statements like, "I'm a Kennedy man, have been
since that nightclub encounter (February 1960 in Las Vegas)
when Kennedy told me he's been a fan of mine for years . . ."

Bishop's bid for some kind of professional independence
was to do his own sitcom, *The Joey Bishop Show*, produced
by Danny Thomas's company, beginning in September 1961.
This was not his first TV show—he'd made his television
debut on CBS's *Keep Talking* in 1958, which had more of a
variety format—but as it carried his name he was more ter-
ritorial about it, much to his assorted co-workers' consterna-
tion. In the series Bishop played a Casper Milquetoast variation as an aide in a public relations firm. He also was given a
brother-in-law (Joe Flynn), who was the bane of his existence—and vice versa.

In their review *The New York Times* nailed down the
problem of the show. "[*The Joey Bishop Show*] completely
misses the humor of Mr. Bishop, which lies in his unexpected turn of phrase and mind. Instead there was substituted
only the canned and predictable artificiality that is the recur-
rent blight of so much [sic] filmed TV comedies." The audience probably would have found the backstage fireworks
more absorbing than the show itself. Who was to blame for
the show's artistic (if not commercial—its lead-in, *Wagon
Train*, gave it respectable ratings) failure depended upon who
you were talking to.

One camp argued that Joey's egomania was to blame for
all the firings, bad feelings, tense atmosphere, and hasty last-
minute rewrites that characterized the behind-the-scenes
desperation of the program. One cast member called Bishop
a "martinet" and suggested that going into work each day was
"like stepping into a mortuary to view the remains." Bishop's
outrages were many: he impulsively altered the story line
just before the pilot was to be filmed, he wouldn't follow the
orders of the show's director and tried to direct everyone

himself, and he fired actor Joe Flynn (and three other cast members) because Flynn was getting more laughs than he was. Flynn, who was only on the show for two months before getting canned, reported, "It was the most unpleasant experience of my life."

When Bishop saw that all the changes weren't having the desired effect, he fiddled with the show so maniacally and rapidly that producer Marvin Marx would come in each morning only to learn that a cast member, guest star, whole stretches of dialogue, most of the gags, and even the entire plot line of the episode had been dumped or revised overnight. For his part, Danny Thomas believed in a hands-off approach ("I have one great talent: I delegate authority and allow it to function"), but he rushed in one day to remind Joey that he was supposed to be playing a character and not doing a guest spot on Jack Paar's program—"Please don't play it that way!" Joe Flynn, best-known as Ernest Borgnine's neurotic superior officer on *McHale's Navy*, theorized that Bishop was "shell-shocked" because he'd always gotten good press before the TV show and was "desperate to be loved." Before too long Bishop's character was no longer a mere aide in the agency, he was the boss.

Bishop had his own theories. He felt the director, David Lowell Rich, was talented but hadn't enough experience in comedy. He was horrified to learn that some of the writers assigned to the show had never seen him perform. "I thought the people I worked with would at least know who I was." The writers were more familiar with TV regular Flynn and therefore wrote their best material for him. When Bishop called in some gag writers from New York (one of whom was director/actor/*Murphy Brown* regular Gary Marshall) they told him Flynn's character was a cliche, and if he didn't want critics calling his show tiresome and cliche-ridden, Bishop had better get rid of Flynn. He did. Along with Flynn went the actress who played Flynn's wife. Not much later Bishop's boss and girlfriend were also replaced. "It was a blood bath," said Flynn.

Bishop contended that the major problem all along was that the character he portrayed simply wasn't right for Joey Bishop. "They wanted me to be a victim of fate, a schnook." That was definitely not the right image for a member of the Rat Pack, who were winners; what would Frank say? "You know what I think Frank thinks?" Bishop said, "I think he thinks I'm nuts." Joey was determined to show the world that he could make it on his own without the help of Frank Sinatra—who never guest-appeared on the sitcom—and he pretty much succeeded; despite all the problems and retooling, *The Joey Bishop Show* managed to last for several seasons.

Meanwhile Frank and Company mulled over their future film projects. Frank Capra wanted Frank, Dean Martin, and Bing Crosby to combine forces in a screen biopic of Jimmy Durante—the four men even announced the project on another of Sinatra's Timex TV specials—but for one reason or another the project never materialized. Instead somebody got the bright idea of putting the entire Rat Pack in another remake of *Gunga Din*. This very loose version of Rudyard Kipling's poem was updated to the American wild west and entitled *Sergeants 3* (1962). The first nominal remake had been entitled *Soldiers Three* and starred Stewart Granger and original Rat Packer David Niven.

Sammy Davis finally married Mai (now known as May) Britt before filming began. Frank Sinatra threw him a wild bachelor party that in some ways resembled a celebrity roast. Milton Berle dressed up as May in *The Blue Angel* complete with black net stockings, high heels, and full makeup and wig, and Peter Lawford and Tony Curtis did a silly duet. After the party was over, Sinatra told Sammy that he knew he and May wanted a family, so he had decided to lower Sammy's advance money for *Sergeants 3*, but to make up for it he was giving Sammy 7 percent of the profits. Frank told him that in all likelihood he would eventually realize a quarter of a million dollars. *Sergeants 3* was a joint production of both Sinatra's (Essex) and Martin's (Claude) production companies.

The Rat Pack packed up and left for Utah, where many of the film's exterior scenes would be shot in the Bryce Canyon and Kanab regions of the state. In Kanab, they discovered that there wasn't going to be a whole lot to do in the evening, especially compared to the situation in Las Vegas while making *Ocean's 11*. To somewhat relieve this deplorable situation the boys took over the top floor of the hotel and had crewmen install connecting doors between each room so the floor would seem like one big suite. There they drank a lot of booze and played cards. Female extras, and a few imported hookers, went in and out of the "suite" at regular intervals, and there were special presentations of old Laurel and Hardy films on 16mm film projectors when everyone was in a less sexy mood. Rat Pack friends such as Henry Silva, Buddy Lester, and Hank Henry were given parts so they could be on hand to amuse the others when these other diversions didn't work.

Previously the only hot spot in town had been a Dairy Queen where the bored teens of Kanab hung out and dreamed, but once Frank and his gang arrived, the hotel's top floor was the in place to be, not that the uninvited would have much luck getting past Frank's security team.

Sammy Davis was thrilled to be making a western—he had always known there were black cowboys and was annoyed that he couldn't convince anyone in Hollywood of that fact—but even here he got cast in Sam Jaffe's role as Gunga Din instead of as a cowboy. This was disappointing to him to say the least. He had almost played an historical role—a slave who helps one of the wives get out of the Alamo—in John Wayne's filmization of the event, but the schedule of *Ocean's 11* conflicted and there was no way he could do both pictures. "I saw my movie breakthrough coming with the Clan pictures rather than playing a small part in a very big Wayne film," he said, but of course there was no way he would have bucked Sinatra.

By the time shooting began, Peter Lawford had packed on a few pounds, mostly from over-indulging in spirits, and as the boys watched the rushes of the film each night Sinatra would tease him and call him "Fattie." Lawford hated this— he particularly hated the fact that Sinatra was right, he really was out of shape by his slender standards—but he would never talk back. He started a regimen of dexedrine on top of alcohol and managed to shed a few of the extra pounds before filming was over. His stand-in—Peter's disabled arm prevented him from doing many of the more physical sequences— wore padding for some scenes so long shots of Lawford's figure would match.

While the rest of the Rat Pack entertained themselves with a variety of women, Peter focused primarily on Joan Arnold, his secretary at his production company, Chrislaw. Joan's father was the head of the camera department at MGM. Each weekend while the gang was on location in Utah, she would come out and hole up with Peter for a little R-and-R. Before long, word of this got back to Peter's wife, and she paid a call on the offices of Chrislaw on one of the rare occasions when Peter was in his office. Pat was no patsy. First she glared at Joan at her desk, looking as if at any second she were going to go over and pull out all of her hair; then she stormed in to see Peter and laid down the Chrislaw. After his wife left, Peter immediately contacted his harried, subservient manager and told him to do the dirty deed: Pat had insisted Joan be fired. Although everyone's sympathy at the time was for Joan—Pat and Peter were depicted as monsters out to destroy a poor working girl—Joan knew that she was messing with another woman's husband and that it was only a matter of time before things exploded. The consensus, however, was that considering how close Peter and Joan had been for some time, Peter should never have delegated somebody else to do the firing.

"I was in an impossible position," he told friends sometime later. "When the wife finds out, you've got to end the affair. How could I have gone on working with her? I'm sure she understood." Peter knew on which side his bread was buttered and if either Pat or Frank—or brother-in-law JFK—demanded something of him, he complied. His breakup with Joan was nothing to the breakup with Sinatra that was just around the horizon.

The director of the film was fifty-year-old John Sturges, who'd directed such films as *Bad Day at Black Rock* (1955), *Gunfight at the O.K. Corral* (1957), *The Magnificent Seven* (1960), and of course Sinatra's *Never So Few* in 1959. A workmanlike professional with little personal style, he worked well with the casual Sinatra, who found that Sturges never "directed" him too much nor expected too many retakes, which was just how Frank and most of the others liked it.

The love interest in the picture was supplied by pretty Ruta Lee. "I had a wonderful time," Lee told one writer, "but, unfortunately, they all treated me like their kid sister." She reported that the Rat Packers drank consistently but never to the point where they were inebriated during filming. Dino was the most fun. "He could always keep calm. He was above it all. Nothing ever got to him. If it ever did, you never knew it." Many more of Martin's co-workers over the years would confirm that this was the impression they got of Dean when he was making a movie or doing a TV show or special. Cool, unruffled, unflappable.

Although told tongue-in-cheek, the transplanted screenplay adhered rather closely to the original story. Sinatra, Martin, and Lawford as the three title sergeants, friends, and

rivals, nearly wreck a saloon in a protracted battle with buf-
falo hunters. From there they head to the town of Medicine
Bend, where they have a climactic showdown with hundreds
of angry, bloodthirsty Indians. In the Gunga Din role (here
called "Jonah Williams"), Sammy Davis is a freed slave who
wants to join the Army. Gunga Din died in the original version; Sammy lives to blow his bugle and then some. Joey
Bishop was handed one good scene as a drunk, and Henry
Silva was one bad "Injun."

Although the picture made money and pleased a few
reviewers, it was essentially savaged by the critical establishment, such as a write-up in *Time* which characterized the
film as "the latest fresh-air outing for Frank Sinatra's gnat
pack." Referring to the cast members of the original *Gunga
Din* of 1939, the *Time* reviewer added, "Sinatra is no [Cary]
Grant, Dean Martin is no [Victor] McLaglen, and Peter
Lawford, a man who looks undressed when not surrounded
by a drawing room, is assuredly no [Douglas] Fairbanks [Jr].
The Clansmen loaf kiddingly through their parts, acquiring
suntans. No one, of course, bothers to look bothered as the
hostiles approach. Such expressions as are evident reflect the
sudsy affability of a pipe fitters' picnic (Hey, get a load of
Dino on a horse!) . . . a $4,000,000 home movie."

It was generally agreed that of the title characters, Dean
Martin played with the most energy (energy was not the forte
of Sinatra, let alone Lawford), and that Sammy Davis out-
shone everyone with his amiability and enthusiasm. "His
contribution to the fun," opined *Punch*, "is to pretend that
he really believes in the character." Some critics admired
aspects of Sturges's direction, which *Variety* found "brisk and
alert." According to the London *Times*, "a number of situations in the first half of the film which curiously recall his
recent *The Magnificent Seven* show him at the top of his
form: the deserted town on a still afternoon, withholding
whatever secrets it may have from the cautious patrol, is

beautifully evoked, and the final action is staged with energy and precision." On the other hand, *Cue* magazine felt this final sequence "approaches a sort of Kipling Keystone Kops on Parade." Other critics admired the sweeping panoramic shots of Utah by cinematographer Winton Hoch.

That same year Sinatra appeared in one of his most talked-about films, director John Frankenheimer's *The Manchurian Candidate*. Clearly a reaction to the McCarthy era, the highlight of this entertaining film is a clever bit when a brainwashing session is intercut with a garden club meeting, which is what the brainwashed soldiers think they're actually attending. Despite fine performances by Sinatra, Angela Lansbury, and Laurence Harvey—and some riveting scenes—the film never quite recovers from its implausible premise: that a famous, nationally-recognizable war hero (Harvey) would be chosen as an assassin when the very success of his mission would depend upon his ability to blend into a crowd! There are those, however, who did not find it improbable that Harvey could go about in public during crucial moments without being recognized.

Sinatra was less interested in making good movies at this point than he was in ingratiating himself with the man in the White House. Unfortunately, JFK's brother Bobby, now attorney general, was getting more and more nervous about Sinatra's Mafia ties, and wanted Jack to distance himself—and hence his office—from the singer. Jackie found Frank so declasse that she forbade her husband to invite him to any White House dinners. But JFK still wanted Frank to introduce him to any number of Hollywood beauties that he had yet to bed and invited Frank to dinner at the White House only when Jackie was out of Washington. Then came the notorious Bing Crosby incident.

Peter had gotten the ball rolling—and paid the ultimate price—when he called Frank and asked if JFK could stay at his house in Palm Springs when he made a trip to Southern

California in early 1962. Anxious to have the President further in his debt, Sinatra not only said "yes!" but on his own initiative spent hundreds of thousands of dollars to turn his estate into a "White House Away From The White House" for Jack. It seemed more or less reasonable when he installed a communications center with extra phone lines and put in extra security devices. When he had several cottages especially constructed for the Secret Service agents, people figured he could also use them for Rat Packers and other guests later on. But when he put in his own private heliport so the President could literally land on his back lawn, everyone figured he had gone a little too far. To make matters worse, the President never even came.

Bobby Kennedy had reminded his brother that if he went to Frank's place he would be staying on the same estate that had played host to Sam Giancana and dozens of other well-known Mafiosi. JFK had only cared about all the women, provided by Frank and Peter, that he'd be getting, but his more sensible brother told him he had to finally think of his image. Jack let Bobby give Peter the bad news. Bobby wanted Peter to tell Frank.

"If there were ever anything in this life that I did not want to do," Peter said, "it was to tell Frank that Jack wasn't coming. He'd spent so much money. The only times I'd ever been afraid for my life were because of Frank Sinatra, and here I had to give him this news, of all things. But I was the one who had asked him in the first place. Frank didn't care that Jack had put me up to it; he didn't care about anything except that the president wasn't coming. He was livid; he was a maniac. Thank God I didn't tell him in person; he might have killed me."

Peter begged his brother-in-law to change his mind, but Jack had been shamed into seeing the stupidity of such an act by his brother. He told Peter that as long as Bobby was investigating so many of Frank's mobster friends, friends who'd stayed at his place in Palm Springs and might even drop by while he, the President of the United States, was on the premises, there was no way he could stay there. Peter tried to save the day by claiming that the Secret Service was worried about security and wondered how safe the Palm Springs pad might be for JFK, but when Frank called Bobby he was told the simple truth: it was his fraternizing with the likes of Sam Giancana that made him an inappropriate host for the President. When Frank found out that JFK would instead stay at Bing Crosby's estate, which was nearby, he nearly became apoplectic. Crosby had not done a thing to help get JFK elected; he was a Republican, for Christ's sake.

Never one to believe in "don't kill the messenger," Frank not only became disenchanted with the Kennedys but completely turned against Peter Lawford. He felt Lawford could have done more to sway the Kennedys' opinions, considering all Frank had done for Peter and his career. He also now saw Lawford as part of the enemy Kennedy camp. He saw the sleek, polished Lawford, who had been admitted (nominally) into the Kennedy family, and then compared Peter's sophisticated style to his own much rougher, less-educated veneer, and felt humiliated. Peter had held a mirror up to him, and he and the Kennedys seemed to be looking at his image and telling him that when all was said and done, he was not good enough to associate with the Kennedys. You did not do that to Frank Sinatra. Except for one occasion, Frank never spoke to Peter Lawford again, and instantly cut him out of all future film projects.

Frank swore that he would have the last word. In the meantime, the Jack Pack was dead.

17

Boys in Texas

In January of 1963, Frank and Dean and Sammy did a trio at the Sands in Las Vegas. Joey was occupied elsewhere and Peter—Peter was O-U-T. The films continued, solo, non-Rat Pack pictures, and the girls kept coming. Dean did a cameo—he played a barely recognizable bum on a street corner—in Frank's picture *Come Blow Your Horn*. Jill St. John had a role in that movie, and she also popped up in Dean's film, another sex-comedy with a suggestive title, *Who's Been Sleeping in My Bed?*

Jill started out as one of Dean's girls, but when he was through with her, he passed her on to Frank, with whom she lasted a little longer. Jill had been just another starlet at Fox until she married millionairess Barbara Hutton's son, Lance Reventlow. "After that, she was given star treatment, to be sure," says Ray Stricklyn, who acted with her in *The Lost World* (1960). Three years later she was being squired around by one member of the Rat Pack after another.

Who's Been Sleeping in My Bed? featured Dean as a television doctor who finds that the wives of his poker buddies come to him for "advice" about their lousy marriages. Carol

Burnett played Dean's psychiatrist's nurse—and came on a little too strong in every sense of the word. Elizabeth Montgomery was more appealing as Martin's fiancee, who's anxious to get hitched to Dino. Despite some comical moments, the film was mostly a mess.

Dean and Frank were together again in a comedy-western entitled *4 for Texas*, which was primarily an excuse for Frank to meet that era's chief foreign sex symbols, the magnificent Ursula Andress (christened "Ursula Undress" by some wags) and the ultra-voluptuous Anita Ekberg (Dean had already worked with her in *Artists and Models*, where she had a bit part, and in *Hollywood or Bust*, where she played the object of Jerry's juvenile affections).

Andress had made her mark playing Honeychile Ryder to Sean Connery's James Bond in the first Bond film *Dr. No* the previous year. Ekberg, who had eye-opening bust measurements to go with her beautiful face, had become an international sensation in Federico Fellini's masterpiece *La Dolce Vita* in 1960 after appearing in several previous films (including the two Martin and Lewis features). Sadly, Ekberg followed this up by appearing in very bad Hollywood movies with every American lech—from the Rat Packers to Bob Hope—who wanted to play with her. As the start of filming approached, Dean and Frank would giggle together like thirteen-year-olds who'd seen their first *Playboy* centerfold at the thought of being on location with these two bodies beautiful.

But Sinatra figured it wouldn't hurt to hedge their bets. Some of the gals they worked with didn't always want to play ball with them, and these two women were in demand; they couldn't be blackballed too easily, not with figures like that. As usual, he and Dino had a house to live in when they were on location, a house that was virtually turned into a brothel. Many of the dancehall girls in the movie were actually high-priced hookers who were shipped in just to service the cast and crew when the day's shooting was over. Frank and Dean, of course, got first dibs on the gals, who were put on the payroll but got paid a lot more than the usual movie extra.

There was some debate as to how to classify these gals so it wouldn't raise eyebrows if anybody looked at the books. As far as the boys were concerned, the prostitutes were essential for morale. There was no way a man could work in close quarters, do love scenes with the likes of Ekberg and Andress, and be able to get to sleep at night without relieving all that sexual tension. The hookers assured that their raging libidos would be satisfied.

Not so satisfied were Peter Lawford, Joey Bishop, and Sammy Davis Jr., all of whom had hoped *4 for Texas* would be another Rat Pack Picture Deluxe. Lawford, of course, was entirely out of the loop by now, but he'd still had hopes. Bishop and Sammy consoled themselves with roles in *Johnny Cool* (1963), which was produced by Lawford's aforementioned production company Chrislaw, formed with his agent Milt Ebbins. (The firm also produced the successful *Patty Duke Show* for television.) Peter's father-in-law, Joe Kennedy, who'd once been involved with motion picture production decades before, was an occasional consultant, although his stroke limited his involvement, which was probably for the best.

Henry Silva, who'd had small roles in *Ocean's 11* and *Sergeants 3*, was cast in the lead of *Johnny Cool*. Elizabeth Montgomery, who'd been with Dean in *Who's Been Sleeping in My Bed?* was cast as the female lead because she was married to the director, William Asher, at the time. Peter importuned his friends—including Sammy and Joey—to take small roles at low pay as a personal favor to him. They were happy enough to comply, as the movie was certainly a change of pace from Rat Pack fare and might get a lot of attention. The character Johnny Cool was a vicious gangster out to get even with everyone who had crossed him, and the film was considered fairly raw by 1963 standards. Elisha Cook Jr.—"he seemed six feet tall for the very first, and last, time," according to Sammy Davis—played the Mafia leader who wanted Cool's head handed to him on a silver platter. Although Sammy was only on-screen for ten minutes, when the film ran in Paris a few years later he was billed as the lead.

Meanwhile, Dean and Frank were up to their usual nonsense in *4 for Texas*. The director of the film was forty-five-year-old Robert Aldrich, who'd just come from producing and directing Bette Davis and Joan Crawford in *What Ever Happened to Baby Jane?* and whose next assignment after *Texas* would be *Hush . . . Hush Sweet Charlotte*, also with Davis. His most famous film before *Baby Jane* had been the brutal meller and subsequent cult film *Kiss Me Deadly* with Ralph Meeker. Aldrich was so anxious to work with the Rat Pack after dealing with the difficult aging ladies of *Baby Jane* that he also co-produced and co-scripted *4 for Texas*. He knew that the youthful faces and knockout figures of Ekberg and Andress would be quite a contrast to Bette and Joan. "God, I'm looking forward to this picture," he was telling everyone in 1962.

Things did not get off to an auspicious start. Aldrich wanted to make certain his beautiful co-stars got the most flattering angles and lighting possible—he was out to flatter them in every way—and he started doing the cinematographer's job for him. Although Ernest Laszlo had done many films with Aldrich, he ended his association with the director well before *4 for Texas* had wrapped. In fact, early in the filming he told Aldrich that he wasn't being given enough responsibility and was subsequently replaced by Joseph Biroc. (Only Laszlo is mentioned in the credits, however.)

In *4 for Texas* Martin plays Joe Jarrod, who takes off with loot that Sinatra (as Zack Thomas) has in turn just stolen from bandits. Dean runs off to Galveston, unaware that it's Sinatra's "kind of town." (Sinatra apparently runs a protection racket for Galveston's business owners.) Hiding the stolen money in his suitcoat instead of his valise (where everyone assumes the money is hidden), Dean manages to deposit it in the local bank. As Frank romances Madame Townsend (Ekberg), Dean hooks up with Maxine Richter (Andress) and helps her transform her boat into a riverside casino. But Frank—via the bank president (Victor Buono)—controls the docks and screws up their plans. In the convoluted ending, Martin blackmails Buono (who hired someone to scuttle his own ship for the insurance money) into giving him the dock rights, and Frank and Dean somehow wind up joining forces to fight Buono and hired gun Charles Bronson.

There's little to say about the performances of Dean and Frank as they basically just play themselves in the Wild West. The film can't make up its mind if it's a parody or a real western—neither can Frank or Dean—and subsequently it doesn't work as either. The film is half-over before Andress appears. "You will give the orders," she says to Dean. "You will be the master." *4 for Texas* is pure male sex fantasy, with Andress as the compliant, exaggeratedly buxom woman who wants her man as the master, as she says, not an equal partner. It is filled with awkward "comedy" scenes such as the fisticuffs that occur when Dean first shows up in town: half a dozen people dopily punching each other and not a laugh in the bunch.

Aldrich was able to put together a few good moments, such as an exciting opening shootout between the boys on a Wells Fargo coach and a group of bandits headed by Charles Bronson. Dean and Frank's confrontation on the docks at the end of the picture is tense and lively, but it leads into a cluttered, messy battle that has too many factions. Dean's men, Frank's men, then Victor Buono's forces, then Bronson's thugs—who can possibly keep everyone straight (or by that point, cares to)?

Charles Bronson was a carry-over from *Never So Few*. This was long before Bronson was a star in his own right, and Sinatra in his patronizing way got a kick out of "the kid." Bronson reminded Sinatra a bit of himself, or at least he reminded Sinatra of the man he was supposed to have been. In Sinatra's made-up biography he had been a Depression kid fighting off animal and human rats in the bitter slums, a tough guy having to get in his licks on a constant basis. But skinny Sinatra had never really looked the part. Bronson did. It wasn't long before producers took notice.

Victor Buono had been in *Baby Jane* and came along with booster Robert Aldrich, who thought he'd be fine in a villainous role. (A year later Buono was to chill audiences as *The Strangler*.) Buono got a kick out of the antics of the Rat Pack, and Sinatra liked him enough to give him another bad guy part in *Robin and the 7 Hoods*. "I always had fun with Frank," Buono said. "There was more drinking and dancing and laughing on the sets than there was working, which was a little strange for me to get used to, as I always liked to be able to concentrate on the work. It was like being in a Vegas nightclub. Frank and Dean and their friends turned every place they went to into a Vegas club. Everyone's eyes were bugging out at Ursula and Anita—who were really very sweet—and there were women hanging around hoping to get a look at Frank and Dean, and Aldrich would have to track them down half the time just so he could get a scene shot; it was madness. Bob was a disciplined director but he'd have to take a shot (of booze) now and then just to keep up with Frank and Dean—or because of them."

When asked about the hookers who had been imported to the set, Buono said, "I personally did not see any hookers, per se, but some of those saloon girls did seem a trifle—licentious, shall we say. I wouldn't put anything past Frank and Dean. If somebody says they had hookers in their hang-out, they probably did."

For his part, Aldrich said, "I never found Frank a problem to direct. He has an instinct for what you want, and he gives it to you. You may have to push Dean a little bit, but the trick is to cast him in a part similar to who he is, and he'll deliver. That's why he worked in *4 for Texas*. Frank gives the same uniqueness to a good line that he does to a good musical phrase; he's an artist whatever he does."

Richard Jaeckel had a small role in the film. At the time of shooting he seemed to be in awe of Frank and Dino. "It's a thrill to be working with them, but they party a little too much for me. Talk about burning the candle at both ends. I don't know how they do it. And they're in practically every scene."

But the true saving grace of *4 for Texas* wasn't Frank or Dean or Victor, or even the bodies beautiful, but a certain trio who made a (very) surprise "guest appearance." "It was Bob's idea to bring in the Three Stooges for a guest shot," said Buono. "He was a big fan of theirs, and he knew that because of Dean and Frank and their not very serious approach to filmmaking—at least this film—that the film had veered from a comedy-western into an out-and-out farce. In those circumstances the Stooges would fit right in. In fact, in my opinion they saved the picture."

Indeed, the Three Stooges liven up the movie for several minutes, playing bumpkins who've been hired to bring a nude portrait of Ursula to her gambling establishment. Ellen Corby and another biddy object to the painting and get into slapfest hijinks with the Stooges. It is the only genuinely funny sequence in the entire movie. Aldrich also hired former talent scout Arthur Godfrey to play a bit as a customer at the casino. He also gave work, with Sinatra's approval, to old-time character actors Fritz Feld and Grady Sutton.

Peter Lawford had had two opportunities to work with Robert Aldrich, but neither had worked out for (officially) different reasons. First, he was originally offered the part of the weird accompanist played by Victor Buono in *What Ever Happened to Baby Jane?* but supposedly turned it down because the role wasn't the "right image" for a Kennedy-in-law, and because he felt the character was beyond his range. Actually, when Aldrich found out he had a chance to direct Sinatra and Martin—not to mention Ekberg and Andress—in *4 for Texas* he began a not-so-subtle campaign of dissuading Lawford from the role. Lawford was smart enough to know what was up, and nice enough to realize that Aldrich didn't want an enemy in Frank. He withdrew from the part and it was given to Buono. There was, of course, no chance of his being in *4 for Texas* because of Sinatra. So because of Frank he lost out on two interesting roles. Peter consoled himself with the fact that the parts weren't that great, that Buono was better playing them than he would have been, and that the movies—even *Baby Jane*—were distinctly second-rate.

It wasn't Aldrich but rather Paul Henreid—Frank and Peter's co-star in *Never So Few*—who was at the helm of the film that Peter did do with Bette Davis, *Dead Ringer*, which was released in 1964. (Ironically, Davis had to ask Aldrich to let her out of a commitment to guest-spot in *4 for Texas* so she could do this picture. One can only imagine Bette Davis and the Rat Pack in one movie together.) Henreid got Peter the part; he was not about to be scared off by Frank Sinatra or anyone else. At the time he scoffed at notions that he was throwing a compassionate bone to someone who was practically a has-been (a term that could have just as easily been applied to Henreid in 1963 when the film was shot).

"Peter is a fine actor," he said. "We need a strong actor, someone who can stand up to Bette, a marvelous, strong actress, in their scenes together. A powerhouse like Bette Davis needs a powerful leading man. That's the only reason Peter is in this part. Because it's a role perfectly suited to his talents."

In truth, no one had ever thought of Peter as a "power-

ful" actor, and he doesn't have much to do in *Dead Ringer*.
It's Bette's show all the way, as she does a variation on her
1946 film *A Stolen Life* and again plays twin sisters—one
good, one evil. The bad one takes the good one's place, but
the cast-off lover (Lawford) of the dead sister notices something is different and threatens blackmail. Bette polishes him
off by siccing an extremely large and vicious dog on him.
That sequence—and Andre Previn's marvelous theme
music—are the only memorable things in the picture aside
from Davis. Paul Henreid was a fine actor, but a thoroughly
mediocre director; he does nothing with a very interesting
premise. *Dead Ringer* gets better as it slowly progresses, but
it never quite catches fire.

Henreid and Davis had their hands full with Lawford,
who was preoccupied with his personal problems during filming and often showed up late and fairly dissipated. Not only
had Frank abandoned him but the Kennedys weren't crazy
about him, either. Henreid did his best to shore up Lawford's
flagging morale, and even Bette—who was predisposed to like
Peter as she was a great admirer of his brother-in-law JFK—
was compassionate. Peter said, "Bette had always had a reputation as a holy terror on the set, and I didn't know what to
expect, but she was understanding, kindly, patient—even
maternal, if that is the word. I suspect she felt sorry for me."

But one person who didn't feel sorry for Peter was Frank
Sinatra, who continued to pretend that Peter didn't exist. On
that shocking day when John F. Kennedy was shot in Dallas,
Frank called and gave his condolences to Pat Lawford, but
never asked to speak to Peter. Peter had been certain that the
assassination of the President—his brother-in-law—would
have been enough to make Frank put things in their proper
perspective, to forget the petty, unfair quarrels of the past,
but it was not to be. JFK was dead, and still Frank was fuming over the slight he blamed poor Peter for.

So you could have knocked Peter over with a feather

when a few weeks later the phone rang and it was Frank Sinatra asking to speak to him. Sinatra was frantic, desperate. "[It] was the only time I'd ever really heard him kind of scared," Lawford said. "He sounded quite frightened." There was no prelude, no apologetic leading up to the request that followed. Sinatra told Peter that his son, Frank Sinatra Jr., had been kidnapped at gunpoint from his room at Harrah's Lodge in Lake Tahoe. He had received a ransom note and was terrified that something might happen to the boy. Could Peter call his brother-in-law, Robert F. Kennedy, the attorney general, and get him to intervene?

Peter was happy to comply. He, too, was worried about Frank Jr.'s safety. He also figured this favor would mean the long drought between him and Frank was over. Frank Jr., who was nineteen years old, had dropped out of school to become a singer, a clone of his father: same material, same style, same jokes. But, unfortunately, not the same talent, the same snap, or the same charisma.

Two twenty-three-year-olds, Barry Worthington Keenan and Joseph Amsler, had taken Frank Jr. from the Lodge, where he had secured a gig, and wafted him away in the trunk of a car to a house in Los Angeles. Peter called Bobby Kennedy, who told him to call Frank back right away and tell him that he would make getting his son back his top priority. FBI agents scoured the area while the state police put up roadblocks. In the meantime, Sinatra paid nearly a quarter of a million dollars in ransom, most of which was recovered when the kidnappers were captured. They had released Frank Jr. upon receiving the money.

Upon the boy's return Sinatra threw a lavish party at his ex-wife's home in Bel Air. The guest list was a mix of original and new Rat Pack members: Dean Martin, the Romanoffs, Jimmy Van Heusen, as well as all of the FBI agents who worked on the case. Peter Lawford was not invited, and Frank never spoke to him again for as long as Peter was alive.

There was much speculation at the time that Frank Jr. may have been kidnapped at the orders of the Mafia to pay Frank Sr. back for some slight or other. Then, during the kidnappers' trial, Barry Keenan claimed that the whole thing had been a publicity hoax planned by none other than Frank Sinatra Jr. The object: publicity for his new act, and some attention and money from his father. The jury completely rejected this story, and years later Keenan himself recanted.

Frank Sinatra Jr. never became the phenomenon that his father was, primarily because he tried too hard to follow in his father's footsteps. By 1963 the music scene was changing tremendously, and teenagers were not particularly interested in listening to the sounds their parents had grown up on. Elvis Presley had already made terrific inroads, as had many black groups. Now there was talk of this group from England, the Beatles, taking America by storm, part of a "British Invasion." The whole world of popular music was undergoing incredible changes. Elvis had taken his cue from some black musicians; rhythm and blues and rock and roll were the name of the game. Strong melody and classy, elegant lyrics fell mostly by the wayside as what some called the "negrofication" of American music began. In truth "old-time" black composers like Duke Ellington were being edged out by the "modern" black songwriters of Motown. The times were changing and only a fool would deny it.

The members of the Rat Pack were getting older, but there was still life in the old bunch yet.

18

Jerry's Revenge

Frank Sinatra had his Peter Lawford; Dean Martin had Jerry Lewis. Jerry was not a member of the coveted Rat Pack, but he was hardly a down-and-outer, either. Dean had done his best to forget the little "monkey," but his ex-partner's pictures kept coming out with appalling regularity. Any vague thought Dino may have entertained as to Lewis's career falling apart without him went unrealized. Now Jerry was not only starring in pictures, he was producing, directing, and writing his vehicles also. Dino knew this was just what Jerry had always wanted: total control.

The amazing thing was that it wasn't just the kids who were in love with Jerry. Becoming the auteur of his own films had turned Jerry into the darling of the film set in France, and not without good reason. Pictures like *The Ladies' Man* (1961), in which Jerry plays a woman-shy handyman in a hotel for would-be actresses, illustrated his fresh approach to comedy. The picture took place entirely on a truly grandiose set, which Lewis showed off in one shot where the camera pulled back to reveal it in all its glory. Lewis's direction was consistently inventive and assured.

American critics, however, weren't so quick to sing Jerry's praises, probably because in such films as *The Ladies' Man* Jerry really didn't play a full-dimensional character as such, and the screenplay was more a series of vignettes than a legitimate story. Therefore it was difficult to care about or get involved with Jerry's handyman or any of the other people in the movie. The French loved his set pieces, his comic flair, his visual style, his clever directorial touches, but the American critics only saw "no story, no picture."

Lewis wasn't crazy about being unappreciated in his own country while everyone seemed so gaga about the Rat Pack. In *The Nutty Professor* (1963) he fashioned a story that would not only involve the audience but tell the world what he truly thought of Dean Martin at one and the same time. In the picture—a comic takeoff on the Jekyll and Hyde story—Jerry plays a professor who drinks a formula that turns him from a buck-toothed geek into a slimy but much better-looking lounge singer named Buddy Love.

There was no doubt in anyone's mind that Buddy Love was meant to be a devastating takeoff on Dean Martin. In his Buddy persona, Jerry takes to the mike in the piano bar and imitates Dean's style of singing. Buddy Love treats women dismissively and contemptuously and is cool and laid-back to the point of insensitivity. As the professor, Lewis is lovable and essentially decent; but as Love—although his looks have improved—he's a real heel and monster: a veritable Mr. Hyde.

Dean heard about the picture but never bothered to see it. He could not have been pleased when *The Nutty Professor* went on to become one of Lewis's biggest hits. Adults in Tinseltown who normally wouldn't have been caught dead at a Jerry Lewis picture rushed to see the film just to see if all the stories about it were true. Dean had been willing to let bygones be bygones, but Jerry just wouldn't let it drop. Dean would get his own revenge, however, a few months later, and he wouldn't even have to lift a finger, let alone make an entire film, to do so.

In the meantime Dean had signed to do a picture, *Something's Got to Give*, with Marilyn Monroe, with whom buddy Frank had had a fling before his brief engagement to Juliet Prowse. The picture was to be a remake of *My Favorite Wife*, with Dean's first wife, supposedly deceased, reappearing after he's remarried. Marilyn had specifically requested that Dean be her leading man, and when Marilyn got fired for her usual round of absences and "illnesses," he refused to do the picture with new leading lady Lee Remick. This was seen by many as proof of how loyal Dean could be to his friends and co-stars, but director George Cukor later confirmed that Dean really refused to do the picture because a) Lee Remick wasn't half as sexy as Marilyn, and b) without publicity hound Marilyn in the movie it would not be as big a hit. Dino had simply decided to get out while the getting was good.

Shirley MacLaine, meanwhile, had gotten over her crush on Dean by the time she signed to do *What a Way to Go!* (1964), which had originally been intended for the now-dead Marilyn. In this Dino was fourth-billed after MacLaine, Paul Newman, and Robert Mitchum, but his role was much smaller. MacLaine plays Louisa Foster, a simple girl who keeps marrying simple, (at first) unambitious guys who suddenly get all fired up and make millions, destroying their marriage to MacLaine by never being home and overworking themselves into an early grave. Dean is her first suitor, the town rich boy Leonard Crawley, but Shirley despises his values and rejects him for homespun Dick Van Dyke. Angered by Martin's condescension, Van Dyke turns his small business into a major concern that wipes out Martin's family department store and puts Dino in the poorhouse.

When Van Dyke drops dead, MacLaine moves on to starving artist Newman (who makes a fortune converting sound into paintings but gets sucked into his machine), airplane tycoon Mitchum (who longs for the simple life on a farm but gets killed when he tries to milk a bull), and Gene Kelly as a pathetic entertainer in a cheap restaurant (who becomes the latest sensation in Hollywood before being inadvertently trampled to death by his own fans). At one point Kelly's manager wants him to co-star with "Frank, Dean, and Jerry" in a remake of *The Four Horsemen of the Apocalypse*. "What do I need those deadbeats for?" says Kelly, "I'll play all four parts myself."

Finally, who does Shirley wind up with but Dean's Leonard Crawley, who has rejected his old values and become a poor-but-simple farmer. There's a brief scare when Dino thinks he's discovered oil on his property ("What a nightmare!" intones the money-phobic MacLaine), but it turns out that his tractor has merely punctured a pipeline. Dean looks good in the film (he was forty-six at the time of filming) and gives a likable, effortless performance. For once that "cool" style of his is appropriate. The movie itself is more silly and loud than funny, but it holds the attention and the various vignettes are inventively told.

By now everyone's schedules were cleared and it was time to make the third of the "major" Rat Pack movies. As Lawford was out, Frank needed someone to play his part, and he zeroed in on a truly perverse candidate: Bing Crosby. Frank and Bing had already appeared together eight years previously in *High Society*, but things had cooled between them because of their political differences. Frank was still furious that JFK had stayed at Bing's Palm Beach estate instead of his own, but he was angrier at "those backstabbing Kennedys" than he was at Bing. Hiring Bing to play the role that had been intended for Lawford was Sinatra's way of having the last laugh.

As director, Frank tapped fifty-four-year-old Gordon Douglas, who had helmed *Young at Heart* in 1954 (as well as the classic giant-ant thriller *Them* that same year) and who'd had a mostly undistinguished career doing "B" movies since the late thirties. Frank found Douglas easy to work with and used him at least three more times in the sixties. He also got Victor Buono from *4 for Texas* for a major supporting role. Peter Falk was signed to play Sinatra's main adversary, and Edward G. Robinson from *A Hole in the Head* was brought in for a small but pivotal cameo.

The film takes place in Chicago in the twenties. Guy Gisborn (Peter Falk) bumps off Big Jim (Edward G. Robinson) so he can be leader of the rackets himself. This doesn't sit well with Robin (Sinatra), who objects when Falk demands 50 percent of every gang's take (25 percent of which will go to the crooked mayor). While Falk and Sinatra take axes to each other's casinos, Big Jim's daughter Marian (Barbara Rush) offers Robin money if he'll "hit" Falk. Instead Robin gives the money to charity—the Blessed Haven Orphan Home, in fact—leading newspapers to dub him "Robin Hood." Rush tries to take over the rackets herself with the help of Little John (Dean Martin) while Falk has Robin framed for the sheriff's murder. When Little John turns on her, Rush then schemes to have Falk wipe out both him and Sinatra. Instead, the two men get rid of Falk. Rush and Deputy Sheriff Alvin Potts (Victor Buono) then try to get rid of Robin and his Hoods by mounting a morality campaign to rid Chicago of crooks. The evil Rush even turns the secretary of the Blessed Haven Orphan Home (Bing Crosby) into her new boyfriend! (The picture, devoid of a climax, simply comes to an end after this final gag.) *Robin and the 7 Hoods* was reminiscent of a thirties crime melodrama—complete with the duplicitous femme fatale—with jokes and musical numbers added.

As Robin or "Robbo," Sinatra shows little pizzazz, as laid-back as he always was during this period. "I'd rather remain your enemy," he tells Falk. "As long as I hate your guts I know I got good taste." As Little John, Dean Martin is again Dean Martin. Going over a list of organizations that are asking for money from "Robin Hood," he notices a "home for wayward girls. I oughta send them something." Although third-billed after Frank and Dean, Sammy Davis has virtually nothing to do in the picture—a few minor lines, a brief bit in one of Bing's song numbers. He had always been grateful for the things Sinatra had done for him over the years, but he was getting tired of being thrown bones. Sinatra liked Sammy, but he had never quite forgiven him for those radio remarks years before. "They always ask me to answer the phone," Davis mutters in one scene, an ad-lib that more or less expressed what he was feeling as well as his character.

Peter Falk gives an energetic if obvious performance as a nasty low-life, while Barbara Rush as Marian, who turns out to be as ruthless as her father ever was, manages to make an impression despite her miscasting. Bing Crosby, Victor Buono, and Edward G. Robinson really score in their smaller roles, as do the always reliable Allen Jenkins (one of Falk's men) and Hans Conreid (a jumpy architect). Frank had given three of Bing's relatives small roles in *4 for Texas* and this time he cast son Phil Crosby in a bit as one of his hoods.

Since Bing now had the part originally earmarked for Peter Lawford, it was decided to include some new song numbers for the crooner and the other boys. How could a film starring four singers not have songs? Naturally, the songs were by Sammy Cahn and Jimmy Van Heusen. One number has Dean and Frank singing to Bing about style and re-dressing him in a variety of outfits. Bing sounds fine during this number, but Frank is oddly shrill, and Dean sounds gravelly and relaxed, as usual. "Don't Mess with Mr. Booze" is sung by Bing at a bogus revival meeting at a casino. Sammy joins in the fun at one point as a pickpocket being "saved" by Bing, but the real hilarity occurs when even Dino joins in to sing about the evils of demon rum.

"That's the Way It Is" is sung by Falk and his boys right after they've killed Robinson. This opening scene is a well-set-up gag, as everyone first drinks a toast to Big Jim at the head of the table and immediately afterward pulls out a gun and plugs him. There's also some amusing black humor when the hoods attend a memorial service for the dead, corrupt sheriff, Octavius Glick. The man was over six feet tall but his body was placed inside the three-foot cornerstone of the new police headquarters. "He was a man who would not bend," intones the eulogist. "We had no trouble," says Falk. Explaining why he became involved with the Orphan Home, Bing tells the boys how he himself was left on the steps of the home with a blanket and a loaf of bread. "How old were you?" someone asks. "Fourteen," says Bing. A bit with gambling tables that conveniently slide into the walls to fool the police was lifted from Abbott and Costello's *Hold That Ghost*.

In spite of these amusing moments, the picture is largely tedious and mediocre. A crucial problem is its lack of a climax. The final encounter between arch-enemies Sinatra and Falk—where Falk winds up in another concrete block that had been intended for Frank and Dean—occurs off-screen. The main adversary has been taken care of, yes, but there still remains a lot that's unresolved; the windup is completely flat.

Victor Buono found that things were pretty much the same on the set of *Robin and the 7 Hoods* as on the set of *4 for Texas*, except there was more to do. "Frank liked to kid around, but I never felt he meant to be cruel. He just liked playing games. Dino was like that, too. I think they were, some of the time, bored and restless, and even melancholy at times, and horsing around took the pressure off. I really sensed that Dean did not enjoy the filmmaking process—the time it consumed, the type of work it was—he found no joy in it. With Frank it was more that he was preoccupied. But I don't know by what."

At the time of filming, Bing Crosby commented that "people compare our voices (Bing's and Frank's) and singing styles; it's apples and oranges. We're different in our styles and projections, but we are similar in that we elicit a real audience response. I don't say that in vanity, I say it with gratitude; the public has rewarded us greatly." He did not go on the record on the subject of Dean Martin's singing, at least not at this time. Bing knew that Dean had "borrowed" much of his style from him just as he knew Dean was never in Bing's league as a vocalist. Asked about Frank's affiliation with the less savory individuals he knew, Bing said, "I guess he felt he had to be decent to everyone who came around. He knew a lot of those guys from the Hoboken days. You can't always choose who wants to be your friend. You try to be nice to people, whoever they are. Sometimes you don't even know who they are." Bing was being very diplomatic, as Frank's Mafia ties were just one aspect of Sinatra of which he mightily disapproved, although he had come to respect him as a singer.

That was what it was like between these two crooners, Crosby and Sinatra, during the filming: mutual respect, cordiality, but not warmth or real affability. Bing got along better with the friendlier, looser Dino, who had always been a bit in awe of Crosby. There were no major incidents, no "scenes" with Sinatra reminding Crosby of the JFK incident, but the two men would never be close friends. Bing, in his own way, was the original Mr. Cool. At sixty-two he was not about to get into feuds and fusses with other entertainers. He would leave that to younger men. If Sinatra wanted to sulk, he would let him. He came in, did his scenes, and left as inobtrusively as he'd arrived.

In January 1964, Frank and Dean opened at the Sands in Las Vegas billed as "Dean Martin and Friend." Again, there was a rolling bar right on the stage, filled with anything that might strike their fancy as they sang and told jokes. While Martin wasn't exactly soused while performing, the drunk act was becoming less and less of an act. Dino was getting older—he was now three years shy of fifty—and he basically had all the money and sex he needed. He was already beginning to feel that he and Frank were antiques in the Age of Elvis, whom they both hated. He only did the act because Frank had asked him to, practically begged him to. Frank was not really alive unless he was in front of an audience, unless he had performing and all of the trimmings, and that included drinking in the lounges till dawn, picking up broads, bar-hopping all over Vegas, giving the peons a thrill, everything.

Dean simply wasn't as interested in making the scene as he used to be. Although he had never been a Boy Scout, he had never been as obsessed with all that stuff, even the booze and broads, as Frank was. He liked to drink more than ever, but he'd just as soon do it alone in his room in front of the TV set than in a crowded bar. The Act simply wasn't very important to him.

The Beatles' "I Wanna Hold Your Hand," "She Loves You," and several others were riding the top of the *Billboard* charts during the weeks "Dean Martin and Friend" played the Sands. Perhaps Dino sensed that the Rat Pack was becoming yesterday's news. Dean and Frank—and Sammy—still had millions of devoted fans who loved them, their style, their music, but youth, in every sense of the word, was passing them by. Dean's twelve-year-old son, Dino Jr., adored the Beatles and seemed to think his own father was passe. That hurt. Particularly when Dean, like Frank, thought the front wave of the British Invasion looked like unwashed "fairies."

But Dino—both of them—were soon to get a happy surprise.

Dean next signed to do Billy Wilder's then-notorious sex comedy *Kiss Me, Stupid* with Kim Novak. In this Dean was cast—a real stretch—as a girl-mad singer named Dino who suggests that he just might develop an interest in a certain songwriter's material if said songwriter allows Dino to bed his buxom wife. The songwriter was originally played by Peter Sellers, who had to quit when he had a heart attack at thirty-nine. Ray Walston replaced him and filming proceeded. At the time even the cast was appalled at some of the double entendres in the script, but in 1998 most of the jokes are no different from what one can hear in the average sex-obsessed sitcom every night of the week. It was a gamy film for the sixties, however, with many critics labelling it "smut."

Director Billy Wilder could be as big a martinet as Otto Preminger, except he had more of a sense of humor. It was that that saved Dean from his wrath when Dean would start directing the picture, telling other cast members in a loud voice that they should do the scene any way they wanted to and not listen to "that cocksucker." When Billy did finally lose his temper at Dean for the latter's failure to say a certain line with the right finesse, Dino snapped, "You should have hired an actor!" Basically the cast and crew giggled and leered their way through the shoot, but the sense of fun didn't carry over to audiences or critics.

Part of the problem (among many) was that Ray Walston, although a fine actor, was a little "heavy" in a part that would have been perfect for Jack Lemmon. Kim Novak managed to be rather touching as the prostitute Walston hires to temporarily take the place of his wife (actress Felicia Farr, who later married Jack Lemmon, is also very good as the real wife), but the film belonged to Dino. He somehow managed to make a sleazy, one-dimensional character seem likable and even relatively inoffensive. He underplays with a casual ease that makes the character's immorality almost seem childlike and innocent—as if he's constantly thinking, "I really don't mean any harm, I'm just horny."

To Dean's surprise—and his son's delight—he had a bigger personal success that summer of '64 when one of his records actually hit the number-one spot on the charts, knocking off the Beatles' "A Hard Day's Night." "Everybody Loves Somebody (Sometime)," which was to become Dean's signature tune, had been written by Irving Taylor and Ken Lane, Dean's bandleader, back in the days when Lane was working as Sinatra's musical conductor. The song had been recorded by a number of singers before Dean got his turn at it, and he did two versions. A jazzier, second version became the hit single, but two of Dean's albums, one of which contained the original version and one the revised big seller, both climbed the charts to the list of Top Twenty LPs. Dean was ecstatic. To hell with the Beatles!

To top it off, Dean's agents told him that NBC was anxious for him to do a weekly TV series for them—and he owed it all to Jerry Lewis.

Jerry had first signed to do a big variety show on ABC, which had spent nearly half a million converting an old theater on Vine Street into a studio suitable for the weekly live broadcast of the show. Jerry, unfortunately, laid an egg, and the show was ignominiously canceled after only three months. So that they could still get some mileage out of the renovated theater, ABC rechristened it The Hollywood Palace and named its new variety program, which would originate from there, after the theater. Martin was the first guest host. "I want to thank Jerry for building this theater for me," he said on the first broadcast, getting one of the biggest laughs of his career. And getting back a little of his own.

Dean hosted the program several times, and TV execs were quick to note his popularity. Suddenly NBC wanted to grab him away from ABC before they could sign him up to his own show, which they felt was inevitable. Dino resisted the offers for awhile, but eventually gave in. He had introduced such long-haired freak acts as the Rolling Stones and the Kinks on *The Hollywood Palace*, and he felt being the star of his own show—while the freaks were relegated to guest appearances—would prove to everybody, even Dino Jr., that there was life in the old guy yet. He was also getting a little sick of Frank and his Rat Pack.

As for Frank . . .

Frank wasn't through with him yet.

19

On the Rocks

Frank and Dean began work on the prophetically titled *Marriage on the Rocks* in 1964. Frank was soon to engage in a disastrous marriage to Mrs. Sinatra number three, while Dean's marriage to Jeanne had been on its last legs for years. Both marriages would be on the rocks by the end of the decade. Frank and Dean's leading lady was to be Deborah Kerr, who seemed a bit too genteel and delicate to be horsing around with the likes of Dino and the Chairman of the Board, although she actually had a ball making the movie.

Kerr at first had serious doubts about doing the picture, which originally had been titled *Community Property*. A strong recommendation to do the film came from a surprising quarter: David Niven. By this time Niven's bad feelings over Frank's treatment of Lauren Bacall had eased a bit (not that Niven had much desire to work with Frank himself) and he figured Deborah would have fun making the picture and it would probably make a lot of money. He also knew Deborah was not a just-widowed gal like Bacall who would fall for Sinatra. Frank also got on the phone with Kerr more than once and finally talked her into it.

In the film Deborah plays Valerie Edwards, a woman who is utterly bored with her businessman husband Dan (Sinatra) and indeed married life itself; she feels Dan takes her for granted and she's sick of it. "I don't have to be romantic," says Dan when she complains. "I'm married." Dan is so unromantic that when he takes Valerie out for their anniversary, he brings his business partner Ernie Brewer (Dean Martin) along with him. Eventually Dan is importuned to take Valerie on a second honeymoon in Mexico, while playboy Ernie "works" with bikini-clad secretaries at his bachelor pad. "Shouldn't we go to the office?" asks one of them (Joi Lansing).

The honeymoon is a disaster, with the result that Dan comes home and Valerie stays in Mexico after receiving a quickie divorce. The two make up over the phone, however, but as Dan is about to fly back down to remarry Valerie, he realizes he must attend a certain meeting and asks Ernie to go in his stead and explain things. Somehow Ernie and Valerie wind up getting married, with Dan moving out of his house and into Ernie's bachelor pad and vice versa. Eventually everything is straightened out and Dan and Valerie are reunited as a happier couple than ever.

Marriage on the Rocks was not well-received by the critics, but it actually turned out to be one of the better movies made by members of the Rat Pack, with Frank and Dean actually bothering to give amusing performances instead of letting the script and supporting cast do all of the work. Director Jack Donahue was a former choreographer (and had directed some of their TV shows), but he was no pushover when it came to Martin and Sinatra, and they did good work under his tutelage. (Also, these roles were more appropriate for their laid-back style.) Frank was ironically cast as a total square and a dull family man, which he was definitely not in real life, even if he did have a family. Dean was in his late forties but at the height of his attractiveness. "I can't stand a woman who can hold her liquor," he says, spoofing his own image/reality. The two men were middle-aged and unlike a lot of actors didn't try to hide it; their characters were not, say, in their thirties and phony-hip—in fact, they react negatively to the new music and dancing of the sixties the way they, and most people their age, did off-screen.

Deborah Kerr was second-billed in between topper Frank and third-billed Dino. Of the filming, she said, "It was so much fun, a joke, and all quite ludicrous. Frank would come in one morning and say, 'We don't need this scene!' and just tear it out of the script and throw it away. Then Dino, perfectly happy and absolutely relaxed, would murmur: 'What a great way to earn a living; what other business is there where you can come in every morning and meet lots of people that you absolutely adore, do something you like doing—and get paid for it?'" As Kerr was actually taller than both of her leading men and spent much of the film clad in a green chiffon evening dress, the two of them affectionately nicknamed her "The Jolly Green Giant." Kerr didn't take the movie at all seriously and didn't think it should have been, but on another occasion she said of Sinatra: "Frank is really an artist. That tough front conceals an understanding heart. And he's vulnerable, although he hates to admit it."

Cy Howard's script was along the lines of thirties-style screwball comedies and had the film been made in that era it would probably have been better received, but the cast did its best to keep things humming. Hermione Baddeley is a riot as Frank's mother-in-law, and one of the highlights is a scene at the bar in the Edwards living room, with Frank, Dean and "Grandma" Baddeley trading lines and drinks with priceless expressions and impeccable timing. Another bit has a stacked blonde in Dean's bachelor pad overhearing Frank telling Dean that he loves him. "Why don't you turn up the music," she says to Dino, "and let the little one lead!"

Cesar Romero, who'd appeared in *Ocean's 11* and had

known Frank and Dean casually for years, played Miguel Santos, a jack-of-all-trades in the Mexican honeymoon village who is manager of the hotel, the doctor, and even a lawyer (for divorces) and justice of the peace (for weddings). "Frank has done a lot of kind things for people down on their luck," he said a few years later, "things no one ever hears about." Of the film he said, "I've never had so much fun doing a picture. Everything was so relaxed, so unhurried, and I think it shows in the finished film."

Also in the cast were veteran funny ladies Reta Shaw and Kathleen Freeman (who appeared in a lot of Jerry Lewis's movies) as Miss Blight, and DeForest Kelley of *Star Trek* fame as a client of Frank's. Dino didn't care that Freeman appeared in Lewis's movies—he knew she was a working actress and had a right to accept any role she was offered, but Lewis wasn't quite so magnanimous. He replaced Freeman with Thelma Ritter in a juicy supporting part in *Boeing, Boeing*. (She was back in his good graces for *Three on a Couch* the following year, however.) Frank also gave a part in *Marriage* to his daughter Nancy, who played his and Deborah's daughter in the film. As Tracy, she exhibited a lot of personality but became more famous for her later hit record "These Boots Are Made for Walkin'" than for her acting.

One problem with the picture is that it has—at least at first—a rather frivolous attitude toward the effects divorce can have on children. (A friend of Dan's son, whose parents are also divorced, tells the boy how he can get lots of presents by playing both parents against each other.) Later on, however, a friend of Tracy's is introduced who is the lonely, messed-up product of a broken home. In a development that mirrored a real-life situation at the time, this character, Lisa (played by a rather weird Davey Davison), becomes involved with Frank's much older character after his "accidental" divorce from his wife. No one could help but think "there goes Frank and Mia."

Sinatra had first met Mia Farrow at Mike Romanoff's restaurant when she was only eleven, in the company of her father, director John Farrow, and her mother, Maureen O'Sullivan (most famous as Tarzan's "Jane"). Two years earlier Mia—the third of the Farrows' seven children—had contracted polio and spent harrowing months in a ward for contagious diseases. When she was thirteen, her nineteen-year-old brother Michael was killed in a plane crash; the anguish of his passing ended his parents' marriage and brought no end of torment to Mia. Inheriting her mother's love of acting (O'Sullivan went back on Broadway after her son's death), Mia moved from New York soaps and off-Broadway productions to a plum role on the nighttime soap opera *Peyton Place*.

Peyton Place was filmed on the lot at Twentieth Century-Fox where on an adjoining soundstage Frank Sinatra just happened to be making *Von Ryan's Express*, the film he did immediately preceding *Marriage on the Rocks*. During her breaks, Mia went to watch him work. "I thought what a beautiful face he had," Mia later wrote, "full of pain and somehow familiar." Mia watched in silence until the afternoon Frank spotted her and asked her to join him and some other men seated to one side of the set. Nervous, she accidentally dropped the contents of her purse at his feet.

Frank helped her pick up her personal items and "it might have been right then, as our eyes met," as Mia put it, "that I began to love him." Frank invited her to a private screening of the film he made—and for the first and only time, directed—before *Von Ryan's Express*, a wartime thriller co-starring his son-in-law Tommy Sands entitled *None but the Brave*. Mia remembered very little about the movie; all she knew was that Frank Sinatra was holding her hand all through it.

When he invited her to his Palm Springs estate for the weekend, Mia was impressed by the heliport he had originally built for JFK's non-visit but now used to fly him back and forth to the studio. The two became lovers on that first visit. Frank Sinatra, age forty-nine, became the first man nineteen-year-old Mia went to bed with. She didn't understand what he saw in her, but she found him tremendously attractive. "I still do," she says today.

From then on the pair were inseparable except for when Frank was working. Even then Mia would go to the clubs with him and stay up until dawn, although more often than not she would fall asleep right at their table long before the sun came up. She and Frank's daughters—Nancy and Tina—became friends, and the gals kept her company when their father was occupied elsewhere. Mia's mother was busy with her career, and her father was drinking himself to death, so Sinatra became a surrogate parent, a sophisticated boyfriend, and an insatiable lover all in one; she was his wounded, affection-starved woman-child—pliable, ready, inexhaustible, unconditionally loving.

The affair became public in late 1964, when Sheila Graham wrote about it in her column, but to everyone's surprise, the press attention did not break up their relationship as Frank alleged it had broken up his relationship with Betty Bacall. The two were finally married in July 1966 at—where else—the Sands in Vegas. Although she put up a happy public front for her daughter's sake, Mia's mother was horrified by the whole business. "He ought to be marrying me!" she said at the time. Frank Sinatra Jr., who was only a year older than Mia, was, if anything, even more appalled. His father's marriage to a woman young enough to be his own daughter only cemented his conviction that his father had no paternal feelings whatsoever.

Another exciting aspect of Frank's life at this time was that, like Dean Martin, he was once again having hit records. "Strangers in the Night," the theme song from *A Man Could Get Killed*, was playing everywhere, and his rendition of

"Send in the Clowns" from *A Little Night Music* also became a jukebox favorite. Dean followed up his success with "Everybody Loves Somebody (Sometime)" with "The Door is Still Open to My Heart" and "You're Nobody 'til Somebody Loves You," songs peculiarly appropriate for his particular style. In fact, Dean had nearly twenty gold albums on Reprise, the successful record label that Frank and several partners had started in 1961. When the two men got together to socialize, there were occasional fireworks, such as a boozy brawl at the tony Polo Lounge that left a third party hospitalized in critical condition. The man recovered but allegedly lost his memory of the incident. His family wanted a further investigation into the matter, but early-morning phone threats intimidated them into letting the whole matter drop. More than once Dean would do his best to keep scrappy Sinatra out of trouble; if he failed to do so, his selective memory as to who threw which punch first would come in handy.

In 1966 Dean made the moderately entertaining *Texas Across the River*—yet another cowboy-and-Indian spoof—with Joey Bishop in a supporting role as a "deadpan" Indian. French heartthrob Alain Delon was also in the picture, but somehow his sex appeal never translated well to American shores. Director Michael Gordon noted, "Dean is great to direct. He appears to be sauntering through a part when he's actually carefully planning each and every movement scene by scene." Half-jokingly, Bishop said around this time that "Dean can be a prick at times, but so can I. I guess it takes one to know one."

Texas Across the River (1966) was one of the better Rat Pack movies, with some genuinely amusing moments. Accused of murdering his fiancée's ex-boyfriend, Delon flees into the Wild West and encounters cowboy Dino, who is bemused by the funny little Frenchman. Their on-again, off-again friendship is put to the test when Delon's fiancée shows up in the town wherein they've settled and falls for Dino. The film ends with a comical duel between the two, who agree that instead of fighting they should just swap girlfriends. Dino is terrific in the picture, enacting the farcical proceedings with just the right light touch, and the interplay between him and Delon is always engaging. Joey Bishop shows up periodically as the Indian who comments sardonically on the events, but he's never really as funny as he probably thought he was at the time.

Both Frank and Dean had noted how successful the James Bond films were, and each decided to do an action film series of his own. For Dean it was the Matt Helm series. The books by Donald Hamilton had more or less been straight action novels, an Americanized take on Ian Fleming's Bond books, but the film versions were more along the lines of *The Man from U.N.C.L.E.* combined with *Get Smart*. As in the Bond films the emphasis was on gadgetry and beautiful women, but the Matt Helm series was campier and more risque: *Kiss Me, Stupid* meets *Dr. No*. Columbia Pictures had ostensibly mounted a "massive talent search" for an actor to play Helm, but Martin had always been the front runner. He agreed to do the first film, *The Silencers*, on the condition that his production company, Claude, get a generous piece of the action.

In *The Silencers*, Helm is a former agent of I.C.E. (Intelligence and Counter Espionage) who has retired to become a centerfold photographer for men's magazines. He is brought out of retirement to combat the deadly Tung-Tze, played by Victor Buono, who plans to use a missile to destroy one of the government's atom bomb testing bases near White Sands. Among the many attractive women embroiled in the "plot" are a klutzy Stella Stevens and an incredibly busty Dahlia Lavi as a deadly double agent. They—and some great sets—are not enough to save the picture from being incredibly pedestrian, tacky, and moronic. Dean saunters through the film in his usual way; whatever it is he "does," he does well.

The picture made enough money to engender three sequels, the first of which was *Murderer's Row* (1966). In this Karl Malden is the villain who holds Ann-Margret's scientist/father captive so he can acquire all the information he needs to wipe out Washington, D.C. with a "helio beam." A faster pace and Malden's fun thesping made the film slightly better than the first. The producers (including Dean) tried to increase the profits of the third in the series, *The Ambushers* (1968), by stinting on the production values, which had formerly been first-rate. In this Helm battles a villain out to steal an experimental flying saucer for his own nefarious purposes. The last film in the series was *The Wrecking Crew* (1969), which concerns a count who attempts to hijack a Danish train for its cargo of gold. Among the many beauties on view are Elke Sommer, Nancy Kwan, Tina Louise, and the ill-fated Sharon Tate, who was murdered by the Manson family shortly after the film's release. Sharon was also supposed to be in the fifth picture *The Ravagers*, in which Matt goes up against a fatal lookalike who's murdered a congressman, but *The Wrecking Crew*'s grosses weren't considered spectacular enough to continue, as far as Dean was concerned. He refused to do the picture and got into all sorts of legal and financial hassles with the studio.

Whatever its flaws, and there were many, the Matt Helm series was undeniably influential. James Coburn starred in a similar series based on the exploits of Derek Flint, who, like Matt Helm, lived in a plush "make-out" pit of a bachelor pad and was surrounded by dozens of nubile females and fascinating gadgets. The series only lasted for two installments, however, *Our Man Flint* and *In Like Flint*.

Coburn played it a bit straighter than Martin. Ironically, the Matt Helm series started out as a spoof of the more serious Bond series, but by the time Roger Moore took over as Bond, the Bond pictures—with their campy characters, absurd gimmicks, and plethora of racy one-liners, most of which were real groaners—had become imitations of Matt Helm.

Sinatra had been approached to play Derek Flint, but he thought all that running around was too much work and couldn't see the point in playing the kind of part Dino could play better. He was the first choice to play Lew (Archer) Harper in the adaptation of Ross MacDonald's *The Moving Target*, but for various byzantine reasons the part instead went to Paul Newman. (Which was just as well if Sinatra wanted a series, as there wasn't another Harper film for ten years.) Sinatra opted to play private eye Tony Rome in the film of that title (1967).

This tough, brass-knuckles private dick was more his speed; Sinatra—with his hoodlum friends—thought he understood Rome's milieu. He got Gordon Douglas from *Robin and the 7 Hoods* to direct, or rather to stay out of his way as he showed up at noon for his close-ups and pretty much did everything just the way he wanted to. Frank gave Jill St. John a role, but it wasn't until she was cast as an honest-to-goodness "Bond girl" in *Diamonds are Forever* in 1971 that she was seen as anything other than a conquest of Frank and Dean's.

Tony Rome had the P.I. hired by a rich man who wants him to investigate the doings of his daughter and her unsavory friends. In the 1968 sequel, *Lady in Cement*, Rome tries to find out who threw a blonde overboard after planting her feet in cement. Gordon Douglas also directed this one, but as usual Sinatra treated him more like an underling than anything else. In both films Sinatra comes off as old, wrinkled, and anemic as he tries and fails to imitate a cool and deadly private detective. Rome was supposed to be a combination of

Broderick Crawford and Ralph Meeker—tough but sexy—but Frank was all wrong on both counts. The knowledge of this—his marriage to Mia was a vain (in every sense) attempt to recapture his youth—made him extremely difficult to work with, and the pictures with their flat pacing, mediocre scripts and stereotyped characters were crass, dull pop-trash.

The marriage between Mia and Frank had not worked out—no one except naive Mia expected it would—and Frank took it out on those around him while shooting *Lady in Cement*. He slapped one actor in the face because he couldn't remember his lines and had Lainie Kazan in tears because she moved too close to him in their scenes together. "Get the hell outa my face!" he told her.

Today Mia says, "I guess we never should have married in the first place. I at that time had no idea what I wanted to be, wanted to do." Except be an actress when Frank wanted a full-time wife, someone who came when he snapped his fingers. She could have a career but it had to coincide with his, she had to make movies only with him. Mia had begun filming *Rosemary's Baby*, perhaps her most famous film, when Sinatra insisted that she walk off the set and come and do a movie—a bad one—with him. When Mia refused, he sent a lawyer directly to the set to serve her with divorce papers.

While this was going on—and afterward—Dean had decided maybe it was time to officially end his long-dead marriage to Jeanne. For one thing, he had met another woman, Gail Henshaw, another beauty queen, and wanted to marry her. Jeanne issued a statement to the press saying she would not contest the divorce. She was—and would be—well taken care of financially, and she was as tired of the sham marriage as he was. By the time the dust cleared, however, Dean and Gail had split up—Dean lost interest—and the "other woman" was now a gal named Catherine Mae (Kathy) Hawn, a beauty salon receptionist from Ohio.

While Frank and Dean—the Dynamic Duo of the Rat Pack—were immersed in all these romantic and cinematic entanglements, the other three members were not exactly being idle. Throw-him-a-couple-of-bones Sammy and ousted Peter Lawford had an alliance that would get them some needed attention-sans-Frank, and Joey was going to tackle the Late Night TV wars years before Jay Leno and David Letterman.

20

In Living Black and White

Citing "irreconcilable differences," Patricia Kennedy Lawford filed for divorce from Peter Lawford in 1966. She had had enough of his boozing, spending, and womanizing, and wanted out. In truth, Peter was as sick of the marriage as she was, but he had one all-important reason for wanting to remain her husband. As long as he was married to Pat, he was still a Kennedy. As soon as the divorce became final, he was totally and completely out of the most famous family in the world. And with that ouster came the loss of the privileges he had known as the brother-in-law of the late JFK.

Peter found that he was fast becoming a has-been in Hollywood. Frank's hatred of him was well-known, and producers were loathe to cast him because they were afraid of Sinatra's wrath. If that boycott weren't enough, his no longer being a Kennedy insider with access to the famous family and their money added the death blow. With the exception of Sammy Davis Jr., who was sympathetic and knew how unreasonable Frank could be, no other member of the Rat Pack would have anything to do with him. He was miserable.

Sammy, on the other hand, was on a personal high. His marriage to May Britt had fallen apart, but as he had always been more career-oriented than family-oriented, the break-up was harder for May than for him. May had never cared that much about her career and didn't miss it; she was much more interested in raising their three children (daughter Tracey, and two adopted boys), but she couldn't deal with the fact that Sammy was never home, that he hardly ever saw their children, and that when he was home he was surrounded by barflies and hangers-on that she didn't approve of and whose company she didn't enjoy. His lifestyle was just what she had been hoping to escape when she married him and dropped out of Hollywood. Their divorce was amicable.

Meanwhile, Sammy was busier professionally than ever. At night he was doing another Broadway show, *Golden Boy*, a musical adaptation of Clifford Odets' drama about a young man who becomes a fighter but really has music in his blood, and during the daytime hours he had started taping his new NBC variety series, *The Sammy Davis Jr. Show*. Seemingly inexhaustible, he then signed to do a feature film entitled *A Man Called Adam*. He pulled some strings and got Peter hired for a small but important role in the movie.

The part Sammy played was originally to have been enacted by the late Nat King Cole, but after his death his associate Ike Jones brought the script to Sammy. Once Sammy got his hands on it, the screenplay was altered to include some of his pet peeves and social concerns, with references and entire scenes crafted to display his feelings on race relations, civil rights, and miscegenation. As with *Mr. Wonderful* and even *Golden Boy*, Sammy was not about to waste an opportunity to educate the public. The trouble was that to make room for this material, much of the all-important characterization and even some drama got excised from Les Pine and Tina Rome's original screenplay. On a brighter note, Ike Jones, who produced along with Sammy's business manager

Jim Waters, became the first black man to receive a producing credit on a major American motion picture.

Sammy played Adam Johnson, a trumpet player (miming to Nat Adderley's horn playing) who has been slowly dying inside because of the guilt he feels over the deaths of his wife and child, who were killed in a car accident when Davis was driving while intoxicated. He also blinded his best friend, Nelson, played by Ossie Davis, in the accident. Trying to help ease his torment is Claudia Ferguson, a lovely young woman played by Cicely Tyson in one of her first roles. Trying to increase his torment is a racist, duplicitous booking agent played by Peter Lawford. Mel Torme had a guest appearance as himself, and Frank Sinatra Jr., still trying to beat Dad at his own game, played a struggling young jazz trumpeter. Rounding out the cast and the characters was no less than Louis "Satchmo" Armstrong as a has-been musician dreaming of the glory days.

The picture was filmed entirely on location in New York, complete with street sounds and traffic noises as background, one of the earliest movies to do so. The nightclub scenes were filmed mostly in Small's Paradise in Harlem. During filming, Sammy told Howard Thompson of *The New York Times*, "As far as I'm concerned this is my very first picture. I'm grateful for *Anna Lucasta*, the three Sinatra pictures and *Porgy and Bess*—but this one is about a man, a musician as it happens, who's dying because of his inability to communicate. He only happens to be a Negro. In a way, there's a lot of me in him. I insisted on that, in the writing. And I insisted, too, that he should die in the end. Why? So the people close to him—Cicely and Ossie—would perhaps have a better knowledge of life for the way he's lived his."

Sammy also thought of *A Man Called Adam* as his "first" picture because he did not have to share the spotlight with anyone; he was the one and only star. Although director Leo Penn did his best to keep Sammy from overdoing things, and Sammy himself commented during filming that "for technical, dramatic acting under a close, microscopic camera, you economize and hold back," many critics thought he overacted. Commented the New York *Morning Telegraph*: "If there are moments . . . when you might feel that maybe (Davis) is punching a little too hard, that maybe a change of pace every now and then, a pause for a deep breath so to speak, would have provided more credibility and more substance, given a more fully rounded depth to the portrait, that's not the Davis way. No matter what he's doing, this is a guy who's always 'on.' You'll have to take him or leave him at that."

The majority of the critics found the film "thinly scripted" due to Davis's tinkering and hogging the spotlight; this time there was no Sinatra or Martin to steal the show and he was going to run with it. The film was recommended strictly for "dedicated jazz buffs and fervent admirers of the talents of Sammy Davis Jr.," as one critic put it. "I don't think the Negro artist will ever be accepted entirely on his own, as a person," Sammy said in 1965 as the film was being shot. Thirty years before a variety of superstars who just happen to be African-American yet have fans of all colors.

Peter Lawford got surprisingly good notices for his work as the venal booking agent. He knew *A Man Called Adam* was Sammy's show but was grateful he had given him a part. He had just finished a chilling bit in the big film *The Oscar* where he was mercilessly cast as a washed-up actor who's had to take a job as a maitre'd in a restaurant just to get by. Peter was terrified that that was to be his fate, although he put a brave front on it for friends. "I'm tired with acting," he would say. "I'm tired of Hollywood. I don't really care anymore; I have enough to get by. If a good part comes along I'll take it, but otherwise I really don't care." In truth, he cared desperately. He hated being out of the spotlight as both actor and Kennedy in-law and was desperate to get parts that would put him back on top again. But whenever he came close the sinister spectre of Frank Sinatra would raise its unforgiving head.

Peter saw that his only way to continue working in high-profile motion pictures was to exploit his past connection to the Rat Pack, but even there the odds were against him. Frank would have nothing to do with him and Dean had never really liked him. Joey Bishop was busy with TV projects, and in any case was a cinema lightweight compared to the others. That left Sammy, who hadn't Sinatra's clout but was better than nothing. Peter just had to be careful that Sammy didn't start treating him the way Frank treated Sammy. There had to be a way they could do a vehicle together but be equal partners this time instead of Peter doing a bit to Sammy's star turn. Peter knew that *A Man Called Adam*, virtually an "all-Negro" movie and cheaply produced at that, would not turn Sammy into a major player, so he would need Peter as much as Peter needed him. The two of them in a movie might recapture enough of that old Rat Pack magic to really make it fly.

While Peter mulled over the possibilities, Sammy was tapped for a small role in the film adaptation of the Broadway musical *Sweet Charity*, primarily through the intervention of his pal—and the movie's star—Shirley MacLaine. The latter was absolutely charming as a dancehall "hostess" who searches for respectability and the perfect man, and dallies with a famous movie star (Ricardo Montalban) and a naive suitor (John McMartin) who chickens out when he learns of her former profession. Sammy was also excellent playing a character much like himself. Based on Federico Fellini's classic *Nights of Cabiria*, *Sweet Charity* is glossy and Hollywood-ish and "pretties up" the situations, yet manages to be consistently poignant.

Sammy and Shirley had a scary incident a couple of years later when Sammy was performing in a club in Mexico

City. During a day off from the film she was shooting at the time, Shirley went to Mexico to catch Sammy's act and say hello to him in his dressing room. Who should she find there but the horrible Sam Giancana, the mobster she had first met when she worked on *Some Came Running*. As usual, Giancana was hiding from the authorities. He had catered a backstage party for Sammy and insisted that Shirley eat some of the pasta. When she refused, he twisted her arm behind her back until she grimaced with pain. When Sammy—with great diplomacy—suggested that Giancana not do that to his friend, Giancana let go of Shirley's arm only to punch Sammy so hard in the stomach that Davis doubled over in agony and started gasping for air. Acting like he had done nothing wrong, Giancana calmly made himself a drink and offered no apology to either of them.

One day a friend of Peter Lawford's told him that he was "salt" and Sammy was "pepper," which started Peter's mind working. First of all, he figured it would be funnier if he played a character named (Christopher) Pepper and Sammy played (Charlie) Salt. Taking his cue from the success Dean Martin had had with his campy, Bond-like Matt Helm pictures, Lawford hired a screenwriter to concoct a girls-and-gadget story to go with the cutesy names. Thus *Salt and Pepper* (1968) was born. Peter had found a way around the fact that no one would hire him. He had his production company, Chrislaw, co-produce the movie and hired himself—and Sammy. As everything English seemed to be "in" that year—swingin' London, mod Carnaby Street, the Beatles, the Stones, a dozen other groups of descending merit—they decided the story would take place in London and environs and they would film on location, taking advantage of all the great scenery and saving money on the sets. As co-producers, Sammy and Peter paid themselves $75,000 each and split the profits fifty-fifty.

There was another great advantage to doing the picture in London. Lawford had been born in England, and Sammy had always been greeted warmly by the (generally) less racist British public, so in England the two men were treated as if they were Frank and Dino instead of the second stringers. Peter still had the second-hand aura of being a former Kennedy, which was the closest thing to being a member of the Royal Family. And the basic excitement of the Rat Pack had infected Londoners as well as Americans.

Peter and Sammy, both then in their early forties, hedged their bets by taking up the "mod" youth movement, which was revolutionizing styles and music in England. They began sporting long hair and muttonchops, Nehru jackets with bellbottom pants, and even the ubiquitous love beads around their necks. In other words, they looked hideous, but it worked. London newspapers gave much precious space to the upcoming picture. Meanwhile the two stars moved into ritzy suites at the fashionable Mayfair Hotel, hired huge trailers to replace the tiny English ones at the Pinewood Studios where they filmed interiors, gave lavish parties at the Mayfair and at the trendy club Alvaro's where most of the guests were half their age, and bedded and shared drugs with dozens of willing young women all too anxious to be in pictures.

Peter and Sammy—like Dino and Frank—had been practicing "free love" for years, but it was fun to know that in the "swingin' sixties" it was the rule more than the exception. They also took to the emerging drug culture like ducks to water—or Frank and Dean to scotch and soda. The latter two Rat Packers thought Lawford and Davis looked ridiculous, and Frank, in particular, always disapproved strongly of the drug culture. They spent so much money on drugs, women, and parties—not to mention giant trailers complete with bathtubs, ovens, and of course, bars—that Sammy had to do outside work while filming just to support himself in the lavish style to which he had become accustomed and which he could not really afford because of his profligate spending.

Things were almost over before they began when Sammy and Peter had a fight over a girl, a white model who moved in with Sammy after a couple of weeks in London. Not content to have her hooks in one movie star, the girl passed her favors onto Peter and apparently fell more for his line than Sammy's; soon she was parked in Peter's suite and Sammy was out in the cold. Production was shut down for a couple of days as everyone wondered if the two would work things out and the filming would continue. It came to a head when Sammy and Peter had a tremendous fight fueled by drugs and alcohol and nearly came to blows. "You're a motherfucker, you know that!" Sammy screamed. "I was in love with that girl." Cool as a cucumber, Peter then replied, "Well then I did you a favor; she's a tramp." The two men then laughed hysterically, had a drink or something stronger, and went back to work. The girl was sent home to mama. Sammy and Peter needed each other more than they needed her, one girl out of a thousand.

Although he would later direct such hits as *Superman*, *Lethal Weapon*, and *The Omen*, in 1968 director Richard Donner was a comparative neophyte. Sammy and Peter had only hired him because Donner had directed an episode of *The Wild, Wild West* that both had guest-starred on and thought he wouldn't be too demanding. Donner hated the experience of making *Salt and Pepper*, primarily because the two stars were totally undisciplined to the point of exasperation, but he couldn't fire them as, frankly, they deserved to be and would have been under different circumstances, because they were the producers and his boss. He just had to put up with their antics, which included showing up four hours late each day so they could nurse their hangovers, never studying the script, and doing a lot of (bad) improvisation on the set, which they and no one else thought was funny. Donner had to let them have their way but he figured he could cut out the truly putrid stuff in the editing room. To his horror and outrage, they fired him once the filming was over. Donner was so angry that he later said that if he had found Peter "it would have made the papers." To make matters worse, when the studio executives saw and hated the cut delivered to them by Sammy and Peter, the two stars blamed Donner's inexperience. The film was taken out of everyone's hands and recut.

In the picture Sammy and Peter play co-owners of a trendy London discotheque. The bane of their existence is a police inspector who cites them for one violation after another. But he is distinctly benign compared to whomever is leaving corpses lying about their Soho nightspot, and whomever later kidnaps Salt and Pepper and places them on a Polaris submarine. The boys become embroiled in a plot by revolutionaries to overthrow Her Majesty's government, but manage to foil the conspirators in a protracted battle in the Military Academy and War Museum. At the end of the film they are knighted (off-screen) and happily return to the psychedelic vagaries and topless delights of their chic disco.

Newsday summed up the general critical response to the picture: "If you have a yen to see Davis and Peter Lawford as an interracial Abbott and Costello, then *Salt and Pepper* may have some appeal. Otherwise, forget it." Another critic noted that Richard Donner's direction seemed like "a weak effort to imitate the (Beatles') *A Hard Day's Night* tempo," and likened the editing job to something the "corner butcher" did with a "cleaver." The photography, particularly of the aforementioned War Museum in the climactic sequence, came in for some praise, however, as did Davis and, to a much lesser extent, Lawford. *Variety* noted that the final bit—"two men running down the road and another, jumping high, following"—was stolen from Mack Sennett and that the accents of too many of the British supporting cast made them completely unintelligible to American ears.

Still, the picture made enough money for there to be a sequel entitled *One More Time* (this time was the last, however). In this Chris Pepper takes the place of his rich, look-alike brother after the latter is murdered and he and Salt have lost their nightclub. Both actors insisted that only one man be hired to direct: Jerry Lewis. The studio was aghast at the notion—Lewis's career was in the doldrums at this point—but Sammy and Peter were insistent. Sammy had been friends with Jerry since the early days and had remained friendly even after Lewis's break-up with Dino. Peter was grateful that Lewis had bucked the trend and given him a good part in his film *Hook, Line and Sinker* (which Peter always referred to as *Hook, Line and Stinker*). Now that Lewis needed a break, both men, who'd had their own career troubles, wanted to give him a chance.

There were troubles, however. Jerry saw this as an opportunity to show the whole world—not just France—what he could do, and he wanted the best of everything, including expensive new cameras, even real antiques in certain sequences. Jerry only got the cameras—they could instantly play back the footage that had just been shot—when he promised to pay the extra costs himself if the film went over budget. But when he started shooting with them he refused to test them first, and a whole day's worth of footage had to be scrapped because of defective lenses. Lewis only realized how stupid it would be to use real antique pieces in the movie when several stand-ins the art department put together got totalled in a fight scene.

Peter and Sammy shared a rented house in London while they were shooting. As usual, there was an endless round of parties that they both hosted and were invited to. One couple they partied with often was Sharon Tate and her husband Roman Polanski. They were shocked when news of Sharon's hideous murder back in the States reached their ears. They knew that if they had not been shooting a movie in London they might very well have been at the party where Sharon met her tragic fate.

Although Jerry did not get along with the real producer, Milt Ebbins, who was trying to keep the costs down while the two stars and nominal producers partied, he and the boys were having a ball. Sammy told Jerry that he and he alone would be the only person he'd allow to direct his just-published autobiography, *Yes I Can* (it never happened). Jerry planned to do a cameo in *One More Time*, but for some reason changed his mind. Every time Ebbins walked off the set, Lewis would do a vicious and very funny caricature of him.

"We all had a great time making that picture," said Lewis. "Next to Dean, Sammy Davis Jr. was the closest friend I ever had. His energy and talent were unbelievable; he was the singularly most talented one-man performer who ever lived. He was like a brother to me, and I was a better person every time I was in his company."

Lewis kept everyone out of the editing room while he put together his "masterpiece." When they saw it, Sammy and Peter had very different reactions. Peter was horrified— to him it looked like they were doing a very bad imitation of Martin and Lewis and he wanted no part of the picture. But Sammy was thrilled—he thought the movie was hilarious and had always been influenced a bit by the comedic style of Jerry Lewis in the first place. Being a black Lewis was not a problem for him. He protested vigorously when the studio took the picture out of Lewis's hands and had somebody else re-edit it.

"Jerry was a brilliant director," according to Sammy. "He did all his homework meticulously and knew exactly what he wanted before he reached the set. He was a very talented young man in those days. It was a crying shame to see what happened to the film after it left his hands. Jerry did not have the final cut, one of the most important aspects of production. Whoever did finally cut it cut all our throats along with the celluloid."

Some of Lewis's touches are still very apparent in the film, which is a silly, mildly humorous farce with a mercifully quick pace. Harmless, but nothing that would convince non-believers of Lewis's genius.

Sammy and Peter's relationship was never the same.

21

Killed in the Ratings

After Joey Bishop's sitcom was put out of its misery, the comedian looked around for another project that would give him the kind of industry status reserved for mega-stars like Sinatra and Martin. His tiny roles in the Rat Pack movies had not been enough to make him a major player in any sense of the word, and supporting parts in other movies such as *Who's Minding the Mint*, *A Guide for the Married Man*, and even the highly publicized *Valley of the Dolls* (all in 1967) did not do much to improve the situation.

He was a frequent guest—and guest host—throughout the sixties on the *Tonight* show hosted by Jack Paar, and continued to appear when Johnny Carson took over as host in 1962. At that time Carson said of Bishop, "Joey has something going for him that a lot of others don't—he's likable." Within a few years Carson would have reason to revise his opinion of the comedian.

It happened in 1967 when Carson got into a contract dispute with NBC and was temporarily replaced on *Tonight* by guest hosts while his lawyers argued with the network's. Bishop had been tapped by ABC to host his own show to compete with the highly successful *Tonight*—it was better than just being a guest host on that program—and the decision was made to present the premiere while Carson was off the air. Carson was not thrilled with the "likable" Bishop— who had guest-hosted for Carson as well as for Paar—when he heard about a closed-circuit telecast Bishop did for the executives of the network affiliates. "The [Carson] show is taken for granted," Bishop told the executives. "There is no excitement in it and no sense of something new happening." Carson was outraged and felt betrayed, just as he would many years later when frequent guest host Joan Rivers began her own competing late-night program, *The Late Show*.

Just as Frank Sinatra had offered his old co-worker and nemesis Fred Tamburro a job as his valet when he had come to Frank asking for a job or a handout, Bishop gave his old partner from the Bishop Brothers—Mel Farber, who still called himself Mel Bishop—a job as his valet and gofer. The difference was that Tamburro had mercilessly bullied Frank, and no such antagonism existed between Joey and Mel. Although he was given the title of "production coordinator," Mel's job included getting Joey's shoes ready, arranging his toiletries in perfect order, and spritzing expensive hair spray on Joey's $5000 hair transplant. (Joey also lived in a $200,000 house in Beverly Hills and drove a Silver Cloud Rolls-Royce to work.) In return for his toadying, Mel was paid a fairly generous salary and got to feel that he was still a small part of the show business he loved.

The new late-night Joey Bishop talk show began its run on the evening of April 17, 1967, and it was not an auspicious debut. To make the premiere outing seem like a rollicking fun fest, the audience was packed with Bishop's good friends and co-workers, including the entire cast of his defunct sitcom, Frank Sinatra's daughter Nancy, Edward G. Robinson, and many others. "Seldom has an audience rocked with such noisy appreciation," wrote *Newsweek*. "Seldom has an opening show, even seen through the sentimental mist, fallen quite so flat on the home screen."

Joey's first guest was Ronald Reagan, then the governor of California, who turned the conversation into a chance for some politicking and to tell the country how great his state was and hint at who was responsible for it. Bishop did little but sit there and look humble and awed. When actor David Hemmings, who'd recently made a splash in the film *Blowup*, came out to chat, Joey asked him such insipid questions as "What are the three things you like about Los Angeles?" Danny Thomas then came out and intoned on the moral quagmire of the modern world: "We're as close to Sodom and Gomorrah as . . . um . . . Sodom and Gomorrah."

To play the Ed McMahon sidekick role, ABC had hired a fairly green comic named Regis Philbin. According to *Newsweek*, Philbin "acted as though he had walked through the wrong door and found himself onstage." The only good news about opening night was that it got higher ratings than *Tonight* with guest host Jimmy Dean.

The situation changed when Carson's contract dispute was settled and Johnny returned to *Tonight* with an annual salary that approached $1.5 million (Bishop was being paid $560,000) and the determination to beat Joey at what he, Carson, knew how to do best. Just like the booking wars that occurred when Letterman took on Leno thirty years later— and Rivers took on Carson—the staffs of *Tonight* and *Joey Bishop* competed to get the hottest guests. As the weeks proceeded Bishop managed to snare Henry Fonda, Raquel Welch, popular comedienne Totie Fields, Robert Goulet, Rich Little, and boxer Joe Frazier, but he also had to settle for Peter Fonda, Don Knotts, and Jackie Vernon.

One near-disastrous evening occurred in early May when Joey had talk-show mentor Jack Paar on as guest; he had coaxed Paar out of semi-retirement to do the show. Instead of just doing ten or fifteen minutes as most guests did, Paar invited himself to sit in for the entire ninety minutes of the program. "Joey thought he'd pulled a coup," wrote one critic, "but (Paar's) pulsating ego so dominated the evening that viewers were wondering who was doing whom a favor." Reverting to his original role as talk-show host, Paar went so far as to go over to Joey's desk and take over the conversation Bishop was having with Juliet Prowse and Ethel Merman. Finally Bishop shrugged and said, "You'll have to forgive me for eavesdropping."

The Joey Bishop Show was not the first time ABC had tried to counter *Tonight* with their own late-evening programming. The now-forgotten—and controversial—Les Crane had failed to unseat Carson as King of Late Night a couple of years earlier. Because of this, there were a lot of ABC affiliates, almost a third, who decided not to carry Bishop and ran movies or sitcom reruns instead. ABC execs begged Bishop to use his friendships with the Rat Pack to not only get the likes of Sinatra on the opening shows but many of Sinatra's high-powered friends. Bishop refused. He was out to prove that he could make it on his own and that was that. When the first week's ratings proved to be unspectacular, however, it was easier to convince Joey to go for the big names, which at that time included Gregory Peck and Omar Sharif and even David Janssen, who came on the show the same night his long-running TV series *The Fugitive* went off the air.

Within six months, Joey's show was not only seriously challenging Carson's, but he occasionally won the time spot in New York, which everyone thought Carson had sewn up. Many of the holdout affiliates began carrying the show, and eventually all of them signed up to air Bishop. The reason for Bishop's success was attributed to the theory that Bishop appealed to a less sophisticated viewer than Carson did: Carson was big city; Joey was the hinterlands—there was room enough for everyone.

But there were still problems. When co-host Regis Philbin didn't get the salary increase he was hoping for from ABC, he walked off the show while it was in the middle of taping. Days later he came back on and apologized to Joey, who, in an awkward, humorless exchange, said he understood why he had done what he did. (The two were never the best of friends under any circumstances.) Occasionally Bishop would have to deal with difficult or prickly guests. Jackie Mason, who'd nearly wrecked his career by innocently giving Ed Sullivan the finger on the latter's variety program, irritated Joey by going off on serious political diatribes instead of sticking to the jokes. Finally the controversy-shy Bishop had to make a tactful on-air comment to get Mason back on the right track. Afterward he said to the comic, "It gets really tough when you get a friend on your show and you have to save his life. If I want intense speeches, I'll hire (Senator Everett) Dirksen." Then there was the time that a man-and-woman singing team started complaining to Joey on camera that their allotted time had been severely truncated by the other verbose guests. "They were bawling me out on the air," he complained. "The whole world is not waiting to hear what they've got to say."

Joey realized that despite having his own reasonably successful TV show, the whole world did not yet think he was a mega-star on Sinatra's level. One afternoon a couple with children asked Joey if they could have "just one picture." But instead of posing with Bishop and having somebody else take the shot, the couple only handed the camera to Joey and had him take a picture of them and their children. "That's the greatest put-down I've ever experienced," he said.

There were worse put-downs ahead, considering what the network was to pull. The show had been on for over two years when ABC renewed it for another two years during the summer of 1969, but four months later the executives changed their minds and cancelled the show in November.

Bishop came in to work one night and was informed of the decision: the ratings were simply not strong enough to keep the show running. Merv Griffin had just started his own late-night show on CBS (Griffin had formerly had a long run in the afternoons), and had more affiliates signed up than Bishop did; ABC felt that with two shows running against Bishop, the competition was just too stiff.

Now it was Bishop's turn to walk off the show during taping. He said a few words to the audience, then turned the rest of the program over to Regis Philbin. Then he left with his wife to go home and have dinner. Guest Vic Damone ran into the Bishops in the corridor and wanted to know where Joey was going. When he heard what had happened Damone said, "This is ridiculous!"

Bishop told reporters that he wasn't through with television, but if they wanted to hear any more they would have to get Johnny or Merv to have him on their programs as a guest.

Although he was a household name during this period, Joey Bishop had failed in his bid for superstardom. After a brief splash with their two *Salt and Pepper* movies, Sammy Davis Jr. and Peter Lawford were floundering. Dino and Frank were doing better. There was really no more Rat Pack, but some of the magic continued to wash over the individual members. And some were at their wits' ends.

Peter Lawford had managed to get cast in a forgettable movie entitled *They Only Kill Their Masters* (1972), in which old co-star June Allyson had a brief but surprisingly powerful bit. James Garner starred as a local sheriff who heads a murder investigation when the body of a woman is found on the beach. The screenplay seemed primarily to be a reaction to the more liberal sexual attitudes of the sixties and seventies, which some people viewed as refreshing and honest and others—such as the screenwriter—saw as a decline in moral standards. When it turns out that the dead lady slept with both men and women, it's the cue for Garner and lady friend

Katharine Ross to make endless quips about "fags" and "dykes" and degenerate "city folk."

Peter hated the picture, which was the very last film ever shot on the old MGM lot, and didn't particularly care for the occasional encounter with other old stars, such as Allyson, who were also cast in the film. "June was bitchy, but also kind of funny," Peter said. "She thought this was her last chance to make a big splash, and I guess it was, but when I said to her, 'But June—the script? And they've only given you one scene. Don't take it so seriously' she told me to go to hell. I only saw her once or twice; we didn't have any scenes together. The picture was a piece of shit, but most of the stuff they were making in that period was shit. The movie had this kind of old-fashioned moral tone to it, which I thought was hilarious considering it was a product of Hollywood."

Peter had remarried by this time. A guest appearance on Rowan and Martin's *Laugh-In,* which was very popular at the time, netted him an introduction to Dan Rowan's daughter, Mary, who was twenty-one to Peter's forty-seven. Mary was swept off her feet, caught up in the Rat Pack and Jack Pack fever that still enveloped Peter and which he continued to exploit whenever he could. For his part, Peter enjoyed being the subject of adulation from such a young woman. Dan Rowan was furious, but couldn't prevent Mary from marrying Peter in October 1971. Fed up with Peter's massive debts, his dependency on Quaaludes and other drugs, and his constant drinking, Mary filed for and received a divorce in 1975.

As for Sammy, after his variety show had run its course, he was tapped to do an interview program entitled *Sammy and Co.* in the seventies. He received bad reviews for the program, in which Sammy would chat with one or two guest stars and then he and the guest might perform a song or two (Sammy would sing solo if the guest wasn't a singer). Years later, watching tapes of the short-lived series, Sammy realized what had got everyone gagging. He was like a star-struck fan, a gushing autograph seeker, with his guests. He laughed too loud and hard at everything. Worse, when he introduced the guests he was back into using the high-falutin' speech that Jerry Lewis had warned him about years before. Wags dubbed the show *Step' n' Sammy* and *See Sammy Sicken*. The program barely lasted a few months. Luckily Sammy was having better luck on the recording front.

Two of his biggest hits were recordings that he had to be talked into making. He always felt that "Mr. Bojangles" somewhat distorted and debased the memory of Bill Robinson, the old-time entertainer it was inspired by, and he thought that "Candy Man," which became the biggest single he ever recorded, was the worst piece of treacle he had ever heard. "It's going to go straight down the toilet and take my career with it," he ranted, but he felt he had no choice but to do it. Motown records refused to release his latest albums because his sound was too "white" and "middle-class" for them; in truth their marketing people didn't know how to reach the target middle-aged audience.

His new producer at MGM records felt that "Candy Man" would sound good on his new album, and Sammy didn't want his refusal to record it to be the deal breaker. No one was more surprised than Davis when it went on to become a number-one record. The song had been written for a Disney film but everyone assumed the candy man of the song was supposed to be a drug dealer. The powers-that-be at Motown let it be known that they were interested in Sammy again, but it was too little, too late.

When doing shows, he was also sensitive about the material he was singing. At one performance, to illustrate how far the country had come in its attitude toward blacks, he sang the original lyrics to *Show Boat*'s "Ol' Man River," which included the word "niggers." Sammy thought it ironic that Oscar Hammerstein, the lyricist, also wrote the lyrics for the antibigotry song "You've Got to be Carefully Taught" for *South Pacific*. But Sammy completely missed the point that Hammerstein wasn't necessarily being racist when he used the word in "Ol' Man River." For one thing, it was historically accurate for black Americans of that period to use the term even as whites did. Also, the song was meant to be an anthem for the downtrodden and oppressed in general, and blacks in particular, and the use of the word was part ironic and part angry and sarcastic. Modern-day recordings of the show are not necessarily considered politically incorrect if they use the lyrics as originally written.

Sammy found that most of his liberal Democrat friends considered him politically incorrect, however, and began frosting him out because he supported Richard Nixon in 1972. It was bad enough when such Kennedy family members as Bobby's widow Ethel Kennedy stopped returning his phone calls, but it hurt even more when long-time friends just shut him out without a word or a chance to explain his side of things. Shirley MacLaine made a special trip to Vegas to confer with him in his dressing room. She couldn't understand how he could support a man who was against so many of the things Sammy had supported all of his life. When she left hours later she still disagreed with his stand, but Sammy was grateful that Shirley, at least, had bothered to ask him why he had seemingly gone Republican.

Sammy had two excellent reasons to stump for Nixon. First, no matter what bad things he had heard about the man, he knew that Nixon was actually doing things for blacks that the liberals had yet to do. Second, after JFK had frozen him out of his inauguration, he knew that "liberal" was often a completely empty word. Besides, Nixon was in office and he was the man with the power to get things done—JFK and Bobby were dead and buried, and there was no other liberal in the White House—so why shouldn't Sammy confer and advise the President on black affairs if Nixon was willing to listen, and more importantly, had both the means and the motivation to effect change?

Sammy was still interested in doing his bit to expose racism and improve relations between blacks and whites, so in 1972 he did his famous guest spot on *All in the Family*. Jean Stapleton had doubts about using a real-life character on the program, but she thought Sammy was great and the episode worked beautifully. In the story Sammy, playing himself, leaves a briefcase in Archie Bunker's (Carroll O'Connor) taxicab and goes to the Bunker home in Queens to retrieve it. In an odd way the half hour exploited the mixed emotions that many less tolerant whites had about Sammy Davis Jr., who was "one of them," but was also a famous entertainer, a celebrity, and, perhaps, one of the "good blacks." Archie lets Sammy sit in his easy chair (which is off limits even to other family members) but won't drink a toast from a glass that Sammy has used. Sammy says to Archie, "If you were prejudiced you'd go around thinking you're better than anyone else in the world. But I can honestly say you've proven to me that you ain't better than anybody!" Then he gives Archie a kiss on the cheek. The episode got a lot of attention at the time because of Sammy's appearance. Though groundbreaking for its time, *All in the Family* was always a rather self-conscious and in some ways overbearing sitcom that appealed to bigots and liberals alike, and now seems remarkably dated and simplistic.

The Rat Pack also seemed dated by 1972. Hairstyles and clothing and music had undergone incredible changes. The drug of choice was not alcohol but marijuana. The melodious ballads sung by Sinatra and the big band sound had been replaced by overly amplified electric guitar music. The day of the playboy or make-out artist seemed passe; in the days of the sexual revolution any geek could get laid without half trying. Having a different lady every night no longer necessarily meant that a man was a big stud—sex was literally every-where. Women no longer needed to be coaxed into bed or seduced by lovely words or alcohol; they were frequently the sexual aggressors in the singles bars, and often went out on the prowl for one-night stands just as men did. Then there was the emergence of Women's Lib and Gay Rights to add new conundrums to the sexual equation. Dean and Frank with their tuxes and short hair seemed antiquated; they were images of yesteryear. Sammy and Peter tried harder to go mod and youthful and almost succeeded. In comparison, Joey Bishop, who had never traded on the "booze and broads" mystique in the first place, seemed to have been born middle-aged.

As a group the Rat Pack was dead.

But the lives of its individual members were far from over.

PART THREE

The Final Years
1972–1998

22

Adrift

Peter Lawford's final years were a miasma of drugs, debts, alcohol, and bad marriages. Although he was haunted by the tragic drug-related death of Judy Garland, it didn't stop him from experimenting with bigger and better chemicals, anything to erase the hurt of being frequently unemployed, out of the Hollywood loop, an ex-Rat Packer, an ex-Kennedy—an ex-everything. He alienated a great many of his friends who were not into the drug scene, and he had very little to do with his four children, whom he thought of as "brain-washed little Kennedys." His hardships often made him bitter and ugly with people he had known for years.

In 1976 he was at a party in Los Angeles where he made the acquaintance of a young wannabe actress named Deborah Gould, who was twenty-five to Peter's fifty-three. Deborah was excited by Peter's lifestyle, all that Hollywood residue, which included meeting celebrities in clubs and going to Hugh Hefner's Playboy Mansion where Peter had a permanent guest room, and, of course, the hope that his contacts might lead to a career in the business. It was at the

Mansion that Peter told Deborah that they should get married. They had known each other for ten days. They flew to Virginia to get hitched in the home of one of Deborah's friends. Peter's son Chris, three years younger than Deborah, came to the wedding, dressed in a natty tuxedo that was a sharp contrast to his father's casual outfit. Many of the guests assumed that Chris was the groom, and were shocked to see Deborah's "father-in-law" take her hand in marriage as the young, handsome guy in the tux stood to the side. Peter got drunk and flirted with the party guests, both male and female, enraging his new bride.

The marriage dribbled on for a few months, but was effectively over just a few weeks after the ceremony. Peter could hardly do anything for his own career; he was in no position to help Deborah. She had no interest in the kinky sex scenes he kept trying to push on her, and the many drugs he was taking created wild mood swings that were difficult for her to put up with. Worse, Peter kept locking her out of their house every time they had an argument. By the time he had taken up with the woman who was to become his next wife, Patricia Seaton, Deborah had had enough. Peter had become convinced that Deborah's only interest in him was what he could do for her career, so his early lust and romantic interest quickly turned to cynical disdain.

Peter had met Patricia (Patty) Seaton, who was seventeen, at another party. He asked her to move in with him right after Deborah exited, but made sure not to divorce Deborah so even if he proposed to Patty while intoxicated there was no way they could make it legal. Patty had had a difficult home life, and moving in with a reasonably famous movie star who had an inexhaustible supply of drugs and glamorous druggie friends seemed like heaven to her. She wasn't with Peter long when he had his manager tell her that she had to move out: his kids were coming for a visit. Patty returned to her mother in tears. Some time later Peter asked

Patty to move back in with him and the relationship continued, on and off, for eight years before they were married when Peter was in the hospital, literally on his death bed. During those eight years Peter had numerous sexual relationships with different men and women.

Many of Peter's friends blamed Patty for his interest in drugs (which had actually begun years before he met her), or for keeping him in the drug scene years longer than he would have if left to his own devices. They also saw Patty as a parasite chiefly interested in what she could get out of a sick and easily manipulated middle-aged man. Even if these assertions were true, it remains that Patty paid a heavy price for her association with a man who by this point in his life was difficult at best and often monstrous at worst. There are other associates of Peter's who say that Patty was actually a very loyal and loving companion to him during his declining years, that she got more grief than anything else, and that Peter failed to appreciate her. "They were both desperate," a friend said. "They used each other. It was truly a pathetic situation."

Peter wasn't getting much work by the eighties, and the ravages of all the drugs he was taking played havoc with his looks. The only member of the Rat Pack who was more in debt was Sammy Davis Jr., but Sammy was earning a lot more money than Peter was. Because of the high price of his cocaine habit, the fees Peter got for appearing on such programs as *The Gong Show* weren't enough to pay his bills, so he resorted to selling most of his precious filmland memorabilia at shops, and writing his memories of old stars such as Judy Garland for supermarket tabloids. When he was finally importuned to go to the Betty Ford Clinic to dry out and detox, he called one of the tabloids himself and sold the exclusive rights to the story of his ordeal. At a party given by original Rat Packer Swifty Lazar, now a big-time Hollywood agent, Lawford dealt drugs to movie stars, something he would do with increasing regularity at more and more parties as the years went by.

Peter tried to make up with Frank Sinatra by sending him a warm, conciliatory letter full of praise and good fellowship, but Sinatra never responded. Peter then went to Las Vegas with Patty and the two went to see Sinatra perform. Peter sent word backstage that he was there, and sat at his table, waiting for the show to begin, convinced that Frank would acknowledge him from the stage and all would be well. Instead came the ultimate humiliation. An embarrassed manager had to tell Peter that Frank would not come out and perform unless he and Patty were ushered out of the room. By this time Sinatra knew all about Peter's drug activities and was more disgusted with him than ever. There was no chance for a reconciliation. Peter grabbed Patty by the hand and stormed out of the casino in rage and mortification.

In the meantime Sammy was having his own problems with money, sex, women, chemicals of varying kinds—and Frank Sinatra. Sammy met second wife Altovise Gore when she joined the cast of *Golden Boy* when the show went to London. He didn't really notice her until the opening night party, when she was all dolled up and looked nothing like she did playing his sister in the show. Altovise was almost immediately won over by Sammy's lifestyle, his energy, the way he had of focusing in on one particular woman and making her feel she was the only one Sammy had ever really noticed in his entire lifetime.

It was in London that Sammy started getting caught up in the whole "swingin' singles" scene of the sixties and seventies. Just like when he'd done *Mr. Wonderful* on Broadway, he needed to be surrounded by an entourage, to always keep moving, to have constant thrills and excitement. He participated in the sexual experimentation of the period, taking two or three girls with him to bed at one time, holding all-night orgies in his hotel suite, occasionally engaging in quickie

homosexual acts just to see what it was like. He bragged end-
lessly about the women he had—as if trying to prove he was
the epitome of the stereotypical Negro stallion—but mostly
kept mum about the times he had sex with men (including a
brief interlude with Peter Lawford). Most of this activity was
done under the influence of drugs—pot, speed, mescaline,
LSD, anything and everything that was verboten and trendy.
He wanted to soak up every single sensation that he could, do
everything that it was possible to do in this world. Most of all,
he wanted to keep loneliness at bay.

He had never really been a family man, but there were
times he missed the closeness he had had with his soulmate,
May Britt, and thought with some regret that he was missing
the chance of watching his children grow up. He thought he
might have found another, more compatible soulmate in
Altovise and asked her to marry him. He had one stipulation:
he already had three children that he shamefully neglected
and didn't want any more. "Altovise had no problem agree-
ing," said Peter Lawford. "She wasn't interested in children,
she was interested in what Sammy could do for her career.
And he did nothing. I think Altovise grew to care for Sammy
a great deal, but that marriage was more about two people
having uses for each other than anything else." To celebrate
his new married life Sammy bought a Beverly Hills mansion
that he had sometimes visited years ago in the days of Bogie
when it was then owned by now-divorced Tony Curtis and
Janet Leigh.

When he thought about them at all, Sammy grew
increasingly guilty about his neglect of his children. To that
end he invited daughter Tracey and sons Mark and Jeff to
visit him in London in '73. His marriage to Altovise had only
curbed his drug use and promiscuity a little, so he tried to
clean up his act a bit before the children came. When they
arrived they discovered that they were to spend most of their
time with new wife Altovise instead of with Sammy. Teenaged

Tracey had had a chip on her shoulder for a long time over their father's neglect of them, but since his remarriage it had gotten worse. She particularly resented Altovise telling her what to do. Because of this, she grew sullen and uncommunicative, difficult to deal with even when her father deigned to see her. Sammy suggested that if she were having that miserable a time she might just as well go home, to which Tracey replied that she would. Her future trips to Europe to see her father were a little more enjoyable for both of them.

"Those kids had a tough time of it," said a friend of the family. "Tracey came off a bit like a bitch at times, but it was because of what she was going through. Her life was more privileged than most, but she was always unnerved and angered—understandably—by her father's attitude. Her brother Mark was a nice kid, but troubled in a lot of ways. Jeff was a real sweetie pie; everybody loved Jeff. Sammy wanted to be a good father on one hand, but on the other—let's just say he wasn't very maternal. Like his idol Frank Sinatra, he was not very much into the whole 'father' thing. He was probably worse than Frank in that respect. Thank God May was always there for those children. They couldn't have asked for a better mother. They owe their character to her, not Sammy, everyone knows that."

Whenever the children visited Sammy in his New York apartment, Vegas suite, Beverly Hills mansion, or somewhere on tour overseas, the ever-present Altovise would try to mother them without success. She knew that the children, especially Tracey, didn't like her and she returned their feelings. One year she gift-wrapped used, dirty clothing and sent it to the children as Christmas presents from their father. Tracey also wondered if her stepmother had developed a drinking problem. By this time Altovise was as caught up in the anything-for-a-thrill lifestyle that Sammy was. And it would only get worse.

But Altovise's haughty air toward Tracey, her bossiness,

and her over-indulgence of alcohol (according to Tracey) bothered Tracey much less than her father's snubs. Sammy broke her heart when he promised her he would attend her graduation but never showed up. The responsibilities of being a father (even an essentially absentee or occasional father) were too much for a man who lived from noon to midnight, took every job that was offered to him, and was generally—in that period—in a haze of drugs, indiscriminate sex, and booze, just like Peter Lawford.

Like Peter, Sammy eventually gravitated to heavy cocaine use. He gave coke parties in his house and handed out little silver spoons people would use to dip into the cocaine which he put in a small bowl (that had originally been used for snuff) that he'd bought in a shop. He told people he was just a casual user, that he preferred vodka. In truth he was virtually addicted to both cocaine and booze and it began to affect his health and his energy, and anything that affected his energy affected his performances. It got to the point that he would go on stage, tell a joke, then tell the same joke again—forgetting he had already told it—and wonder why nobody laughed. All the booze was giving him a pot belly for the first time in his life, and he hadn't the vigor to work it off. Worse still, his timing was off, his memory was shot—and Frank Sinatra wasn't returning his phone calls.

Frank wanted nothing to do with Sammy. Booze was one thing, but to Sinatra cocaine was something long-haired, no-account, country-hating hippies—and Peter Lawford—did. Sammy wondered why Frank kept blowing him off—they'd been such good friends for years—and finally asked one of Frank's "bodyguards" what was what. He was told it was the coke. Sinatra wanted nothing to do with cokeheads. There'd been too many stories of people going to shit because of drugs. It was the wrong image. Sammy was told Frank wouldn't have anything to do with him until he was off the cocaine.

Frank was also nursing a grudge because of Sammy's association with Peter Lawford, the movies they'd made, the things they'd been up to in London. He'd even heard about orgies where men had sex with women and then with other men. He thought that Peter must have corrupted his buddy, Sammy. He figured to hell with both of them.

Sammy was angry at Frank. Who the hell was he to dictate anyone else's behavior? Did he think getting rip-roaring drunk and getting into one scandalous bar fight after another was the right "image"? He decided if Frank was going to be like that he'd have nothing more to do with him either. The silence between them lasted for three years, much longer than it had when Sammy spilled his guts on the radio program. Altovise ran into Frank's third wife Barbara Sinatra one afternoon and the two of them decided to end the frost. The two couples were going to have dinner together and that was that.

Sammy melted as soon as Frank walked into the restaurant and told him how concerned he was for him. Frank argued that if he stayed on the drugs he could lose everything that he'd worked so hard for, which, they both knew, had already happened to many other celebrities. Sammy swore to give up the drugs, and the two embraced, friends forever.

Eventually Sammy had to give up booze, too, when he developed liver damage so severe that his stomach was even more distended than usual. Not only was his liver dangerously enlarged, but so much liquid had backed up in his system that the doctor had to remove three and a half quarts of it with needles. Sammy was told in the bluntest possible terms that if he continued drinking the way he'd been doing he would come to a horrible end. From then on, except for the occasional drink, Sammy sipped Orange Crush soda pop from noontime till dawn.

But then there was a new crisis. Sammy had been dancing so energetically—some might say maniacally—nonstop for so many years that he began to develop agonizing pain when he was performing. The doctor gave him the worst news Sammy could have heard. The situation was serious enough to require surgery; he needed a hip replacement. Worse than the pain he felt was the fear that if he went through with the operation, it might severely affect his dancing abilities. He was nervous that the whole procedure might not even work. Shirley MacLaine was among the friends who called and told him he should go ahead with the surgery. With it, there was a chance. Without it, there was none. How could he continue performing when he was in so much agony? Sinatra asked for the name of Sammy's doctor and said he would check him out; if Sammy wanted, Frank would get the best bone specialist from Switzerland for him.

Sammy went ahead with the operation, but during the long convalescence when he was either on crutches or in bed, he was a holy terror. He took out his fear of permanent physical impairment on Altovise and virtually everyone who came to see him. Finally Shirley MacLaine called and talked some sense into him. He had lost an eye and managed to go on after that, hadn't he? When he married May, hadn't he thought the reaction to the interracial marriage might destroy his career? Hadn't there been other trials and tribulations over the years and hadn't he triumphed over all of them? Why was he being such a wuss about this? She advised him to stop feeling sorry for himself and accept the fact that even if his dancing days were over—a big if—he would go on as an entertainer. His millions of fans were rooting for him.

Sammy used a cane in his act but didn't do any fancy footwork for awhile. He sang so much he sang himself hoarse and worried if his voice would ever come back. It did. It wasn't too long before he was nearly back to his former glory; he was nearly sixty, after all.

He may have avoided physical disaster, but financial

armageddon was always looming. Sammy's attitude toward
money had always been completely irresponsible and ludicrous. He spent money as soon as he made it, buying expensive items he really didn't need, picking up huge tabs so he
could seem the big spender, having to have the best of everything for his all-precious image. He gave lip service to his
worry over less privileged black people than himself, but in
one week he could easily spend more than ten average
American citizens made in a year or more. Most of the Rat
Packers were this way with money, but Sammy bought too
many unnecessary items—including a private jet—even in
times when he couldn't afford to, which was basically
throughout the latter years of his life. He once threw a
$75,000 lavishly catered party in his home just so people
wouldn't think he was broke. Most of his salary—as large as
it was at times—was immediately gobbled up by the jaws of
the IRS, to whom he owed millions in back taxes.

It got so bad that the IRS was threatening to take away
Sammy's Beverly Hills estate and other properties. Even after
he and Altovise went on an economy kick—fish from the
farmers' market instead of a high-priced food store on Rodeo
Drive, for instance—Sammy just didn't seem to get it. He
wanted to reward Altovise's pennypinching by buying her a
necklace from Gucci's that cost over $10,000. Fortunately
his business advisers talked him out of it. Their efforts, however, seemed to come to nothing when Sammy would celebrate paying off one bill by going out to an expensive restaurant with half a dozen friends or picking up the tab for 800
people in a club one night (the bill came to nearly $17,000)
because he was too hungover to continue his performance
(this was in the days when he was still drinking).

Sammy claimed that he was solvent by the late eighties, but he never really caught up with what he owed. Even
considering how much of his salary he'd had to give to his
father and "uncle" in the earlier days, there was no excuse

for his unbelievable debt. He should have been able to live very comfortably on what he made—and then some. "It isn't just that Sammy sucks as a businessman," Peter Lawford once said during his own dark days of debt, "but he really doesn't care."

Peter could well have been talking about himself.

Sadly, there were worse things to come for both of them.

23

Cannonballed

Although Frank Sinatra had officially "retired" in 1971, he couldn't stay out of show biz—or politics—for long, and combined the two by coming out of retirement to perform at benefits for his favorite political candidates. Fed up with Kennedys and Democrats, Frank supported Reagan in his re-election for governor. He was still smarting from the Palm Springs/JFK/Bing Crosby business. Frank had once told Shirley MacLaine that he thought Reagan was "a stupid bore who couldn't get a job in pictures, which was why he went into politics." But Reagan's opponent was a Bobby Kennedy loyalist, which was enough to earn him Sinatra's enmity and gain Reagan Frank's support. Frank also became fast friends with outspoken veep Spiro Agnew, and infuriated many—as did Sammy Davis Jr.—by stumping for Nixon for his re-election bid in '72.

Sinatra had always hated Nixon, and his motives for supporting the man were entirely different from Sammy's. Sammy felt Nixon could get things done for blacks (Sammy was also getting some not-so-subtle pressure from Frank), but Frank had become friends with Nixon when the latter

congratulated him on his performance before the House
Select Committee on Crime, whose members Frank scorned
as "publicity-seekers." Frank's daughter, Tina, and even the
wife of his long-time lawyer Milton Rudin called him a "monster" for going Republican. (This, among other things, led to
a divorce for the Rudins.) Frank officially ended his "retirement" in 1973 with a splashy TV show that made little
impact with reviewers or in the ratings.

In the meantime Frank had begun a relationship with
the wife of Zeppo Marx of Marx Brothers fame. Her name
was Barbara, and she had formerly modelled for Mr.
Blackwell, he of the infamous "worst-dressed" list. Forty-
three-year-old Barbara was utterly smitten with Frank, and
he found in her the kind of woman he had always been looking for. Unlike Ava or Lauren or Juliet or any number of others, she had no career. She could just be there for him, to
satisfy his needs, whenever it was required. Even friends
reported that Barbara was not exactly a class-A intellectual.
"Barbara was perfect for Frank," said one. "She couldn't
intimidate him the way classy, highly intelligent people
could. They brought out Frank's worst side; Barbara didn't."
Barbara divorced Zeppo, but it took three years for Frank to
finally produce a ring in 1976, when they were married at
the California estate of Walter Annenberg. Zeppo seemed so
unruffled by the way Frank had basically stolen his wife of
thirteen years away from him that there were reports Frank
had laid a generous "settlement" on the man, in effect, buying Barbara from Marx.

During the long on/off engagement period, Frank
became friends of a sort with someone who had formerly
loathed him: Jacqueline Kennedy Onassis. By this time
Aristotle was dead, and Jackie was impressed with the classy
way Frank sent a note of condolence to her table at "21" and
asked if he might see her instead of blundering over and forcing his presence on her. Could he have picked up some pol-

ish over the years? Frank was also a symbol of a period in Jackie's life that had as many golden memories as nightmarish ones; he was someone who understood Camelot as few of her other friends and acquaintances did. (She had never been that close to the Kennedys.) Frank became Jackie's escort at a number of events, and friends wondered if the Widow Onassis was entertaining the notion of shocking the world by marrying another famous and monied individual. After the crudities of her Greek shipping magnate, Sinatra must have seemed positively dignified to Jackie. But it was not to be. Barbara Marx had her hooks in Frank, and Jackie and Frank were basically oil and vinegar.

The year 1977 was the worst of Sinatra's life, for in January of that year his beloved mother Dolly was killed when a jet Sinatra had hired to fly her and a friend to his opening night in Vegas unaccountably went off course in intense precipitation and slammed into the San Gorgonio Mountains. When he heard the news, Frank clung to the faint hope that his mother had survived. He cancelled his engagement and waited at his Palm Springs estate for further news. Rescue efforts were hampered by horrendous weather, and Frank was tormented by thoughts of his mother, injured, lost, and alone, struggling to survive in the snow. When helicopters managed to find the wreckage and mangled bodies, it was clear that there was no hope and that Dolly and the others aboard had been killed on impact.

Frank's success, talent, money, and achievement suddenly all seemed very hollow if none of them could have saved his mother's life. He retreated into himself, into the religion he had paid scant attention to over the years, trying to find solace. It wasn't just his mother's death—it was the violent way she died, torn literally to pieces, cruelly slung out of the broken plane like so much flotsam. His mother had hardly been perfect. She was often rotten to his wives (Barbara included) and could be irascible to say the least, but

he loved her dearly, and those feelings were strongly returned. She had encouraged him from the very first; she had
stood by him through thick and thin. She scolded and argued
and gave unwanted advice, but she had always had his best
interests at heart. Francis Albert would not have become
Frank Sinatra were it not for his mother.

His old friend Jimmy Van Heusen and Rat Packer Dean
Martin were two of the pallbearers. For many months Frank
was disconsolate.

Dean didn't quite become a Republican like Frank did,
but he had publicly stumped for Governor Reagan as part of
a Democratic group called Californians for Reagan. Unlike
Sinatra, Dean had no great love of politicians, no need to
curry favor, nor a thirst to be seen as close friend to the
power brokers. He was his own man—not the Kennedys', not
Reagan's or Nixon's or anyone else's. Occasionally he would
get involved if talked into it; he would come entertain at
assorted inaugural galas if invited—that was singing, not
stumping—but that was about it.

By the seventies, Dean still made movies, more than
Frank did, but he was essentially a TV star. His hugely popular TV program was basically a burlesque show with many
pretty girls and crude jokes and oddball comedians, and after
awhile all the risque humor attracted the attention of the network standards people and prim and prissy social critics.
Women's liberation also made much of the humor on the program, which was geared mainly toward the middle-aged,
seem dated. Most of the jokes were, like Dino himself, undeniably and delightfully vulgar, but also sexist, involving boobs
and derrieres and more than a hint of impropriety. All of it
was ludicrously harmless except to the humorless, too tiresome and silly and mindless—like the old burlesque skit carried out for the thousandth time—to be truly offensive. As if
he were sticking out his tongue at the naysayers, Dino
replaced the long-legged troupe of dancing girls known as the

Golddiggers with four Ding-a-Ling Sisters who were dumb as well as busty. The series exploited Dino's image as playboy, heavy drinker, and man-about-town, and it put a leer on NBC's peacock.

Producer Greg Garrison briefly cleaned up the act after all the protests, but when he felt the heart and soul had been cut out of the show he ordered the writers to become even more tasteless and suggestive. But by the eighth season the old formula was positively creaky, and the ratings plummeted, and it was that—and not a peep from the protestors such as N.O.W. (the National Organization for Women)—that wrote finis to the show, at least in its original format. There were those who felt that Dino's divorce from Jeanne had turned off many of his fans, particularly older women. It was one thing to play at being a playboy, and quite another to actually leave your wife for a younger woman. (By this time Dean had divorced Jeanne and married the aforementioned Kathy Hawn.)

Dean's next TV gig for several years was to host a series of weekly "roasts" of major and minor celebrities. Amusing at first, soon they also degenerated into a formula, with the audience aware of what the jokes would be even before the comics on the dais opened their mouths. Red Buttons would do his routine about how he "never got a dinner"; Foster Brooks would do his fabulous drunk act. The viewers at home never realized—although the choppy editing may have helped them suspect—that the "roasts" never really occurred in "real time." Often the different celebrities' five minutes or so of gags were taped days apart in completely different studios in different cities.

Nick Tosches writes amusingly of "Dean Martin's Celebrity Roasts" in his book, *Dino*: "It was a dais of despair. They sat at banquet tables at either side of the podium: the undead of dreamland and the fleeting stars of the television seasons, each rising in turn, at the beckoning of Dean or his bloated sidekick, Orson Welles, to deliver the moribund jokes consigned to him for the occasion."

Eventually the roasts ended their weekly run and became a series of occasional "specials."

Dean divorced Kathy Hawn in 1976—Kathy would receive generous alimony payments—then started seeing a variety of women, among them Peggy Crosby, a thirty-eight-year-old cocktail waitress who was the ex-wife of Bing Crosby's son, Phillip; a nineteen-year-old student at UCLA named Andre Boyer; Phyllis Elizabeth Davis, an actress who appeared in the TV show *Vegas*; and Joni Anderson, another actress.

Contrary to popular opinion, Dino and Jerry Lewis had crossed paths more than once over the years, but they had never really reconciled their differences; when one spotted the other he would do his best to avoid a meeting. They hadn't seen each other in sixteen years, however, when Frank Sinatra got the notion to go on Jerry's telethon in 1976 and bring Dino along with him. Something about it appealed to Dean's perverse sense of humor or he would never have done it; perhaps even he was getting nostalgic and figured he and Jerry were too old not to make up. Frank's motives were his alone: he had never mended fences with Peter Lawford. Perhaps he also had a perverse need to see what would happen. He figured it would get good publicity, and it did.

On the air, Jerry was overjoyed to see Dean and Dean seemed happy, if more reserved. It did not lead to any kind of real reconciliation or friendship, however. When Jerry would call Dean, sometimes to talk about going on a future telethon, either Dean would be "out" or an associate would take the call. He didn't respond to any of Jerry's letters. He finally agreed to meet with Jerry—through a third party—but never kept the appointment. Dean had been happy to make up with Jerry, but he had no intention of becoming buddies with him or making him part of his social circle. His days with the monkey were over.

By this time Dean was drinking worse than he ever had in his life. He was also addicted to Percodan, which he had taken as a painkiller—for alcohol-induced headaches, among other things—for years. When he did club engagements he often showed up inebriated; ditto for the golf course. The drinking-for-show had been replaced by drinking-for-real with a vengeance. He was also developing ulcers and severe liver problems—but what else was new?

Since his retirement Sinatra hadn't been in any movies until the well-received television film *Contract on Cherry Street* (1977). He had played a private eye in the two Tony Rome films, and a police detective in *The Detective* (he would play a police detective again in *The First Deadly Sin* in 1981), but in *Cherry Street* he was improbably cast as a cop taking on, of all things, the mob. Why all these cop roles? For one thing, Frank had developed that certain chip-on-the-shoulder toughness that characterized some cops (at least in the movies). For another, Frank thought it might dispel those pesky Mafia rumors if he portrayed the good guy for a change. By this time, mob contacts like Giancana and Luciano were long gone, and Frank didn't know or like their younger replacements all that much.

Dino had done *Airport*, a couple of westerns, and seemed tired and disinterested as a criminal lawyer in *Mr. Ricco* in 1975. It was six years before he appeared in another film, *The Cannonball Run*, in 1981. The director, Hal Needham, had been a stunt man and stunt coordinator who decided to get behind the camera to the regret of audiences everywhere. In all of his action films and action-comedies, the stunt work was always excellent, but there's more to a well-crafted film than stuntwork. In many ways Needham's films, which he usually made with good buddies Burt

Reynolds and Dom DeLuise, were like Rat Pack movies: the final product was much less important than the fact that everyone have fun during the shoot with booze and broads and all the trappings. It was one big party. For more of that Modern Rat Pack glamour, Sammy Davis Jr. was added to the cast, which included Roger Moore, Peter Fonda, Jimmy the Greek, Terry Bradshaw, Bianca Jagger, and—the only one of the outre supporting cast who could really act—Molly Picon.

Dino and Sammy were sixth- and seventh-billed, respectively, in this picture about a zany cross-country automobile race where the drivers are as nutty as they come. Dean and Sammy masquerade as priests in black robes and big black cowboy hats throughout most of the movie. The trick is to disobey the speed laws without getting stopped by the police, so our boys pretend they're speeding to give someone last rites, for instance, while Reynolds and DeLuise drive a souped-up ambulance with a bogus patient in the rear; Jackie Chan has a computerized car with fancy evasion techniques; and so on. Typical of the humor is when Dean, still dressed in priest's garb, whispers something naughty to buxom competitor Adrienne Barbeau, all the time eyeing Barbeau and her shapely female co-driver. "That's a no-no," says Barbeau saucily. "It hasn't been allowed for a thousand years." To which Dean replies, "We're a liberal branch. How about just one?"

Needham's direction was, as usual, too hands-off to make the film exciting, and the truly amusing moments were few and far between, with the cast having much more fun than the audience. This was made clear in the series of out-takes—Dino and Burt cracking up over assorted flubs—shown over the closing credits, which are funnier than anything in the movie. The picture even commits the sacrilege of using a badly reorchestrated and execrably played rendition of Rossini's "William Tell Overture" for one of the racing scenes. Sammy Davis exhibits great personality throughout the proceedings, but Dino just seems stewed as usual. Proving H.L. Mencken's adage that "nobody ever went broke underestimating the taste and intelligence of the American public," *The Cannonball Run* became one of the biggest box office hits of the year.

Sinatra and Shirley MacLaine were spared being a part of the Needham debacle—but only until the sequel. In the meantime MacLaine was having better luck in *Terms of Endearment* (1983), for which she won a Best Actress Oscar. The overrated picture cast (or rather miscast) the Rat Pack mascot as the mother of Debra Winger and detailed the two women's troubles with men and each other over the years. Perpetrated by triple-threat producer/director/screenwriter James L. Brooks, the picture rarely rose above the level of the sitcoms that Brooks had formerly been involved in. Even the picture's teary finale, with Winger dying of cancer, hadn't the impact it should have, although a devilish Jack Nicholson stole every scene he appeared in. Perhaps critics overpraised *Terms of Endearment* because it seemed like a masterpiece next to tripe like *The Cannonball Run*.

Speaking of which, Hal Needham gathered his pals together—Burt, Dom, Sammy, and Dino—and set about making *Cannonball Run II* in and around Vegas in 1983. Shirley accepted a role in the film before she won her Oscar, and was mortified when her very next film after *Terms of Endearment* was Needham's dreadful opus. When Sinatra heard that three of his pals were doing the movie, he let it be known that he was interested in a part, and the producers hired him for a cameo playing himself.

The slightly more involved plot of *Cannonball Run II* has a sheik (Jamie Farr) putting up one million dollars as prize money for another race. When mobsters from the Cannelloni family hijack Farr's car to steal the loot, the Cannonballers question the wisdom of asking the Sheik's father, the King, for help when it's well known that the King can't stand his son. "He's not the only king!" cries Dino. "We got kings in America." To which the Cannonballers respond by paying a call on the real Frank Sinatra in his office in Vegas. "How much this time?" Frank asks Sammy, Dino etc. as they walk in excitedly (or what passes for "excitedly" in this picture). "It's not for us," Sammy assures him. "Not this time." Frank orders underlings to help his pals, but it's all to no avail: the contest—and money—is won by an orangutan (mistakenly referred to as a chimp all through the movie). The orangutan gives the best performance.

Martin and Davis were billed third and fourth, respectively, after the team of Reynolds and DeLuise, while MacLaine came in six after fifth-billed Jamie Farr (most famous as "Klinger" of *M.A.S.H.* on TV). After these six headliners, Sinatra was billed alphabetically as one of the additional "stars." Sammy and Dino played the same characters as in the first movie, only at one point they trade in their priests' vestments for policemen's uniforms. Martin (as Blake) is making martinis for a blonde in his bed when Sammy (as Fenderbaum) provides some *coitus interruptus*. Dino is again partially soused while Sammy seems to be doing an imitation of Lou Costello, but at least they both look good. MacLaine and pal Marilu Henner play showgirls in *The Sound of Music* who are mistaken for real nuns—of the Order of Immaculate Charity—by not-too-bright Burt and Dom.

Sinatra managed to have his cake and eat it, too. He had half a day of fun with the fellas while actually maintaining his dignity, which is more than can be said for the rest of the cast. Wearing a sharp, stylish suit, he sits behind a massive power-desk and does what he does best: be himself. As usual, he did no retakes, and none were necessary. Sammy and Dino and the others clowned with Frank before and after shooting the scene, but while the cameras were rolling no one dared flub a line. Everyone knew Francis Albert did not like to shoot a scene twice. Frank also turns up very briefly in a car at the end of the picture. Dino would always resist whenever Frank would ask him to go out on the road or do a club date with him; now Frank wondered why Dean should put up such resistance when he didn't mind appearing in garbage like this (and Martin had to do a lot more running around in the movie than Frank did).

Things were relaxed on the set, to say the least. Shirley scolded Dean for putting several teaspoons of sugar in his coffee, and the following day he opened a five-pound bag of the stuff and threw it all over her trailer. Martinis were served every afternoon, and the boys flirted with all of the comelier female extras. When Needham wasn't setting up a particular stunt—generally involving a car crash or three— he'd hang around with Dom and Burt as they all tried to make like a poor man's Rat Pack. Sinatra's bit was so short he came in one afternoon and left by five. There was none of the old magic.

"There's a higher purpose involved, officer," MacLaine says at one point, "only the Lord knows what it is." Which might be one way of describing the antics of *Cannonball Run II*, which MacLaine later called "a disgrace." To be fair, although the picture is mostly an excuse for good stunt work, it does have its amusing moments. Sammy says to Dino, "You're gonna drink milk? Aren't you afraid it's gonna curdle when it hits your liver?" To which Dean replies, "My liver died last year." Sammy, Burt, and Dom are fun in harem drag, lip-syncing to the Supremes' "Stop in the Name of Love." There's some more or less good-natured gay humor when lisping Charles Nelson Reilly admires Sammy's jewelry and asks him if he can buy him a drink. But the best bit has Dom DeLuise doing a terrific Brando-as-the-Don imitation as the head of the Cannelloni family.

But when all was said and done, the two *Cannonball* movies were far below the level of *Ocean's 11* and *Robin and the 7 Hoods*, no world-beaters themselves.

For some of the Rat Packers, there was nowhere to go but up.

For others, unfortunately, there was nowhere to go at all . . . .

24

Death and Taxes

Peter Lawford was the first to go.

By 1984 Lawford was hopelessly addicted to drugs and alcohol, and all attempts to get him clean and sober were futile. The situation was so bad that even during his stay at the Betty Ford Clinic he used his credit cards to hire helicopters to fly cocaine into the desert behind the Clinic. Once out of the Clinic he began drinking heavily again. He was in and out of the hospital with bleeding ulcers and liver problems. During one stay he officially married his common-law wife, Patty, and made out a will leaving her everything, which, aside from insurance money, was mostly debts. He was hired to play a small role in the television film *Malice in Wonderland* (about the rivalry between gossip mavens Hedda Hopper and Louella Parsons), but was so sick on the set that he couldn't finish his scenes. Patty found him nearly unconscious on the floor of his home a few days later and he was admitted to Cedars-Sinai. There he died of total kidney and liver collapse on Christmas Day 1984. He was sixty-one years old.

Sammy Davis Jr. was the only one of the remaining four who really mourned him. As far as Frank Sinatra was concerned, Peter Lawford had died a long, long time ago.

Sinatra had never quite recovered from the death of his mother. In March 1987 Dino was going to get an even worse shock, the worst news any parent could possibly get.

Out of his several children Dino had perhaps always been closest to his namesake, Dino Martin Jr., a.k.a. Dean-Paul Martin. Sister Claudia had briefly attempted a singing career, but only Dino seemed determined to follow in his father's footsteps. He had formed a one-hit band—Dino, Desi and Billy—with Desi Arnaz and Lucille Ball's son Desi Jr. and another friend back in the days of the Beatles, and starred with Ali MacGraw in the tennis film *Players* in 1979 (which pretty much finished his film career). By 1987 he was a twice-divorced captain in the Air National Guard. (His ex-wives were actress Olivia Hussey and skater Dorothy Hamill.)

Dino Jr. was flying maneuvers in a F4-C Phantom jet near San Bernardino when it hit a sudden blizzard, lost altitude, and smashed into the San Gorgonio Mountains, the same range that Dolly Sinatra's plane had tragically encountered. Although Dino Jr.'s superior officers at first thought that he and his weapons officer might have bailed out in time, it turned out that they hadn't. Dean and his ex-wife Jeanne, Dino Jr.'s mother, spent many hours huddled together waiting for word, but five days later knew the worst when the wreckage was found in Wood Canyon. Dean was shattered by the news. He lost even more of his zest for life, which had been slowly eroding as he got older, and started drinking even more heavily than before. Sinatra could do nothing but offer his sympathy, as did Sammy Davis Jr.

In late 1987 Barbara had invited Sammy and Dean to appear with Frank in a telethon to raise funds for a new wing of the Eisenhower Medical Center. They were sitting around Frank's pool in Palm Springs when Sammy reminisced about all the fun they'd had during the Rat Pack days. "We should do something like that again," Sammy said. Frank opined that it wasn't enough just to get together in Vegas again, because there were literally millions of people who never got to Vegas and might never have a chance to see them. "How's about we do a tour?" He suggested they travel from town to town by a special train, but later realized it didn't make much financial sense to pay all the bandmembers and so on for each day they travelled with them on the train when they'd only need them for one show a week. Instead they'd travel on planes. Two planes, as Frank liked to arrive in a city about an hour before the show began, and Dean and Sammy liked to be in town the night before to relax and see what was what.

Dino was not that enthused. Frank had approached him with less ambitious variations of this idea a few times over the years and he had never been interested. They had done an act together in Tarrytown in 1977, but such occasions were rare. Dean was seventy years old at this point; Frank was seventy-two, Sammy ten years younger. Dean was still grieving over the death of his son, and he didn't need the money or the adulation from fans. He was old and tired. But he knew that there was no real Rat Pack as such without him, and he wanted to be a pal. Frank and Sammy were much more into the whole showbiz thing—all the preparation, the costumes, the planning. Dino would show up with his tux, watch TV while he drank scotch, and show up on stage at the alloted time. To him it was a chore, done quickly, done simply, done and over with.

It was to be officially called the "Together Again Tour," but everyone called it the Rat Pack Tour. They made the announcement at Chasen's, where, for once, Frank played ball with the press (now that he needed them) and charmed them. Dean asked, "Is it too late to call the whole thing off?"

Rehearsals were held at the Ren Mar Studios in Hollywood, with the orchestra led by Morty Stevens, who'd once been conductor for the Will Mastin Trio but now was head of the music department at CBS. Sammy noticed that there were only three black musicians, so for the sake of political correctness, as we'd call it today, nine white guys were fired to make room for more blacks. Yet Sammy did not object to the billing, which was "Frank. Dean. Sammy." He was still bringing up the rear, yet he was smart enough to know that as big as he was, he wasn't really as big as his two buddies. If his movie career had really taken off it might have been a different story, but he was neither the Sidney Poitier nor the Denzel Washington of his time.

American Express was the sponsor, Home Box Office would run one of the shows months later, and the tickets were sold out weeks in advance. The opening night was in Oakland at the Coliseum, where Dino wondered what the hell they were doing in a stadium where rock-and-rollers played when they were supposed to be intimate Las Vegas lounge acts. Sammy wondered why they were giving up lucrative club bookings for a tour that might blow up in their faces. The papers ran nasty columns ragging the Clan, wondering what these "senior citizens" were trying to prove. Frank's lips were set in a determined frown, only crinkling now and then at the corners. He reminded them that in this one opening night they'd be performing in front of more people than saw them the entire time they played the Copa room at the Sands back in the *Ocean's 11* days.

The show at the Oakland Coliseum was successful, but during the last set when the three entertainers came out and sang and clowned together, Dean missed a few cues, sang a few bars behind the others, didn't really seem to give a damn about what he was doing. This did not sit well with Sinatra, who lit into him about it backstage. It got worse when they flew into Chicago for the next week's gig, and Dean told

Frank that he wanted to stay in his room and watch television instead of hitting all the bars they way they used to. Dean was fed up with Frank, the way he was still behaving as if he were thirty years old, pushing his weight around. When they arrived Frank had had a fit because their suites weren't all on the same floor, when Dean didn't give a damn where he was. He also resented the way Frank told him he wasn't singing as well as he used to, that he wasn't giving his all to the tour. Frank wanted to recreate the Rat Pack magic, but times had changed. Sammy wasn't drinking anymore, and Dean was drinking too much. But he wanted to do it alone.

Frank thought Dean was ungrateful. Part of the reason he and Sammy were doing this tour was because they hoped it would bring Dean out of the shell he'd been in since his son's death, and to tell the truth, for a few years before that. But there was an essential difference between Dean and Frank—and Dean and Sammy—that Frank just couldn't understand. Dean had never been driven like Frank was. He wanted to be successful so he could have money for nice things and booze and broads, but he'd never cared about being an artist. Now that he was old and had all the money he needed, the career meant very little to him. Frank's career meant everything to him. He knew he was an artist and it was something he was reluctant to let go of even when the Voice had lost much of its lustre.

Dean sat eating spaghetti in his hotel room while Frank tried to talk him into going out with him. Half humorously and half seriously, an exasperated Sinatra finally picked up the plate of spaghetti and let the strands that remained fall on top of Dean's head. He waited for Dean's reaction, expecting him to laugh like the good buddy he'd always been. But Dean simply sat there for a spell, didn't even look at Sinatra, and finally got out of his chair and walked into the bathroom, slamming the door behind him. The next day—after only one week—he left the tour.

The HBO special had to be cancelled. Although performing was not something Dino really cared to do at this point, he was so outraged at "frog-voiced" Sinatra's negative remarks about his singing that he agreed to do a solo gig at Bally's Grand in Vegas after a brief stint in the hospital. Each night he would "perform" on stage drunk. Sammy and Frank did a few shows by themselves, then asked Liza Minnelli to join them for their European engagements. As "Rat Pack Tour" was no longer applicable, it was rechristened "The Ultimate Tour" and hit eleven cities.

Even with Liza there were problems. She had to cancel in Helsinki when she got an ear infection. In Stockholm she was informed by the authorities that she had broken Sweden's quarantine laws by bringing her dog, a Scottish terrier named Lily, into the country with her. When told that the dog was going to be deported, Liza threw a fit and refused to do the show unless the dog was allowed to stay overnight in the hotel with her. Finally she wound up spending $50,000 just to charter a jet to fly the problem-causing pooch to Paris.

Joey Bishop resurfaced—somewhat—in the 1990 film *Betsy's Wedding*, another of the mediocre movies Alan Alda kept directing in the hopes of recreating the success of his highly likable *The Four Seasons*. The movie was a tedious, generally unfunny tale of a father (Alda) arranging his daughter's wedding while inadvertently getting involved with mobsters in his construction business; at one point in this desperate turkey he's even caught in a Mob shootout. Joey Bishop—second-billed after Alda because the billing was alphabetical—played Alda's late father, who pops up twice (for a total of three to five minutes) to comment on the action and talk to Alda. Looking fit and lean—not drugged up and hungover like the other Rat Packers—Bishop made the most of his brief appearances, but the best line went to Anthony LaPaglia, who's courting Alda's other daughter and wonders what her tastes in music might be like. "Maybe she likes classical," he asks himself. "Like Sinatra."

Sammy was the next to go.

He was diagnosed with throat cancer—ironically the same thing that killed Humphrey Bogart—in 1989 when The Ultimate Tour was over. He was brave about it and felt certain that a few weeks of radiation therapy would cure him. It did not. After an initial remission, and a final burst of energy, the cancer came back stronger than ever and sapped all of his strength. Checking into Cedars-Sinai, he learned that Dean Martin—being treated for numerous ailments related to his heavy drinking as well as prostate trouble—was just down the hall. The two were in no condition to visit each other. The particularly tragic thing about Sammy's condition was that unlike Dino and Peter he had followed his doctor's orders and cleaned up his act, gotten off drugs and liquor, and still it did him no good. He gave up the things that had been killing him only to be felled by something else.

By this time Altovise had been in and out of the Betty Ford Clinic for treatment of her alcoholism, but nothing seemed to work. The news of Sammy's condition—it was terminal at this stage—only made it worse; there were only rare moments when she was sober. Sammy's first wife May was also devastated by the news, as were his children. Sammy did not want to spend his last days in the drunken chaos of his home in Beverly Hills, but his family told him it would be better than the hospital, and they would do everything to make things comfortable for him.

Things had not improved between Altovise and Sammy's daughter Tracey, who was married by this time. She threatened Altovise with bodily injury if she did anything to make her father's passing more difficult or occur sooner than it had to. Altovise was shocked to learn that her husband owed five million dollars to the IRS; between that and Sammy's condition she was nearly insensate. The Beverly Hills home was turned into a temporary hospital complete with nurses and monitors. When Sammy came home from Cedars-Sinai, Altovise greeted him at the door in a near-alcoholic stupor. Tracey, completely unable or unwilling to see the woman's side of it, her desperation and grief, was livid.

Just as Frank had come to see his dying friend Humphrey Bogart, he came frequently to see Sammy. The two had seemingly known each other forever, and no matter what hurts or misunderstandings there had been in the past, Sinatra was deeply affected by the sight of Sammy wasting away in his bedroom. When he left after his visits, he would bow his head and look at no one. Another visitor was Liza Minnelli, but she wasn't able to take it, the sight of Sammy, the hopelessness of it, more than once. By the time Tracey's son was born—she was happy her father had lived to see his grandson—Sammy was down to around seventy pounds. By that time he and his embittered daughter Tracey had come to terms with one another, but the hatred between Tracey and Altovise was never reconciled.

Sammy Davis Jr. died at five in the morning on May 16, 1990.

Throughout his life Sammy Davis Jr. had tried to be fair when it came to black-white relations and attitudes. He admitted that black people weren't the only ones who were poor and suffering, telling one interviewer that when the near-starving Will Mastin Trio waited in booking agents' offices looking for work, there were plenty of white folks in the same desperate spot sitting on the benches beside them. At other times he'd become so bitter at being constantly labeled a "Great Negro Entertainer"—why not just a Great Entertainer Period?—that he figured as far as some white people were concerned the lowest, dirtiest, most diseased and unbearably filthy white wino was better than any black man.

But he also had problems with the attitudes of certain blacks, particularly as the black militancy movement came into prominence. The word "black" had originally been perceived as an insult, but James Brown changed all that with his record "Black is Beautiful." Sammy went along with that all right, but he couldn't get behind those blacks who burned down their own neighborhoods and refused to take responsibility for their own actions—and their own fate. He had always believed that hard work was the answer to getting out of the ghetto, and too many of the young blacks he met seemed more anxious to whine and blame "Whitey" than work or do anything positive about their situation. He was a black man who was against the black tendency toward "victimization" long before it became fashionable.

Naturally this got him in dutch with black newspapers and militants, who generally saw him as an establishment type who had forgotten he was black. Editorials denounced him for staying away from his old neighborhoods, for staying in uptown hotels and living in ritzy, predominantly white areas. Sammy countered that he hated being in a ghetto even when he had no choice, so why should he want to live in one now that he had other options? The very people criticizing him wouldn't live in the ghetto (and many of them didn't) if they didn't have to, so who were they to judge him? Like Sinatra and Dino, Sammy hated people telling him how he should live his life.

The Black Panthers thought Sammy was a jive-ass joke and didn't mind telling him so. In a meeting he arranged with some of them he argued that he didn't like to be judged by people who didn't even know him—he'd felt this way ever since he'd first been called a "nigger" as a child—and he was sure they felt the same, right? The militants studied this odd creature from behind their shades (Sammy thought they were equally odd) and agreed that he had a point, but they'd never see eye to eye. Sammy was always distressed that there was no real unity in the black community, and knew that that was part of the problem that couldn't be laid on white people.

Sammy was appalled that he had a hell of a time getting black businesspeople to give money to Martin Luther King's movement; they just didn't want to be bothered, or else they felt King was wasting his time. They had given up, as far as he was concerned, before they'd even started. He felt the blacks should use the Jews as an example: after the Holocaust, the survivors didn't lay down and die, they didn't give up—they built Israel. He discovered that blacks could be just as mean-spirited and bigoted as any white person.

Because of his hatred of any kind of oppression, some of his sexist and borderline homophobic remarks can be taken as products of their time. When he refers in a hypocritical, rather negative way to "a dreadful crew of fags, prostitutes . . . (etc.)" in his book on Hollywood, it is likely the line was actually written by a ghostwriter. Sadly, during that period of his life Sammy was probably too busy or hungover to bother vetting the manuscript.

By this time (the seventies) Sammy had converted to Judaism, which became an endless source of jokes about him, but which he always took very seriously. The conversion had not come about overnight, and he had carefully considered what it would mean every step of the way. He had always found the Jews an inspiration. "The Jews had been oppressed for three thousand years instead of three hundred," he wrote. "After thousands of years of waiting and holding on and fighting, they finally made it." He always hoped that the black people would make it, too, and was deeply disturbed by the black-on-black violence—brother against brother, guns, drugs, stabbings—that was epidemic in the inner cities.

He could be proud that he had helped, had, in some small way, and in some ways not so small, made things better for the black man and woman in America. He had always loved his country. England may have had less discrimination against the black man, but he knew that the greatest opportunities lay in the land of his birth. It was America that made him a star, and he never forgot it. "I'm tired of black people complaining about what we don't have here in the United States," he once said. "Why can't we ever concentrate on what we do have?"

He knew that no other country in the world could have possibly spawned the phenomenon that was Sammy Davis Jr.

25

Blue Eyes Descending

Frank Sinatra was seventy-seven years old. Sammy was dead. Joey was basically retired. Dino refused to work with Sinatra. In 1992 Frank had no choice but to call on the old club mascot, Shirley MacLaine, and ask her if she would go on tour with him.

It was to be an event similar to the tour of 1988, except there would only be the two of them. His son, Frank Sinatra Jr., was the bandleader. Frank Jr. had always had a rather tense, even combative relationship with his father—he boycotted his wedding to Barbara—but this was an opportunity not to be missed. They played a multitude of indoor stadiums, flying from city to city in Frank's private jet. Because of his failing memory, the lyrics—even to songs he had sung thousands of times—had to be relayed on monitors to the side, but this did little good as he couldn't read the monitors. Half the time he forgot MacLaine's name, so she came out sans introduction.

As there was no rehearsal, no two shows would ever be quite the same. Once Frank walked off the stage in the middle of a show because his son had begun playing a number before he was ready. Another time Shirley came out to do her set, introduced Sinatra—only to learn that at the last minute he'd decided he was having throat trouble and even at that very moment was flying off in his jet without having bothered to tell her. MacLaine never knew what to expect, but usually Frank was a trouper and somehow got through it; the audiences loved their banter on stage as much if not more than the singing. The two, plus their entourage, would eat at shady Italian restaurants run by ex-gangster friends of Frank's—there was at least one in each city—where, according to MacLaine, this multi-millionaire would secretly pocket and walk off with the silverware.

MacLaine had never quite forgiven Frank for dumping her those many years before, and she'd always felt that Dean Martin had treated her better. She wrote a very unflattering portrait of Frank in one of her memoirs after the tour—making him seem like a half-demented, senile, lonely old hoodlum—which deeply hurt and angered Sinatra. "I thought that broad was a friend of mine," he told an acquaintance. "That shows what happens when you try to do someone a favor, let 'em get too close. I trusted her, too." She was off his Christmas list for good.

Betrayal of a different if related sort came from closer quarters that year. For some time Sinatra had wanted to write his autobiography, but all of the prominent writers he contacted refused to work on a fluff piece or whitewash him. His daughter Tina, itching to work in television, was given the assignment of turning his life into a major miniseries, which she produced in 1992. If Sinatra expected that his daughter would highlight his virtues and leave his vices unsaid, he got the biggest surprise of his life. While the entertaining *Sinatra* emerged as superficial as any fifties Hollywood biopic, it did not gloss over Sinatra's faults: his heavy drinking, endless philandering, and nasty treatment of friends and underlings got full exposure. The Frank Sinatra depicted in this "authorized" movie came off as a highly unpleasant individual. The talk in Tinseltown was that Tina had never forgiven her father for leaving her mother and for his childhood neglect of her and her siblings. On the plus side, the film also presented Sinatra as the magnificent singer that he was.

Philip Casnoff did a great job impersonating Sinatra, capturing those certain mannerisms and mouth movements and even looking like the singer in some shots, though critics noted that he was a lot handsomer and sexier than the real thing at any age. As Ava Gardner, Marcia Gay Harden, unfortunately, lacked the real woman's beauty and voluptuousness, making her an odd casting choice. The first half of the miniseries, focusing on the early years of Sinatra's career, was far superior to the shorter but plodding second half, which involved him with the Kennedys and others in the later days. Associates tried to remind Sinatra that the network would not have accepted a sanitized version of his life, but he raged for days after seeing the show, blaming the TV executives more than his daughter. To counteract the miniseries and recent tell-all biographies of her father—and some say to court Daddy's favor in regards to inheritances and such—daughter Nancy wrote a very flattering book about Sinatra. Reportedly Nancy and Tina did not speak for some time while Frank Jr. stewed that his career, while hardly a failure, had never taken off on the level of his father's.

To Sinatra the miniseries was just another example of how the press and indeed all media were out to get him. His hate affair with the press, which started during World War II, had if anything intensified since he'd taken over the Rat Pack, although he did have his side of it on more than one occasion. Some journalists and gossip columnists would deliberately bait him, hoping for some juicy copy and quotes with plenty of expletives deleted, then feign shock and outrage when Frank complied. For instance Maxine Cheshire, society columnist for *The Washington Post*, asked him about his mob connections outside a State Department dinner in the hearing range of many of his important political friends. Cheshire certainly had a right to ask the question, but many felt she was overdoing the wounded female bit when she complained that he had "attacked her as a woman" when he later called her a "cunt." "What did she expect?" said one colleague, "that Frank would kiss her? Besides, just about everybody who knows her thinks Cheshire is just what Frank called her." He also got into feuds with Rona Barrett and Rex Reed, who ridiculed Sinatra in his review of his televised Madison Square Garden concert and on several other occasions. Sinatra ranted about Reed in front of several associates. "He says I can't sing anymore! That asshole can't write. And what the hell has happened to his face? Did you see the way one side of it hangs down like he's had a stroke? And he has the nerve to make fun of me!"

Frank also had a right to be bitter about the way he was constantly being used by politicians who dropped him due to his unsavory connections once they were in office. You'd think Frank would have learned once he'd been manipulated by the Kennedys, but he was either a glutton for punishment or so desperate to be buddies with the world's true power people that he was willing to risk further snubs. Sinatra did a lot of fund-raising and performing for Ronald Reagan's presidential campaign. He even organized a massive inaugural gala that was dismissed as "vulgar" by most of the press, but when it came time for the inauguration itself the following day, Sinatra discovered that he was not to be one of the chosen One Hundred allowed to stand on the steps of the U.S. Capitol as the President was sworn in. Sinatra did not bother flying into a public rage—instead he simply marched up the steps and joined the One Hundred whether they liked it or not.

It was an old story. Politicians always wanted Frank to use his showbiz connections to get entertainers from all across the world to campaign and entertain for them, but once they were in office their advisors would remind them of Frank's pesky mobster ties. In other words, Sinatra had served his purpose and it was time to give him his walking papers. No wonder Frank was embittered. Had the politicians been more ethical they would have either rejected Sinatra's offers of support from the get-go—"all or nothing at all," as Frank would sing—or give him the continued friendship that they knew perfectly well had been his tacit goal all along. Of course politicians were only too happy to go to bat for Frank if he helped raised money for them, which was the case with Governor Hugh Carey of New York, who dismissed talk of Sinatra's mob connections as a "filthy assertion unworthy of comment" after the singer gathered one million for Carey's expenses.

Throughout the latter years of his career more stories circulated of the "benevolent monster" who could be so generous to strangers and so miserable to friends. One difference was that news of his many charitable activities was now being released to the press, whereas before the gift-giving had been done primarily in private. A *Washington Star* editorial opined that "Mr. Sinatra's charities are rather like Mr. Rockefeller's dimes—good for the old blue-eyed image. They are not to be taken seriously by any except those who receive them." It was also theorized that the charitable deductions were mostly used as tax write-offs because of his formidable income. Nevertheless, he continued to help out numerous friends who had fallen on hard times.

Although he certainly didn't need any money, it seemed like old friend Dean Martin had fallen on hard times of a different sort himself. There were increasing reports of ill health and Dean's continued desire to shut himself off from the world. "A lot of spirit went out of him after (his son) Dino was killed," said Bob Newhart. "He lost a lot of his drive." By 1994 he had stopped working altogether, and his social life seemed to consist of trips to his favorite restaurant, La Famiglia, in Beverly Hills. "He brings his own music," said the owner, Joe Patti, "he gets bored listening to anybody else." He and ex-wife Jeanne had grown closer since Dino Jr.'s death and he would have dinner with her at La Famiglia each Saturday night.

Eventually Dino's assorted health problems got to be too much for him. He had been drinking heavily for too long, he was frail, the memory was shot. There were the ulcers, the liver, the prostate. . . . He slipped into the long night in early January of 1996. Sinatra felt a tug at his own mortality when he heard the news; Shirley MacLaine broke down and cried. By this time Shirley was heavily into all of her reincarnation/New Age beliefs, and she was soon telling friends that she was "talking" to Dean in the spirit world at least once a week. Sinatra could just shake his head and mutter, "poor, crazy Shirley."

Sinatra had his own health problems to worry about. In late 1996, as his eighty-first birthday approached, he was admitted to Cedars-Sinai for a pinched nerve that was causing him agonizing pain. He was also diagnosed with pneumonia and an irregular heartbeat. The brief hospital stay provided wife Barbara with some much-needed rest, because Frank was difficult to tend to at home even on his better days. Sixty-six-year-old Barbara complained to friends that all Frank did all day was sit in front of the TV set like a zombie, not even bothering to change the channel, or play his recording of "New York, New York" over and over and over again. He forgot the names of the servants, his children, and occasionally his wife, referring to third wife Barbara as Nancy, or even Ava, on occasion.

Meanwhile more melodrama sprang up over a huge eighty-first birthday party Barbara was planning for Frank for early December. Relations between Barbara and Frank's three children had been more strained than ever since

Barbara sold Frank's $4.9 million Palm Springs estate in 1995 without informing them first. Now she insisted that Nancy, Tina, and Frank Jr. make appointments to see their ailing father, letting the tabloids know that it was because, according to her, they upset their father by asking for bigger and bigger percentages of their inheritance—which was conservatively estimated at $500 million. Barbara was actually furious at the way Frank was giving away cash trust accounts, stocks and shares, and expensive properties to his children in an effort to legally outwit the IRS and keep their hands off the 55 percent of his estate they might get if he left everything in a will. Frank had already given his son a Lake Tahoe estate worth $1.2 million, Nancy a $5.3 million Beverly Hills home, and Tina a $4.8 million beachfront property in Malibu.

Tina and Frank were angered that Nancy also had been given another $27 million in assets, and Barbara was the most furious of all. She was supposed to be the executor of Frank's will, but all this fancy financial maneuvering gave her a very hollow crown. She was also outraged that her own son (by Zeppo Marx) would be comparatively left out in the cold with a mere $600,000 trust fund. (Her absurd plans to have the son, an adult man named Bobby, adopted by Sinatra never came to fruition.) Now she decided to tell fifty-five-year-old Nancy, forty-seven-year-old Tina, and fifty-one-year-old Frank Jr. that they were not welcome at their own father's birthday party. To top it off, one week before the party Frank accidentally took too much prescription medication and had to be rushed to the hospital to have his stomach pumped.

In January of 1997 he checked into Room 8003 of Cedars-Sinai under the name Robert Blakeley. His doctor, Rexford Kennamer, told reporters, "He appears to have had an uncomplicated heart attack and is undergoing tests, observation and treatment." Some friends observed that it was probably all the fighting between Barbara and his children that brought on the heart attack. It was reported that he was definitely suffering from a deteriorating mental condition known as dementia, but that it was not absolutely certain that the condition, in his case, was caused by Alzheimer's disease, as it often is. Within days he was demanding to be let out of the hospital. The prognosis was good for a full recovery of the heart problems if not the dementia.

The prognosis was not so good for the family feud, however. When it was announced that Sinatra was going to receive the Congressional Gold Medal from President Bill Clinton—one of many honors Frank received over the years—Barbara was told by Frank's daughters that she should not expect to stake a claim on the medal after her husband's death. Sinatra was increasingly unaware of and unconcerned with what was going on around him. In February he was diagnosed with bladder cancer and told that he needed heart bypass surgery, which was not recommended due to the fear that he was too weak to survive the operation.

As of this writing, Frank Sinatra, Leader of the (Rat) Pack, Chairman of the Board, spends his days either in a wheelchair or in bed, waiting for the day when his body will be laid to rest in the coffin he has had custom-made from drapes and fittings taken from the late, lamented Sands Hotel and Casino.

Individually—and as a group—the members of the Rat Pack had a long run, but it was over.

Yet there is still enormous interest in the Rat Pack. When the Museum of Television and Radio presented *The Rat Pack Captured* in the summer and fall of 1997, the screenings received an incredible amount of attention from the press. Radio personality Mark Simone told the *New York Post's* "Page Six" column that he had even rarer footage, an actual film of one of their performances at the Copa Room of

the Sands, made in 1963. That same year hi-fi audio recordings were made of an act they did at the urging of Sam
Giancana at the Villa Venice in Chicago. The material was
considered too strong to be commercially released—in the
act the boys would often sing altered risque song lyrics to old
standards—but bootlegs have been available for some time.

The time of the Rat Pack is long gone, of course. Even
Las Vegas is no longer the way it was. Then it was a swingin'
city for babes and bachelors, but now the casinos are full of
entire families, couples with strollers, old folks with bags of
quarters and bottles of Maalox. The whole boozy, sexy mystique is all but gone, which is certainly true of Atlantic City,
which Frank and Dino started playing in the eighties. From
Fun City Las Vegas has turned into one big theme park, day
care center, and retirement home all rolled into one. More
middle-class than the middle-class. No wonder Frank and
Dino got disillusioned. In the old days the smell of the rot of
the crooked gambling institutions was covered up by booze
and cheap perfume: now it's hidden by wine coolers and
baby formula.

As for the Rat Pack: Second Generation, it's interesting
that the only child of a Rat Packer who is currently acting is
Peter Lawford's forty-two-year-old son Chris. In 1997 Chris
executive-produced and appeared in the independent film
Kiss Me, Guido about a man who answers an ad for a room-
mate but thinks GWM means Guy With Money instead of Gay
White Male. Married with several kids in real life, Chris plays
a sleazy gay actor in a picture rife with gay and Italian-
American stereotypes. Although most critics thought *Kiss
Me, Guido* was the sort of stuff the Rat Packers wouldn't have
touched with a ten foot pole, it wasn't all that far from *Kiss
Me, Stupid*.

There have been futile stabs to create the excitement of
the Rat Pack with new groups over the years, but neither the
Hollywood Brat Pack of several young actors or the New York

Brat Pack of several young writers had a long run. Each of the actors either fled for the shelter of sitcoms or faded into obscurity after they were—quickly—washed up in pictures, and the equally short-lived writers were dubbed "MTV authors" by one astute wag. Their staying power and contribution to either films or literature was rather meager compared to the achievements of the members of the Rat Pack.

Frank Sinatra, the Voice, influenced an entire generation of singers—and even generations beyond that (witness Harry Connick). Black Americans might still be banned from nightclubs where other blacks are appearing on stage were it not for his efforts and the uncompromising attitude of Sammy Davis Jr. Joey Bishop's late-night talk show challenge of the Mighty Carson paved the way for other competitors who came years later. In his films, stage shows, and television programs, Dean Martin pushed the envelope as to what was or was not acceptable for a mass audience, and in his own way was in the forefront of the move toward less censorship and more frankness on TV. Peter Lawford was always seen as "the Kennedy with class," a gentleman to his fingertips regardless of his private nightmares, and his son carries on in his footsteps. Individually each member of the Rat Pack has left a small legacy, and collectively they galvanized an entire nation. They were not just entertainers: as the Jack Pack they did their best—rightly or wrongly—to influence world affairs, pointing the direction for the politically involved celebrities of today. They were movers and shakers, people who made things happen, and the "happening" that was their era still resonates today in the fascination they hold for so many people.

Acknowledgments

The authors wish to tender their appreciation to Mike Emmerich, Holly McGuire, Anita Edson, Jim Green, Lynn Brooks, Jason Rath, Jim Donovan, Caroline Schoell, the staff of the Billy Rose Theatre Collection at The Library of the Performing Arts at Lincoln Center, and the individuals—those quoted in the text or mentioned in the notes as well as those who wished to remain nameless—who spoke to one or both of the authors about the Rat Pack either in recent interviews specifically for this book, or in contemporary interviews when the Rat Pack was at the height of its glory. (A film journalist and editor of film publications during this period, Lawrence J. Quirk conducted interviews on the sets of several of the movies that members of the Rat Pack appeared in as a group or individually, while William Schoell, who was only a child when the Rat Pack was at its zenith, conducted most of the more recent interviews.) The authors also tender their appreciation to Jerry Ohlinger and his staff, MGM, Canterbury Productions, United Artists, Ted Allan, Castle Films, CBS-Television. The photos in this book come from private collections.

Notes

PART ONE

The relationship of Humphrey Bogart and Lauren Bacall was well-documented in contemporary press reports. Other sources for their relationship and films include Lauren Bacall, Delores Moran, Walter Brennan, and Howard Hawks. In addition, Miss Bacall wrote candidly of her life with Bogart in her memoir *By Myself*. Confidential sources were also consulted. Sources for Frank Sinatra's early life and career include Tommy Dorsey, Harold Evans, Phil Silvers, Richard Whorf, Mary Wickes, Shelley Winters, and confidential sources. Fred Zinnemann, Burt Lancaster, Donna Reed, and Ernest Borgnine went on the record as to Frank's behavior while making *From Here to Eternity*. James Mason spoke candidly in a 1960 interview with Lawrence Quirk about his dinner with Frank and Ava; Peter Lawford also provided much information. Other confidential sources were tapped for more details in the relationship between Sinatra and Ava Gardner. Kitty Kelley's *His Way* was also consulted for additional information on Sinatra's career and marriage to Ava. Sources for information on the Holmby Hills Rat Pack include David Niven and Sammy Davis Jr. William Holden offered his minority viewpoint in 1954. Sources for the early life and career of Dean Martin (and Jerry Lewis) include Lou Costello, Eva Gabor, and Paul Henreid, as well as many who spoke off the record. Nick Tosches's *Dino* was also consulted. Sammy Davis Jr. spoke of his life and career in interviews; also consulted were his two candid autobiographies, and the (auto)biography written by his daughter. The source for most of the information in the Peter Lawford chapter was Peter Lawford himself, culled from many conversations with Lawrence Quirk. James Spada's *The Man*

Who Kept the Secrets was also consulted. Joey Bishop told of his life and times in private and published interviews.

PART TWO

Lauren Bacall wrote of her relationship with Frank Sinatra in her memoirs, and there were numerous press reports at the time; other sources were Peter Lawford, David Niven, and confidential sources. Sources for stories of Sinatra's generosity and malevolence and other sections of Chapter Eleven include Peter Lawford, Shirley MacLaine, Lee J. Cobb, William Holden, and others who wish not to be named. The tragic death of Deputy Sheriff Richard Anderson and Sinatra's alleged role in it was widely reported upon in the press, as was Sinatra's involvement with various members of the Mafia. *His Way* and official documents were also consulted. Sources for material on *Some Came Running* include Arthur Kennedy, Vincente Minnelli, and Shirley MacLaine, among others. Sources for material on *Never So Few* and other sections of Chapter Thirteen include Sammy Davis Jr., Frank Capra, Peter Lawford, Paul Henreid, Gina Lollobrigida, Joey Bishop, and Richard Johnson. Sources for *Ocean's 11* and additional material in Chapter Fourteen include Juliet Prowse, Peter Lawford, Lewis Milestone, Joey Bishop, Dean Martin, Angie Dickinson, Shirley MacLaine, and Akim Tamiroff. Primary source for information on the Jack Pack in Chapter Fifteen is Peter Lawford, as well as confidential sources and numerous press reports. Peter Lawford was primary source for material in Chapter Sixteen on his breakup with Sinatra, their activities while making *Sergeants 3*, and his affair with his secretary at Chrislaw; other details were provided by Bobby Kennedy in interviews with Lawrence Quirk at the time. *The Man Who Kept the Secrets* also provided some information. Information on Joey Bishop's sitcom was gleaned from Joe Flynn and published reports on and reviews of the series. Sources for *4 for Texas* and related material include Robert Aldrich, Richard Jaeckel, Victor Buono, and Ray Stricklyn. Sources for material on

Dead Ringer were Lawford and Paul Henreid. The kidnapping of Frank Sinatra Jr. was detailed in numerous press reports of the period. Sources for *Robin and the 7 Hoods* include Victor Buono and Bing Crosby. Sources for *Marriage on the Rocks* and additional material in Chapter Nineteen include Deborah Kerr, Cesar Romero, Michael Gordon, and Joey Bishop. Peter Lawford provided many of the details in Chapter Twenty. The hoopla over Joey Bishop's talk show and his competition with Johnny Carson were the subject of many press reports. Books consulted for this section include those by Kelley, Spada, Torsche, Quirk, and MacLaine.

PART THREE

Peter Lawford talked bluntly of the difficulties of his later years with Lawrence Quirk. Sammy Davis wrote candidly of his own difficulties, drug troubles, and the like in his memoirs; some information was also gleaned from his daughter Tracey's book (particularly pertaining to Sammy's cancer and death), as well as from press reports and confidential sources. Frank Sinatra's marriage to Barbara Marx was heavily reported on in the press, as was his relationship with Jacqueline Kennedy Onassis, the tragic death of his mother (as well as the death of Dean-Paul Martin), and his various political activities, as well as Dean Martin's. Videotapes and reviews of Dean Martin's various TV programs were consulted. Shirley MacLaine wrote of her experiences in *Cannonball Run II* and on tour with Sinatra in 1992 in one volume of her memoirs; other confidential sources were also consulted. The 1988 "Together Again" and "Ultimate Tour" shows were covered extensively in the press at that time, as was the *Sinatra* miniseries; confidential sources were also consulted. Frank Sinatra's assorted press feuds were covered in the press and in *His Way*; other confidential sources were consulted. Sinatra's assorted illnesses and the relationship between his wife and children have been reported upon extensively by the press. Other books consulted include those by Tosches, Spada, and Quirk.

Selected Bibliography

Arnold, Edward T., and Eugene L. Miller. *The Films and Career of Robert Aldrich*. Knoxville: University of Tennessee Press, 1986.

Bacall, Lauren. *By Myself*. New York: Alfred A. Knopf, 1979.

Braun, Eric. *Deborah Kerr*. London: W. H. Allen, 1977.

Davis Jr., Sammy, and Jane and Burt Boyar. *Yes I Can*. New York: Farrar, Straus and Giroux, 1965.

Davis Jr., Sammy. *Hollywood in a Suitcase*. New York: William Morrow and Co., 1980.

Davis Jr. , Sammy and Jane and Burt Boyar. *Why Me?* New York: Farrar, Straus and Giroux, 1989.

Davis, Tracey, with Dolores A. Barclay. *Sammy Davis Jr.—My Father*. Los Angeles: General Publishing Group, 1996.

Kelley, Kitty. *His Way*. New York: Bantam, 1986.

Leigh, Wendy. *Liza: Born a Star*. New York: Dutton, 1993.

Lewis, Richard Warren. "The Show Is Over at 1 a.m." *TV Guide*, February 24, 1968.

Levy, Shawn. *King of Comedy*. New York: St. Martin's Press, 1996.

MacLaine, Shirley. *My Lucky Stars: A Hollywood Memoir*. New York: Bantam, 1995.

Millstein, Gilbert. "Portrait of a Well, Well, Well Comic." *The New York Times Magazine*, January 1, 1961.

Murphy, Mary. "The Days and Nights of Dean Martin." *TV Guide*, July 16, 1994.

Neibaur, James L. and Ted Okuda. *The Jerry Lewis Films*. Jefferson: McFarland, 1995.

Quirk, Lawrence J. *Robert Francis Kennedy*. Los Angeles: Holloway House, 1968.

Quirk, Lawrence J. *The Films of William Holden*. Secaucus: Citadel Press, 1973.

Quirk, Lawrence J. *Lauren Bacall: Her Films and Career*. New York: Carol Publishing.

Quirk, Lawrence J. *Fasten Your Seat Belts: The Passionate Life of Bette Davis*. New York: William Morrow, 1990.

Quirk, Lawrence J. *The Kennedys in Hollywood*. Dallas: Taylor, 1996.

Quirk, Lawrence J. *Paul Newman*. Dallas: Taylor, 1997.

Schoell, William. *Stay Out of the Shower: 25 Years of Shocker Films Beginning with* Psycho. New York: Dembner Books, 1985.

Spada, James. *Peter Lawford: The Man Who Kept the Secrets*. New York: Bantam, 1991.

Thompson, Howard. "Golden Boy Turns to the Trumpet for Film." *The New York Times*, November 26, 1965.

Tosches, Nick. *Dino: Living High in the Dirty Business of Dreams*. New York: Dell, 1992.

Periodicals consulted include *Variety, The New York Post, The New York Times, The Daily News, TV Guide, Filmfax*, and others.

Filmography

(Includes films in which two or more of the five main Rat Pack members and mascot Shirley MacLaine appeared. Major Rat Pack films—in which three or more main members appeared—are capitalized.)

It Happened in Brooklyn. 1947. Sinatra and Lawford.

Artists and Models. 1955. Martin and MacLaine.

SOME CAME RUNNING. 1958. Sinatra, Martin, and MacLaine.

Career. 1959. Martin and MacLaine.

Never So Few. 1959. Sinatra, Lawford.

OCEAN'S 11. 1960. Sinatra, Martin, Davis, Lawford, Bishop, and MacLaine.

All in a Night's Work. 1961. Martin and MacLaine.

SERGEANTS 3. 1962. Sinatra, Martin, Davis, Lawford, and Bishop.

Johnny Cool. 1963. Davis and Bishop.

4 for Texas. 1963. Sinatra and Martin. (NOTE: This was to have been a major Rat Pack movie—like the other three films there is a number in the title—but Sinatra was through with Lawford and neither Bishop nor Davis participated.)

What a Way to Go! 1964. Martin and MacLaine.

ROBIN AND THE 7 HOODS. 1964. Sinatra, Martin, and Davis.

Marriage on the Rocks. 1965. Sinatra and Martin.

Texas Across the River. 1966. Martin and Bishop.

A Man Called Adam. 1966. Davis and Lawford.

Salt and Pepper. 1968. Davis and Lawford.

Sweet Charity. 1968. Davis and MacLaine.

One More Time. 1970. Davis and Lawford.

The Cannonball Run. 1981. Martin and Davis.

The Cannonball Run II. 1984. Martin, Davis, MacLaine and Sinatra. (NOTE: Sinatra only has a cameo in this picture, preventing it from being a "major" Rat Pack event—among other reasons.)

Index